FROM WORLD WAR
TO WALDHEIM

Culture and Politics in Austria and the United States

Edited by

David F. Good

and

Ruth Wodak

Berghahn Books
NEW YORK · OXFORD

Published in 1999 by

Berghahn Books
Editorial offices:
55 John Street, 3rd Floor, New York, NY 10038 USA
3, NewTec Place, Magdalen Road, Oxford, OX4 1RE, UK

Library of Congress Cataloging-in-Publication Data

From World War to Waldheim : culture and politics in Austria and the
United States / edited by David F. Good and Ruth Wodak.
    p.   cm. – (Austrian history, culture, & society ; vol. 2)
    Includes bibliographical references and index.
    ISBN 1-57181-103-6 (alk. paper)
    1. United States–Relations–Austria. 2. Austria–Relations–United States.
3. Culture diffusion–Austria. 4. Culture diffusion–United States.
5. Austria–Civilization–American influences. 6. Political culture–Austria.
7. Political culture–United States. 8. National socialism–Psychological
aspects. I. Good, David F. II. Wodak, Ruth, 1950–   . III. Series.
E183.8.A8F76 1998
306'.09436–dc21   98-3726
                                         CIP

British Library Cataloguing in Publication Data
A CIP catalogue record for this book is available from
the British Library.

Printed in the United States on acid-free paper

Cover Illustrations: 1. Vienna 1945. Courtesey of Peter Croÿ.
2. Chancellor Bruno Kreisky being presented with a peace pipe on occasion of the
establishment of the Center for Austrian Studies. Photo by John Ryan. Courtesy of
the Center for Austrian Studies. 3. Fred MacMurray and Barbara Stanwyck.
Publicity shot from Billy Wilder's *Double Indemnity.*
4. Kennedy-Krushchev summit in Vienna. Courtesy of Kennedy Library.
5. President Kurt Waldheim. Courtesy of M. Wenzel-Jelinek.

CONTENTS

Part Three: America and Austrian Political Culture

Preface

The essays in this volume have their origin in a symposium, "A Small State in the Shadow of a Superpower: Austria and the United States since 1945," which was organized by the Center for Austrian Studies and held at the University of Minnesota in November 1994. This event was preceded by two other symposia that also adopted a small-state perspective in examining key issues relating to cold-war Europe: "The End of the Cold War: Security Policy in Austria, Finland, Sweden, and Switzerland" in fall 1992 and "The End of the Cold War: European Reintegration and Institution-Building in Austria, Denmark, Estonia, Finland, and Hungary" in fall 1993. Established in 1977 with the generous gift of one million dollars from the Austrian people on the occasion of America's bicentennial, the Center for Austrian Studies serves as a focal point for the study of Austria in its wider geographical and intellectual setting. By transcending the narrow boundaries of present-day Austria, these three symposia typify the strategy used by the Center to pursue its mission as an international, interdisciplinary institution.

Coming just before the fiftieth anniversary of the end of World War II, the fall 1994 symposium offered an occasion to reflect on the legacy left by the bipolar system of international relations that defined the cold-war era. By adopting a small-state perspective, the papers that were presented at the symposium showed how the power of the United States was at once profound and limited and how the dependency of Austria still permitted considerable leeway for independent action. In addition, the papers provided valuable insights into the mechanisms through which culture is transferred across political boundaries and the role of politics in shaping this transfer.

We asked participants to revise and expand their conference papers with these perspectives in mind. The resulting volume presents an interdisciplinary look at how power and forms of cultural representation interacted in the context of Austrian-American relations during the cold war. Taken as a whole, the contributions challenge naive notions of cultural imperialism according to which small "peripheral" areas are at the mercy of hegemonic powers. To be sure, much of Austria's post-1945 experience is a story of its "Americanization" and its political dependence on the United States in the shadow of the Eastern bloc. These chapters, however, offer a far more complex and nuanced picture. Local forces were crucial in shaping Austria's "Americanization," and Austrian elites enjoyed considerable leeway in pursuing "Austrian" political objectives in the context of the superpowers' confrontation. More importantly, the relationship between America and Austria was not solely unidirectional. With the expulsion of Vienna's cultural and intellectual elite after Austria's incorporation into Nazi Germany, the United States, more than any other country, fell heir to the rich cultural legacy of "Vienna 1900," which profoundly shaped politics and culture in both its "high" and popular forms in post-1945 America. The story of culture and politics in these two countries reached a climax and came full circle with the unfolding of the controversy surrounding Kurt Waldheim's wartime role in the German Wehrmacht, which forced both Austrians and Americans to rethink the meaning of the Nazi era for their respective histories.

The authors wish to thank the Austrian Cultural Institute in New York for providing major funding for the symposium that formed the intellectual foundations of this volume. In addition, they gratefully acknowledge the financial support of several institutions at the University of Minnesota: the Center for European Studies, the College of Liberal Arts, the Continuing Education and Extension Program Innovation Fund, and the Frederick R. Weisman Art Museum.

The contributions of the Center for Austrian Studies go far beyond its role in organizing the fall 1994 symposium. In addition to absorbing some of the direct costs incurred in the editorial and production phases, the Center also subsidized the time of Kenneth H. Marks, who, in his role as assistant editor, managed the manuscript brilliantly from beginning to end and copyedited it with extraordinary care and expertise. Above all, the authors wish to thank the cooperation and strong support of Marion Berghahn and her staff at Berghahn Books. We are pleased to present this volume as the second in Berghahn's Austrian History, Culture, and Society series.

David F. Good   Ruth Wodak
Minneapolis   Vienna

THE SOUND OF FORGETTING MEETS THE UNITED STATES OF AMNESIA

An Introduction to the Relations between Strange Bedfellows

Reinhold Wagnleitner

Relations between societies across national, cultural, ethnic, religious, linguistic, social, and economic lines are usually complicated and often ambiguous, ambivalent, and even paradoxical. These connections may be hidden, but they are nearly always there, somewhere below the surface. This is especially the case with Austria and the United States of America.

The original title of the symposium that was hosted by the Center for Austrian Studies at the University of Minnesota in November 1994 and forms the basis for this volume was "A Small State in the Shadow of a Superpower: Austria and the United States since 1945." In the case of the United States, many Austrians would probably argue that where there is shadow there is light, but the rather dark thematic reference of the title does contain an important element of analytical weight. Austria's twentieth-century history is necessarily interpreted against the background of (mostly fallen) empires and the resulting multitude of traumatic identity crises: the empires of the Habsburg monarchy and Nazi Germany (and the complicated role played by Austria—or, more correctly, many Austrians—during that period), the (military) empire of the Soviet Union, the (economic) empire of the Federal Republic of Germany, and, last but not least, the (informal) empire of the United States.

The connections between the United States and Austria during the last half century were so pervasive that a random selection of topics shows the scope of any such undertaking: the Anschluss and the expulsion and mass murder of Austrian Jews and many other "undesirables" (some of whom, though not nearly enough, found refuge in the United States); the fighting and bombing during World War II; the liberation and occupation of Austria by the "Four in the Jeep"; *The Third Man*; the cold war; the Marshall Plan; the Berlin airlift; NATO and the Warsaw Pact; the Austrian State Treaty and neutrality; the flood of refugees after the Hungarian revolution of 1956; the summit meeting between John F. Kennedy and Nikita Khrushchev in Vienna; the Cuban missile crisis; the wars in Indochina; the occupation of Czechoslovakia; the moon landing; the visit of Richard M. Nixon and Gerald Ford to Salzburg; Bruno Kreisky's independent *Ostpolitik* and Middle East policy; the creation of United Nations offices in Vienna; the signing by Jimmy Carter and Leonid Brezhnev of SALT II in Vienna; Ronald Reagan's "Star Wars" program, the deployment of medium-range nuclear missiles in Europe, the peace movement, and détente; Ronald Reagan and Mikhail Gorbachev; George Bush, the New World Order, and the war against Iraq; Kurt Waldheim; the opening of the iron curtain; and a "permanently neutral" Austria that is moving (full circle?) closer and closer to NATO.

While it is hard to imagine that any single volume could address all of these topics, the situation becomes even more complicated when analyzing other significant aspects of Austrian-American relations during the cold war. However important the political and economic cold war may have been, American relations with the rest of the world are befuddled by the plethora of images, symbols, and codes created and distributed by the American culture industries. From Humphrey Bogart to Arnold Schwarzenegger, from Marilyn Monroe to Meryl Streep, from Frank Sinatra to Whitney Houston, from Miles Davis to Joe Zawinul, from Elvis Presley to Public Enemy, from Ford to Chevrolet, from Chesterfield to Marlboro, from chewing gum to Coca-Cola, from New York to Chicago, from Los Angeles to San Francisco, from Buffalo Bill's (*and* Karl May's) Wild West to Route 66, American icons and myths have turned into an international soundtrack, a quasi-ubiquitous global household Muzak, and a second vernacular culture that symbolize for many the good life of consumption, youth, wealth, power, sexiness, optimism, and fun.

The fact that Arnold Schwarzenegger and Joe Zawinul are Austrian born does not make distinctions any easier, especially in the case of Schwarzenegger, who is a born-again American. But then, what does it matter that the World Wide Web is a "European" invention when the hypertext mostly hypes (real or imagined) Americana? While the question has recently been raised quite often whether the (political, military, economic) American Century isn't coming to an end, there is very little doubt that the passing parade of the American Pop Culture Century is going stronger than ever.

The following seven vignettes (lively scenes or deadly sins?) from the Austrian-American multiplex kaleidoscope serve to demonstrate the point:

1. When Robert Wise, the director of *The Sound of Music*, was criticized for having the Trapp family leave Salzburg for Switzerland by climbing up and over the Untersberg, he quipped: "In Hollywood you make your own geography." And history! (See chapter 7.)
2. In a 25 October 1948 memorandum to director Carol Reed and author Graham Greene about the bleakness of their depiction of Viennese life in *The Third Man*, Hollywood mogul David O. Selznick suggested that they read an article on Vienna in *Life* to get a *realistic* picture of the situation! (See chapter 7.)
3. After having watched the road-show engagement of *The Sound of Music* in Detroit with her eighth-grade classmates in 1965, the American historian of Austria, Laura Gellott, recalls the following: When she listened to the student reports of the show, she heard each of them telling the story of the communist invasion of Austria—in 1938! Her attempts at correction were met by an utterly confused teacher who said it didn't matter—it was all the same thing anyway. (Personal communication with the author.)
4. Only the concerted protests by the International Alliance for Women in Music (Union of International Congress for Women in Music, American Women Composers, and International League of Women Composers) and other American women's organizations seemed to be able to change the males-only policy of the Vienna Philharmonic Orchestra. Of course, the potential loss of revenues might have been much more embarrassing than a few lonely posters reading "A Woman's Place is in the Orchestra," "VPO Needs a Lesson in Harmony," and "I Am Woman, Hear Me Play" before the concert halls in Los Angeles and New York during the February-March tour of 1997.
5. The weapons no one felt sorry about. When about eighty secret American arms depots from the early cold-war years were discovered in Austria in 1996, creating an embarrassing situation between the United States and a (probably not so very) neutral country, the whole affair had to be downplayed as a little, juvenile cold-war adventure. Upon being informed about the typical gold-fever greed of many Austrians who dreamed of hidden Nazi treasures, U.S. Ambassador Swanee Hunt, a public-relations genius, appropriately remarked: "Sorry, no gold, guys!"
6. In 1996 the Austrian Association of Musicians, Composers, and Authors (MKAG) reported that the share of Austrian pop music on the pop radio station Ö3 had hit a new all-time low between 6:00 A.M. and

12:00 P.M., 1.44 percent; the remaining 98.56 percent was devoted to international pop music (read: American and British). Of all CDs, cassettes, and albums sold in Austria in 1994, 78.1 percent were international pop music, 8.2 percent Austropop, 4.6 percent *Volksmusik*, and 9.1 percent classical music. Between 1987 and 1992, the share of international pop in Austria rose from 71.8 to 76.8 percent, while Austropop sank from 12.2 to 8.5 percent. The Austrian market may be small, but it is not insignificant: in 1995 the turnover was 4.149 billion schillings (Renger 1995). The situation in the film, television, and video markets is comparable. All over Europe, American movies nearly crowded out local products during the 1980s and accounted for about 85 percent of movies shown. Between 1985 and 1990, the international market for American films grew by 124 percent, while the domestic market grew by a meager 39 percent. The explosion of private cable and satellite channels more than tripled the European market for American films and other forms of entertainment during the 1990s (Wagnleitner 1994). But even better days are yet to come: in 1997 Blockbuster Video and Pizza Hut are opening their doors to Austrian customers, and Austrian neo-Nazis are receiving support from their "Aryan resistance" brethren in the United States via the Internet.

7. The highly fascinating cultural crosscurrents in the cinematic representation of Austrian (and American) history are not only visible in Austrian (*Heimat*) films but also in their Hollywood models (*Vor-Bilder*). Hollywood casting, which was more than friendly toward "the typical Austrian," was maybe less considerate to Austrian actors. After all, it seems more than significant that Leon Askin, an *Austrian* actor, who had been kicked out of the country in 1938, assumed prominence in two "typical" roles, no doubt brilliantly acted: as the *German* general Albert Burkhalter, a character in the cult TV series *Hogan's Heroes*, and the Soviet commissar Peripetchikoff in Billy Wilder's cold-war cult comedy *One, Two, Three* (1961), who was no less clumsy than General Burkhalter but more drunk. Dr. Strangelove as an Austrian seemed wildly off the mark, and it should not come as a surprise, however unfortunate, that Austrian central casting proved even milder.

These vignettes and the contributions of this volume must be seen against the backdrop of the Marshall Plan, which stands as the single-most concerted effort to shape the world in the American image in the postwar era. For Austria in particular, the importance of the plan should not be underestimated. The American aid of thirteen to fifteen billion dollars under the European Recovery Program (ERP), which in Austria still amounts to nearly thirty-two billion schillings in ERP reserves from the Counterpart

Funds, was deeply rooted in the conviction that the political blunders and economic disasters of the interwar period were to be avoided at all costs.[1] Marshall Plan measures do appear to have strengthened the potential for long-lasting coalitions and compromises between formerly antagonistic groups (Kindley 1994), and Austria is among a handful of European countries whose citizens have enjoyed consistently low rates of unemployment and inflation, high rates of economic growth, and a high degree of social peace. Yet the Social Partnership, the institutional symbol of Austria's postwar settlement, has been attacked violently in the mid-1990s, especially after the decision to join the European Union. More importantly, most contemporary modernizers on both sides of the Atlantic seem hardly aware—or at least do not want to be reminded—that the Austrian, European, and American economic miracles were not only a result of hard work and market forces but also of large-scale economic planning, the New Deal being the original example. Why else would Austrians, who received approximately one billion dollars as a gift, be strangely mute about the Marshall Plan in the year of its fiftieth anniversary?[2]

The Marshall Plan may have made Austria even more Austrian by strengthening some aspects of corporatism (Kindley 1994). Yet, the presence of the Red Army and the question of German external assets (which differentiated Austria from all other small states receiving ERP funds), the participation of many Austrians in Nazi war crimes, the reality that most leading Austrian politicians and trade-union leaders had learned their (political and economic) lessons, all of this, too, has to be put into the equation along with direct and indirect American interference. It was precisely the economic interference and budgetary control initiated by the Marshall Plan and its economic governing bodies that made the "neocorporatism" of the Second Republic so different (and, especially, so successful) when compared with the institutional legacy of corporatism from the Habsburg monarchy and the corporate system messily propagated by "Austrofascism," which was hardly built on coordination, consensus, and compromise.

John Bunzl's contribution shows that the problem of deciding what is Austrian has an even longer history, both inside and outside the United States. Since the period of the Habsburg monarchy, Austrian immigration to America did not result in a hyphenated interest group with a vocal lobby for the old country. On the contrary, the majority of immigrants came from ethnic groups that fostered the image of the "prison of peoples," while

1. Only the economic basket case Austria and civil-war-struck Greece received ERP funds as grants; all other participating countries received ERP aid as loans.

2. Granted, the Austrian official silence on the occasion of the fiftieth anniversary of the announcement of the Marshall Plan in June 1997 may perhaps be explained by the fact that the actual program for Austria did not start until 1948.

many members of the smaller group of German Austrians tended to seek adoption by the much larger group of German Americans. This, ironically, only mirrored the nationalist allegiances of many of those who stayed in the old world.

For the victorious powers after 1945, of course, interests in Austria were always dominated by global considerations, especially for the new Western superpower, the United States. Wartime plans and the wartime necessity of weakening (Nazi) Germany soon were washed away by the "global containment" of communism. Wartime necessity transformed into cold-war reality; strengthening the former adversary against the former ally promoted European anticommunism. The feat of keeping West Germany and Austria out of the Soviet sphere may only have been possible by cooperation with sympathizers of the former powers. Still, it must be noted that despite the vociferous recent accusations from the (not so) New Right, which claim that denazification resulted in an American brainwashing of Germans and Austrians (and other Europeans), the historical record is somewhat different. Vigorous early attempts at denazification were soon followed by a quick accommodation between the new masters and many followers of the Nazi gospel. Denazification withered away, and the new situation became part and parcel of another global confrontation, the cold war. Radical antifascists soon found themselves in the awkward position of appearing to favor Soviet power, whereas the old Nazi party members and collaborators had the best anticommunist record.

These cold-war strategies are part of the real story behind the making of Austria into the first victim of Nazi aggression, the other part, of course, being that millions of Austrians, predominantly but not exclusively Jewish Austrians, really were victims. The all-important need to keep Austria neutral but still within the Western camp overrode Jewish claims for restitution and played into the hands of those who wanted to put a blanket over the horrors of Austrian participation in the Third Reich. But the history of collaboration is not only a peculiarly Austrian problem; it has a European dimension, as even the "gnomes of Zurich" and French art museums are now finding out with some difficulty.

The image of a depoliticized and dehistoricized Austria as a kind of *Sound of Music* Disneyland created by the American media industry was more than welcome in the former Ostmark, even though hardly any Austrian liked the film itself. But then even kitsch that is deemed "alien" has a hard time in the land of *gemütlicher Walzerseligkeit*. But the media's image of "harmlessness" found favor in this small state, which was busily creating a new national identity and concentrating on rebuilding from the rubble of war—a state that had the Red Army on parts of its territory for ten years and was partly surrounded by the iron curtain for nearly forty years more.

Only revolutionary changes in the international scene—who, besides many Austrians (this one included), would want a neutral Austria after the breakdown of the Soviet Union?—and domestic developments within the United States following the Americanization of the Holocaust led to drastic changes of the perception of Austria in the United States. Moreover, Bruno Kreisky's mediation policies in the Middle East and his attempts to deepen trade relations with COMECON states (including goods that had been banned as strategic by Washington), Kurt Waldheim's insistence that he had only done his duty, and the massive popular support during his presidential "campaign" provided all the ingredients for the reversal of roles: Germany as the enlightened NATO ally, Austria as the new pariah. Future developments, for example, a decline in American support for a muscle-flexing, German-dominated European Union as a result of a shift in American global interests, must await later historical analysis.

Whatever period in the postwar era they scrutinize, analysts will always have to bear in mind the complex web of the global ramifications of "American national interests." An American diplomat in Vienna, Martin F. Herz, clearly had this in mind when he commented on the massive lack of any feeling of guilt for World War II by most Austrians in an Information Services Branch opinion poll in early 1947: "Since as a matter of national policy we encourage a separate Austrian nationalism, we cannot be surprised, and should in fact find comfort in the fact that most Austrians deny ever having had anything to do with Germany" (Herz 1984: 132). Of course, Herz, who had strong personal and cultural roots in Austria, was the last to share any sympathy for Nazism, but cold-war realpolitik won the day: "It stands to reason that the emphasis on Austria's separateness from Germany results in a corresponding feeling of guiltlessness" (Herz 1984: 132). In the same way, one does not have to agree with the implications of Geoffrey Wheatcroft's correct, if somewhat exaggerated, claim that for every single American citizen who knows about the Holocaust a million are fans of *The Sound of Music* (Wheatcroft 1988).

Oliver Rathkolb's piece on Bruno Kreisky's perceptions of the United States demonstrates the limits of independent foreign relations for a small country caught within the tight web of American global considerations. Kreisky was clearly untainted by fascism as a result of his socialist roots—most evident in his role as political prisoner and exile in Sweden in the late 1930s and his important contributions to Social Democratic diplomacy and politics starting immediately after the war. Yet his critical views on American domestic issues, for example, the situation of African Americans, and on foreign policy had already raised suspicions when he became Austrian foreign minister in 1959. Kreisky was a confirmed anticommunist who thought that American power was necessary to defend Europe and who regarded the

Marshall Plan not only as the most important answer for Europe's economic chaos but also as a model for massive solidarity programs for the Third World.[3] Despite these views, Kreisky maintained his critical intellect and dared to express some doubts, as well as offer some alternative solutions, about certain aspects of American foreign policy in coping with the communists. Kreisky's early *Ostpolitik* and initiatives on behalf of détente, as well as his insistence on the necessity of continuous talks between the superpowers and on strengthening economic ties as trust-building measures for a peaceful deescalation of East-West (and North-South) conflict, were not looked on with favor by successive American administrations, at least not as long as Austria took the lead.

Consequently, Kreisky's conflicts with supposed American interests became most evident not when he began to build bridges toward former Austrian National Socialists but when he initiated his Middle East policy in the mid-1960s, already ten years before the oil shock of 1974 woke up the rest of Europe and many other parts of the world. His conviction that only the official recognition of the PLO would lead to a long-lasting solution was anathema to the United States and many of its Western allies. Rathkolb is convincing in showing Kreisky's effectiveness as a mediator: despite grave ideological differences with the Reagan administration, in his last years as chancellor (and afterwards), he supported the Reagan plan (1982–84) as well as the Arab Fez plan, which sought the integration of the PLO as an official player, a policy that slowly but surely became conventional wisdom in the United States and the European Union.

While Bruno Kreisky's relationship with the United States was not free from friction, he still was, for most of his career, the most diligent Austrian student of modern American politics. His brilliant use of the power of the media and his suave handling of public opinion resembled the much admired style of John F. Kennedy. After all, Kreisky was the first Austrian politician to hire a PR man for his highly visible lecture tours through the United States in the 1960s. It may be typical of Bruno Kreisky's multifaceted personality and intellect—and of the complicated relations between Austria and the United States more generally—that he, more convincingly than most, represented the last major politician to be deeply rooted in and socialized by Austrian (and European) culture and history while at the same time becoming the first brilliant example of "Americanized" politics in Austria.

3. The initiatives of Bruno Kreisky and Willy Brandt on behalf of financial, economic, *and* moral support for the "underdeveloped" world had as much to do with their understanding of the development of underdevelopment as with the necessity of finding an economic balance for "First World," especially American, postwar policies, which, at least since the Korean War, very much resembled international military-oriented Keynesianism (Chomsky 1993: 106–7).

Suave handling of the media would have been necessary, but certainly not enough, to stave off the greatest crisis of Austrian-American relations after World War II: the unprecedented act of placing Kurt Waldheim, president of a friendly country, on the "watch list" of undesirable aliens under the 1981 Holtzman amendment. Richard Mitten's meticulously researched and thoughtful analysis represents a state-of-the-art study of the politics of remembering and forgetting, especially the long-range implications of how it was used politically in the context of cold-war geopolitics.

While there is no doubt that Kurt Waldheim's inept reactions and unreliable statements fanned the flames of criticism inside and outside Austria, the gravely deficient and inadequate historical knowledge of many journalists dealing with the affair proved that "Waldheimer's disease" is not only an Austrian but an international condition. Notwithstanding the clear political and moral issues, none of the historical and juridical commissions that examined the evidence found that there was a case for criminal proceedings against Kurt Waldheim. Even the watch-list decision was issued because his Balkan activities fell under the terms of the Holtzman amendment, not because they were criminal under American law.

The double standards of the Reagan administration become even more vividly clear in Mitten's analysis of the handling of President Reagan's visit to the Bitburg cemetery in 1985 and the treatment of Waldheim in the following years. The power of the Federal Republic of West Germany as well as its importance as a military ally pushed aside all critical arguments. The willingness of the West German political elites to "assume the burdens of history" had long silenced questions about the quiet reintegration of many former National Socialists, especially high-ranking Wehrmacht officers and secret-service specialists brought into service under the pretext of "defending the West." Moreover, West German presidents with interesting Third Reich biographies had escaped closer American scrutiny in earlier decades, at least in public.[4]

It may be stretching the argument too far to say that after Bitburg Washington saw the Waldheim affair as a useful vehicle for demonstrating its vigorous commitment to fight Nazism; no real political price had to be paid because it involved Austria, and "politics" and "morality" could converge again. In addition, the most important question could be evaded: How could Kurt Waldheim, if he had been what he was made out to be, become a career diplomat and secretary general of the United Nations when he only could do so after having been cleared by Allied, especially American, secret services after the war? All of a sudden Austrian historians were attacked in

4. These, of course, are historical and political arguments better not mentioned when promoting the inclusion of former Warsaw Pact states as well as neutral Austria as new members of NATO.

the United States for having been asleep. They answered that they had been asking for relevant American documents for a long time, but the files remained closed to them. Richard Mitten's biting assessment of this Western morality play, which cast Kurt Waldheim as a symbol not entirely commensurate with either his shortcomings or his importance, reminds us that we still need much more knowledge about continuities in the history of fascism and collaboration during the cold war, not only within Austria but on a global scale as well.

Egon Schwarz's chapter reaches the core of the book by touching on the heart of Austrian-American relations since the 1930s. Schwarz is a perfect illustration of the notion that what was Austria's loss has become America's gain. Like many others in his youth, Schwarz was hounded out of Austria with his family. His personal story belongs to that short but probably most extreme period of contemporary history when Austrians (as Germans) indulged in what amounts to the most massive and violent export of culture, scientific knowledge, practical expertise, artistic quality, and human beings in history! After all, what other country would kick out all Nobel Prize winners active in its universities?

The German emigrants, refugees, and exiles had had a couple of years of warning, so most of them did not experience the brutality that was suffered especially by Viennese Jews. The persecution in what was formerly Austria started relatively late, which meant that only the least desirable destinations remained open for many Austrian Jews who were forced out of the country. Their final settlement in the United States had to take a circuitous route.

Egon Schwarz's story is chilling: his family's flight to Bratislava, their deportation to the no-man's-land between Slovakia and Hungary, their lucky escape to Prague, their even luckier acquisition of Bolivian visas, their journey to South America via Paris, the port of La Rochelle-Pallice, and the harsh conditions during the transatlantic trip on a freighter, including their feelings of not really being welcome at their final destination. Just as chilling is his reference to the conference of Evian in 1938, which could not produce any satisfactory solution for the many thousands of European refugees and proves that contemporary history really is contemporary.

More horrible than the corporeal abuse, Schwarz reminds us, "was the mental agony: the feeling of impotence, the sense of humiliation, the loss of dignity, the lack of recourse, the terror of an unimaginable future." His individual story was experienced by many who represented the cream of Viennese intellectual life: economists, psychoanalysts, musicologists, the Vienna Circle of logical positivists, writers, musicians, actors, and directors; (more than three thousand) physicians; art historians, architects, and social scientists; one-third of empirical and all theoretical physicists; and many in the school of positivistic jurisprudence, technicians, and engineers. Corresponding to what Stuart Hughes calls the *"de*provincializing" of American intellectual life (quoted in Coser 1988: 100; emphasis added), the provincializing of Austria was to be felt for several decades.

This rupture in one prototypically modern discipline lies at the heart of Bernhard Handlbauer's chapter. Probably more than in any other field, the exiling of the most creative thinkers of modern psychoanalysis left a vacuum in Austria that remains to this day. The consequences for American intellectual life in the second half of the twentieth century were just as deep. Many students of major figures like Sigmund Freud, Alfred Adler, and Karl Bühler became prominent and successful doctors, pedagogues, and social workers and exerted an enormous influence on the development of psychoanalysis, individual psychology, and other schools of psychotherapy after the 1940s, especially in New York and California but also in Boston and Chicago. About 40 percent of the Austrian psychoanalysts who emigrated were women whose qualitative contribution to the field was at least as important as their numbers.

The proverbial lack of roots of the *conditio Americana* certainly contributed to the tremendous success of these Viennese psychoanalysts in the United States. As the vanguard of the modern life-style, they were particularly qualified to understand the problems of life in America because, Handlbauer reminds us, many of the later emigrants had already experienced an earlier migration from the periphery of the former Habsburg Empire to Vienna. This double exile and double (e)migration certainly motivated these psychoanalysts who had lost their roots to dedicate their lives to the restitution of those who were uprooted emotionally, and their personal traumas at the same time significantly influenced the development of psychoanalysis itself.

It seemed that psychoanalysis had arrived at the right place at the right time, soon popularizing notions of repression, the unconscious, the oedipus complex, dream analysis, Freudian slips, infantile sexuality, defense mechanisms, castration fear, penis envy, identity, and identity crisis became household words that permeated both American popular culture and academic disciplines from ethnology to history, from sociology to literary studies.[5] But chicness has its price, and psychoanalysis underwent dramatic transformations in its new haven. It seems that with the transplantation to the new world psychoanalysis itself experienced a deep identity crisis, as few analysts dared to criticize openly the social conditions of cold-war America.

The former outsiders became prestigious insiders, and their goals of therapy shifted from liberation to adjustment, from emancipation to correction, from revolt against the norms of the old culture to submission to the new. The Americanization of psychoanalysis resulted in the removal of Freud's

---

5. Erik Erikson's concept of identity and identity crisis perhaps owed as much to the situation of uprootedness as to the political culture of the cold war.

cultural critique—no more the pessimistic notion of a death wish. Handlbauer views the petrification of American psychoanalysis, with its glorification
of the past and orthodoxy, as the main reason for the present anti-Freudian
mode in the United States. His most acerbic and provocative critique, however, is hidden in a note: "Where 'liberal' has become an invective, where new
prisons and the death penalty are the ultimate answers to social disintegration,
and where Prozac is the general solution to depressing conditions of life, there
is no longer fertile ground for psychoanalysis to thrive."

Jonathan Munby's chapter concerns another group of Austrian-Jewish
exiles who dealt with the problems of modern existence on quite another
level of expression, although their understanding of Freud and psychoanalysis is quite evident. The connections between Austrian and American
psychoanalysis are common knowledge, but the indebtedness of Hollywood's darkest film genre to Austrian-Jewish artists is known only to the
most avid film buffs. Even those French critics, who coined the term "film
noir" after having seen five American thrillers in 1946, were completely
unaware that three of these films—*Laura, Double Indemnity,* and *Woman in
the Window*—had been created under the direction of exiled Austrian-Jewish directors: Otto Preminger, Billy Wilder, and Fritz Lang.

Just like most psychoanalysts, the artists who achieved prominence in
postwar Hollywood experienced a double exile—from Vienna via Babelsberg (Berlin) or Paris to New York and Hollywood—and just as in the case
of the psychoanalysts, their emigration did not result in a simple trans-
planting of European modernist sensibilities to American soil. Still, Munby
clearly shows that behind this visually dark and thematically pessimistic
body of film work that was deeply influenced by these exiled directors—and
subsequently attacked as "un-American" by the House Un-American Activities Committee—lay the horrors of the gas chambers, the mass destruction
of two world wars, and the "red scare" of the early cold-war years.

For Munby these Austrian-Jewish artists represent modernity's chosen subjects, who, in the context of antisemitism in Vienna, had experienced the crisis of the individual earlier and more threateningly than others. The films
noir—with their dark moods and feelings of displacement, alienation, disillusionment, and an inescapable conspiring fate—formed the avant-garde of
a sentiment that was typical for many European artists but became implanted
in America only when the possibility of nuclear annihilation had to be faced.

The contribution of Austrian-Jewish directors to the modernist critique of
modern (American) life as dehumanizing was central within American film art
and may even be as important as the Austrian contribution to American psychoanalysis. After all, there can be no doubt that throughout the twentieth
century American film and television have been the dominant institutions for
the creation and dissemination of America's self-image both at home and

abroad. It certainly was no mean feat, therefore, that Billy Wilder and his colleagues identified Hollywood as the prime site of American self-deception.

Jacqueline Vansant deals with one of the most important examples of this self-deception in her chapter on *The Sound of Music*. As is true for most films with a historical setting, this Hollywood musical tells us more about the period and society in which it was produced—the United States in the mid-1960s—than about Austria before the Anschluss. While the American self-deception has been working ever since the opening night of the movie and *The Sound of Music* still belongs to the top ten of all-time movie hits, the deception of the "other" did not function as well: the movie was a complete flop in the Austrian and German markets.[6]

Hollywood's construction of a particularly idyllic Austria with Austrian characters (and scenery) removed from, if not outside of, history was rooted in a long *American* tradition of depicting Austria as an aristocratic fairyland of waltzes and frivolous decadence, a tradition going back as far as World War I. Robert Wise (and the writers of the movie) did indeed create their own history and geography. While the geography was purely European, albeit cut by Hollywood scissors in the best Wilsonian tradition, the history was not. To be sure, the studio created a *Heimatfilm*, but the *Heimat* (homeland) at stake was the United States, not Austria!

In 1965, *The Sound of Music* was a respite from a highly complicated and unstable world. The problem, however, was not the Anschluss—remember, West Germany had God on its side now, too—but the escalating war in Indochina and the burning inner cities in the United States. The absolute loyalty and unquestioned patriotism of the Trapp family represented a bulwark against conflict over civil rights and antiwar protests, and the hymn (*Hohelied*) for the virtues and strength of the patriarchal family was especially timely in an age of exploding divorce rates. While it is true that quite a few Austrians have been and still are pretending to exist outside of history, many Americans keep them good company. *The Sound of Music* is at least as much a film about the *American* longing and search for the "good old days" as it is about the escape (!) of an Austrian family. It is a revealing indication for the "revolutionary" character of the 1960s that this film is the single most important and successful product of popular culture of the decade and not, as some would have it, Jimi Hendrix's "Star Spangled Banner."

In the Austria of the 1960s, the Trapp family was anything but a predominant model, and many Austrian women, just like their American sisters, faced

---

6. In Salzburg the film is still shown every day in one cinema during the summer holiday season—but exclusively for tourists from the United States, Australia, New Zealand, the United Kingdom, and Japan. It may be hard to find a Salzburger who has not yet been asked whether "Edelweiss" isn't the Austrian national anthem. The enthusiastic tourists are ever so surprised to find out that most Austrians do not even know the song.

quite different problems. Similar social trends in both countries—more and better educated women in the workforce, rising divorce rates and sinking marriage rates, and the availability of new forms of contraception—brought the demands of women for control over their reproductive rights to the center of public debate.

In her chapter on the abortion conflict in Austria and the United States, Maria Mesner discusses the enormous influence of the "new" American women's movement in Western Europe, especially in West Germany and Austria. The pro-choice stance, which was adopted by the National Organization for Women (NOW) only in 1967, became a highly symbolic issue for women's liberation on both sides of the Atlantic, while the opposition manned the ban on abortion as the symbolic dike against all evils of decadent and materialistic modernity. It is hardly a coincidence that the final decisions to legalize abortions on demand during the first term of pregnancy—*Roe vs. Wade* on 22 January 1973 and the Austrian law of 23 January 1974—were issued exactly within a year of each other.

At the same time, the political conflicts over abortion and the dissimilar strategies of the debates in Austria and the United States allow interesting insights into two alternative weltanschauungen based on different political traditions and cultures. Very similar demands came from women's organizations with quite different histories. While the American women's movement was deeply rooted in Evangelical Protestant moral movements that had promoted temperance and the abolition of slavery, demands for the liberation of Austrian women had mostly been issued within traditional party structures, especially by Social Democrats.

While NOW hesitated until 1967 to adopt the abortion issue and achieved success by grassroots lobbying and addressing the courts, Austrian feminism could build on much earlier traditions that focused on political solutions through parliamentary legislation. Nothing proved more different than the further development of the issue: while abortion lost its symbolic relevance—outside of a small group of (mostly Catholic) traditionalists—and was put on the back burner in Austria, the Evangelical tradition as well as the activist policies of the Catholic Church in the United States fueled the conflict toward a bitter confrontation and heated polarization of society that has resulted in terrorism and even murder.

Edward Larkey's chapter on the impact of economic and cultural hegemony on Austrian identity serves as an excellent conclusion to the volume. Like people from other small states (and not so small states, like Canada), Austrians had to construct identities within the cultural framework of the world system. Yet the Austrian case is even more complicated; the construction of a modern Austrian, that is, non-German, identity after World War II had to be managed in the shadow of two hegemonic powers, the United States and West Germany.

While it can be argued that the Austrian culture and economy are now effectively dominated by German capital, the resulting cultural identities contain interesting ambiguities. For many, the crafting of a non-German cultural identity in the face of German hegemony achieved a central political, ideological, and even moral importance after the Holocaust. But the de-Germanization of Austrian popular culture could be achieved only by introducing the homogenizing tendencies of global cultural industries. The Catch-22 of this murky situation contained a further ironic twist: much of the de-Germanization (Americanization) of Austrian popular culture was actually managed under the economic tutelage of the American cohegemon, West Germany.

Austropop is a good case in point. For Larkey, this genre, which achieved popularity in the early 1970s, primarily represents a discourse strategy that provided a political foundation for aesthetic judgment: combining American pop music idioms—from orchestration to instrumentation, from blues to hip-hop—with lyrics in various dialects of Austrian German helped, at least in the best cases, to achieve an artistic emancipation from the German tradition of *Schlager* (hits) and *Schnulzen* (tearjerkers). It is no secret that this strategy sometimes achieved highly problematic and ambiguous results. Re-creating Austrian popular music strengthened and affirmed the more general (economic) hegemonic framework and allowed a critical cultural distance from within the system.[7]

In this context, Americanization stands for a cultural strategy that aimed at promoting the good life by connecting leisure, relaxation, and entertainment with a consumerist social utopia. This strategy was reintroduced in Europe after World War II by the United States, the world's most powerful capitalist society, but neither capitalism nor consumerism is an exclusively American invention. The development of these cultural processes, which had actually begun much earlier than 1945, may best be termed "creolization" (Kroes 1993: 302–18). But we should not forget that America was first to be creolized by Europeans before Europe could become creolized in turn. It is no wonder that to this day the best remembered Coca-Cola advertisement campaign during the hardworking days of reconstruction and the nascent economic miracle is "Mach mal Pause!" (Take a break!). Even historians must pay heed to this summons, whatever they will eventually imbibe.

---

7. It is also no secret that some of the most popular interpreters of German *Schlager* and *Schnulzen* are Austrian artists.

References

Chomsky, N. 1993. *Year 501: The Conquest Continues.* London.

Coser, L. 1988. "Die österreichische Emigration als Kulturtransfer Europa-Amerika." In *Vertriebene Vernunft II. Emigration und Exil österreichischer Wissenschaft. Internationales Symposion 19. bis 23. Oktober 1987 in Wien,* ed. F. Stadler, 93–101. Vienna.

Herz, M. F. 1984. *Understanding Austria: The Political Reports and Analyses of Martin F. Herz, Political Officer of the US Legation in Vienna, 1945–1948.* Ed. R. Wagnleitner. Salzburg.

Kindley, R. W. 1994. "International Trade, Domestic Bargaining and the Structure of Corporatist Arrangements: The Marshall Plan and Institution-Building in Postwar Austria." Paper presented at symposium, "A Small State in the Shadow of a Superpower: Austria and the United States since 1945," 3–6 November, at the Center for Austrian Studies, University of Minnesota.

Kroes, R. 1993. "Americanisation: What are We Talking About?" In *Cultural Transmissions and Receptions: American Mass Culture in Europe,* ed. R. Kroes, R. W. Rydell, and F. J. Bosscher Doeko, 302–18. Amsterdam.

Renger, R. 1995. "Audio-Industrie." In *Medien in Österreich. Medienbericht 4 interaktiv,* ed. Institut für Publizistik- und Kommunikationswissenschaft der Universität Salzburg. Vienna. CD-ROM.

Wagnleitner, R. 1994. "American Cultural Diplomacy, Hollywood, and the Cold War in Central Europe." *Rethinking Marxism* 7, no. 1 (spring):31–47.

Wheatcroft, G. 1988. "Absurd Reich." *New Republic,* 28 March.

Part One

THE POLITICS OF AUSTRIAN-AMERICAN RELATIONS

Chapter 1

....

AMERICAN ATTITUDES TOWARD AUSTRIA AND AUSTRIAN-GERMAN RELATIONS SINCE 1945

John Bunzl

Historical Background

Unlike most European immigrations, Austrian immigration has not produced ethnopolitical interest groups and lobbying efforts in the United States. Before World War I almost one quarter of immigrants arriving on the shores of America originated from lands then ruled by the Austro-Hungarian Empire, yet no common awareness of an Austrian identity developed among newcomers. Immigrants identified with the ethnic group from which they stemmed inside the Habsburg Empire, and if German speaking, they tended to identify with other Germans in the United States. Also, by means of "Americanization," they tended to shed any trace of "Austrianness" that may have survived.[1]

The generally bad reputation of the "prison of peoples" and the tendency for Americans to identify with the struggle of oppressed nationalities against Habsburg rule fueled this process.[2] The reactionary image of the Austro-Hungarian monarchy, however, should be distinguished from American attitudes

1. For the evolution of Austrian immigration into the United States up to World War I, see Spaulding 1968, Jones 1960, and Schwegel 1904.
2. The reactionary image of the Habsburg monarchy is described in Bailey 1946, Matsch 1990, and Wittke 1952.

toward Germany at the time of World War I. While Germany did engender feelings of enmity and rivalry, Austria did not elicit such feelings among Americans. This explains attempts by the American government during World War I to lure Vienna away from Berlin and to decrease Austrian dependence on Germany.[3] The policy continued in the interwar years, but there was no consensus within the American government on the political future of Austria, especially with respect either to an anschluss, which would strengthen the Catholic south of Germany, or to a Danubian federation.[4] No firm American commitment existed to preserve Austria in its interwar borders.

The establishment of an authoritarian regime in 1934 yielded no sympathy for Austria, especially in the context of America's isolationism and economic crisis. This explains in part why there was no mobilization either of public opinion or of official policies against the impending Anschluss despite outspoken warnings by Washington's diplomatic representatives in Europe.[5] After 1938 the sudden influx of thousands of refugees had little impact on American attitudes toward Austria. Most had no intention of working for the rebirth of a country that had humiliated and rejected them. Also, rivalries among a politically motivated minority of these refugees made it difficult to find a common ground. Unlike members of other occupied countries, Austrian émigrés formed no government in exile.[6] American interest in Austria, whether within government or among the public, came only in World War II, especially after 1943. Before then, no clear-cut Allied policy in favor of an independent Austria existed, and when it did emerge, its main goal once again was to weaken Germany through patriotic resistance and the deannexation of Austria.[7] There was, however, no ideological commitment to Austrian independence.

The Postwar Treatment of Austria in Theory and Practice

Toward the end of the war, government officials in the United States developed principles for coping with Nazism after the victory over Germany. Policy toward Austria was to be distinct from that toward Germany, but it

3. On American policies toward Austria in the era of World War I, see Mamatey 1957, Schmid 1968, Hausmann 1972, Zelter 1961, and McClelland 1987.

4. For a description of American policies toward Austria during the interwar period up to 1934, see Luchak 1987 and Pucher 1980.

5. For American views on the Anschluss question and on the establishment of the authoritarian regime in Austria, see Hofer 1931, Clough 1933, Slosson 1930, Low 1985, and Meysels 1960.

6. For a discussion of Austrian emigration circles in the United States after 1938 and American attitudes toward them, see Eppel 1992, Mikovits 1992, Wimmer 1992, Goldner 1977, and Beer 1992.

7. American attitudes toward Austria and Germany during World War II are discussed in Fellner 1972 and Keyserlingk 1988.

shared some common assumptions. According to Richard Mitten (1993: 18), an "administrative purge [of elites] represented the lowest common denominator" for different planning agencies, of which the Office of Strategic Services (OSS) with Franz Neumann and his associates proved most influential. This common denominator "served to define the presumed conceivable limits of 'de-Nazification' in Germany, and *a fortiori* in Austria" (Mitten 1993: 25). In addition, a fundamental identity between National Socialism and Germanness was assumed, while Austria was starting to be seen as having a cultural profile of its own and thus capable of "de-Germanizing" itself. Finally, neither the "Jewish question" nor the Holocaust was a main concern for American political and military leaders, who did not regard antisemitism and the persecution of Jews as a central feature of Nazi Germany. This was even more so in the case of Austria; if Nazism as an ideology and as a system was imported and implemented from outside, it made no sense to demand special reparations from the Austrians. In short, the "Americanization" of the Holocaust as an explicit factor in foreign policy had not yet begun.

Once the deannexation of Austria became an Allied objective in the war against Germany, American authorities started to ponder measures of denazification and to formulate policies aimed at introducing Western democratic structures after Austria's liberation from German control. In this context, an important directive of the Joint Chiefs of Staff stated clearly (April 1944) that Austria should be treated differently from Germany:

> The political aims of occupation of Austria will differ *fundamentally* from those of the occupation of Germany in that their primary purpose will be that of liberation.… The attitude to the Austrian population should be more friendly than in Germany.… you should be prepared to give more latitude to political activity in Austria than in Germany. (quoted in Leidenfrost 1986: 49; emphasis added)

Austrian independence, economic well-being, and patriotism would prevent any future take-over by Germany. The establishment of an Austrian government was anticipated at the end of a democratization process (Fellner 1972: 86).[8] Western attitudes toward an independent Austria rested on pragmatic necessity, not on ideology, while opposition to Nazi Germany had roots in principle: it was Hitler who brought the United States to Europe and to Austria.[9]

The United States differed from the other Allies because it initially emphasized removing not only the remnants of Nazism but also of "Austrofascism" from public life. This was mentioned for the first time in a State

8. Western postwar planning for Austria is discussed at length in Bischof 1990.

9. An excellent treatment of American policies toward Nazi Germany can be found in Junker 1988.

Department memorandum "The Treatment of Austria" (June 1944), which became one of the guidelines for the emerging military government (Leidenfrost 1986: 405). When John George Erhardt was nominated to become political adviser on Austrian affairs at the State Department in autumn 1944, he became the object of various lobbying efforts by Austrian exile politicians, among them the Socialist Julius Deutsch, who was credited by observers with considerably influencing the image of Austria among State Department officials (Leidenfrost 1986: 410; Beer 1992: 47). The "Provisional Handbook for Military Government in Austria" of April 1945 distinguishes between "mandatory removal categories" (that is, Nazis) and "discretionary removal categories," which were to include, among others, "fascists" (quoted in Leidenfrost 1986: 470). Fascists were defined as members or sympathizers of "totalitarian Austrian organizations" whose ideologies or programs resembled the Nazi Party in Germany or the Fascist Party in Italy. The Vaterländische Front (the only political organization allowed between 1934 and 1938) and the Heimwehr (the militia of the Christian-Social Right), two pillars of the Austrian authoritarian regime between 1934 and 1938, were explicitly mentioned. In these early stages, American planners were not content with "de-Germanizing" Austria.

But the realities of early postwar Austria—the demands of reconstruction, the necessity of cooperating with local bourgeois elements, and especially the overriding goal of denazification—made such directives irrelevant. Allied recognition of Austrian political parties and of the Renner government (October 1945), the subsequent elections in November, and growing tensions with the Soviet Union had a large impact on American policies. Austria was to be deannexed from Germany but not become dependent on the Soviet Union or dominated by Stalin. For their part, leaders of the two major parties, the People's Party (ÖVP) and the Social Democratic Party (SPÖ), saw an alliance with the United States as a main instrument for counterbalancing a perceived Soviet threat. In this way, measures dealing with the consequences of Nazi rule became part and parcel of a new global confrontation. American officials regarded Austrian reparations payments to Moscow, for example, as threats to the economic viability and independence of Austria. American policies of reeducation and denazification have to be seen in this context (Stiefel 1981: 21; Wagnleitner 1991; Rathkolb 1984: 302–25).

Most of the Allied proposals were accepted by the Austrian Parliament, but the general public never liked them. A special report on denazification written in 1948 by the director of intelligence for American forces in Austria states flatly: "Most Austrians regard the de-Nazification laws as dictated by the Allies" (quoted in Stiefel 1981: 113). Because National Socialism was, as a rule, not experienced as a foreign yoke and the discovery of Nazi atrocities did not reverse public opinion, there was no readiness for radical measures to cope with the "brown" legacy. This was the main domestic reason for the failure of denazification. At the same time, starting already in 1946, reducing Austrian dependence on the Soviet Union became more important for the Western Allies than denazification. General Clark had this to say: "The Soviets here … use de-Nazification as a means for justifying large numbers of troops in Austria, I … will not allow the Soviets to make immediate political capital of this subject…." (quoted in Rathkolb 1986: 88, 89).

This shift put radical anti-Nazi forces in Austria in the difficult position of appearing to favor Soviet power and denazification laws, both being highly unpopular options (Knight 1986: 51). From this point, the Western powers became interested in preventing the Soviet Union from using denazification as a means for intervening in Austrian affairs. Thus, the paradox occurred that the one occupying power that had initially proposed the most radical denazification measures ended up being midwife to the "fourth party," Verband der Unabhängigen (VdU), which was registered in 1949 and became a collecting point of former members of the Nazi Party (NSDAP). While American policies originally envisaged the "destruction of the Nazi-party through a total exchange of elites" (Rathkolb 1984: 305), they now granted a kind of general pardon in 1949. As Rathkolb (1984: 315) states, "The new slogan was 'Westintegration'—ideological reorientation at all cost—instead of re-education."

In short, although "reeducation" was to be implemented in the whole former Reich, it took milder forms in Austria than in Germany. Some American officials did doubt the wisdom of Austria's "special treatment." Martin Herz (1984: 132), an American diplomat in postwar Vienna, once called it a "fiction" that all Austrians were innocent. In addition, he observed: "Since as a matter of national policy we encourage a separate Austrian nationalism, we cannot be surprised, and should in fact find comfort in the fact that most Austrians deny ever having had anything to do with Germany" (Herz 1984: 132).

But Austria's special status was reiterated by the United States in October 1946, when the Truman administration declared Austria "a liberated country, comparable to the status of other liberated areas and entitled to the same treatment"(quoted in Bischof 1993: 358). Such declarations strengthened the Austrian government in its rejection of Jewish demands for reparation and restitution.[10] In 1948, the State Department confirmed that the American government "does not consider the Austrian government responsible for the acts of the Nazi regime or its representatives during the effective period of the Anschluss" (quoted in Keyserlingk 1988: 182).

10. For an extensive report on internal Austrian government deliberations on issues of Jewish interest, see Knight 1988.

Nevertheless, Jewish concerns could not be totally ignored in the United States, so a directive was given to the U.S. high commissioner in Austria in November 1950 pointing for the first time to certain obligations of Austria with respect to the victims of National Socialism. Subsequently, the United States urged Austria to negotiate with Jewish organizations. The State Department made it clear that ratification of the Austrian State Treaty would be positively influenced by satisfactory results from such negotiations (Albrich 1994: 159, 161–63). In spite of these signals, Jewish interventions with the Austrian government as a rule failed. Western priorities were clear. As Albrich (1994: 156–57) argues, "Resistance against Soviet demands for reparation and securing economic recovery and political stability for Austria prevailed over other considerations, including justified Jewish claims and Austria's moral obligations."

On Neutrality and Independence

Global considerations continued to dominate American attitudes toward Austrian affairs. After World War II the United States sought to promote Austrian independence so as not to give the Soviet Union a pretext for perpetually stationing its troops in the country. But the cold war complicated the negotiations that were to lead to the Austrian State Treaty. They became a function of superpower rivalry and did not concern Austria as a problem in its own right. The Marshall Plan had little to do with Austria's Nazi past and everything to do with the country's strategic role vis-à-vis the Soviet Union. The same could be said for the question of "German property" in Austria. United States support for nationalizing these assets was, of course, motivated neither by a sudden departure from free-enterprise ideology nor by a new evaluation of Austria's past; it reflected the American interest in preventing the Soviet Union from taking control of them.[11] Austrian politicians in this period were more interested in achieving independence than were their American counterparts. But the period after Stalin's death in 1953 provided a window of opportunity for Austria to use the idea of neutrality as a path to independence. Before 1955, the United States was highly skeptical about Austrian neutrality. As John Foster Dulles put it, "The Russians may have cooked something up acceptable to the Austrians, but not to us" (quoted in Luchak 1987: 174). Doubts were fueled by the fear that Austrian defense capabilities were insufficient to deal with a potential Soviet threat. Such insufficiency would affect NATO planning. One observer noted that

11. On American positions vis-à-vis the Austrian State Treaty and neutrality, see Rauchensteiner 1979, Stourzh 1985, Rathkolb 1988, Cronin 1986, Bischof 1992, Rathkolb 1990, and Luchak 1987.

withdrawal of occupation troops before Austria can organize, train, and equip reasonably adequate security forces would create a military vacuum in Central Europe in which the Communists ... may be expected to seize power and dominate the country, thus creating a Soviet salient in the East-West line.... the peace treaty for Austria should become effective only after the US is assured that Austrian armed forces are reasonably adequate to perform all tasks envisaged in the treaty.[12]

In addition, there was concern that a neutral Austria might create a precedent for Germany. In 1953 the National Security Council warned the administration: "Vigorously resist the neutralization of Austria as contrary to US interest, particularly as a possible precedent for a German settlement" (quoted in Rathkolb 1988: 393).

But in 1955 the advantage of seeing the departure of Soviet troops from Austria outweighed other considerations. Dulles made it clear in June 1955 that he saw neutrality as a tactical move only: "I think that one can recognize that in the case of small countries such as Austria and ... Switzerland, there is a legitimate place for independent neutrality. I do not think that the principle is a sound one for general application" (quoted in Cronin 1986: 157). The American desire to pull Austria out of the Soviet sphere of influence prevailed over other concerns like Austria's relationship to Germany or Jewish claims for reparations (Knight 1991). The United States ultimately signed the Austrian State Treaty, which dropped the clause of the Moscow Declaration (1943) that had indicated Austria's coresponsibility for the war on the side of Nazi Germany.

Austria's Image before the Waldheim Affair

Consistent with official American policy, the public image of Austria in the United States differed sharply from that of Germany. In the period before 1955, the American print media portrayed Austrians primarily as "heroes of the cold war" (Koppensteiner 1976: 133). After the departure of American troops, political interest in Austria dropped markedly, and the image of the country became more depoliticized and characterized by cultural clichés

12. Louis Johnson to Dean Acheson 1949 (quoted in Cronin 1986: 77). "By virtue of its geographical location, Austria is an important strategic link in the defense of Western and Southern Europe. Any weakening of our present military position in Austria, such as would be brought about by a substantial 'neutralization' of Austria, the creation of a military vacuum in Austria, or, as the most adverse possibility, the Communization of Austria, would have a serious impact upon the entire NATO defense concept. Therefore, maintenance of the status quo would be preferable to acceptance of a treaty which would deny the United States its security objectives with respect to Austria" (General Staff to Ministry of Defence 1953; quoted in Cronin 1986: 122).

relating to *The Sound of Music*. While Austria appeared as the "Disneyland of Europe" (Koppensteiner 1976: 135), there was still an undercurrent that drew attention to remnants of its Nazi past, for example, antisemitic incidents and acquittals of war criminals.[13]

These issues were taken up once again with the election of Bruno Kreisky in 1970.[14] Some considered it remarkable that a politician of Jewish extraction won the sympathies of so many Austrians; others criticized Kreisky's conciliatory gestures with respect to former Nazis (Koppensteiner 1976: 137).[15] Kreisky's controversial Middle East policies proved a backdoor for opening up the "undercurrent" once again. It appeared that Kreisky was "appeasing" terrorists, for example, in the Schönau incident, by putting obstacles in the way of Jewish emigrants from the Soviet Union to Israel, which led to accusations of "Jewish self-hatred" and similar invectives.[16] But the Schönau incident also provided an occasion for remembering the Anschluss, wartime collaboration, acquittals of former Nazis, and the absence of restitution for Jews (Wechsberg 1973). While there does not seem to be a direct connection between resentment against Bruno Kreisky and the Waldheim affair, Austria's Middle East policies might have contributed to a politically negative image of Austria in the United States, especially among Jewish Americans. Compared to Waldheim, of course, Kreisky was much less identified with Austria as a whole. At the end of Kreisky's chancellorship, Peter Marboe, then director of the Austrian Cultural Institute in New York, noted that problems of image in the United States continued to be of major concern ("Österreich-USA. Zuviel Schmuserei?" 1983). He summarized the issue by observing that Americans lacked knowledge of Austria, that kitsch remained a central component of the American image of Austria, that Americans insufficiently distinguished Austria from Germany and did not recognize sufficiently that Austria belonged to the West, and that the image of Austria suffered from the presence of "shadows of the past."

A further deterioration in image occurred in 1984 and 1985 with the scandal surrounding the handshake between then Minister of Defense Friedhelm Frischenschlager and released Nazi war criminal Walter Reder, which reanimated traditional clichés about Austria. Because of its later role in the Waldheim affair, it is significant that the World Jewish Congress (WJC) held for the first time since 1945 its annual meeting in Vienna during the

---

13. See, for example, *Atlantic Monthly*, 1 February 1968.

14. The Kreisky period is dealt with in Luchak 1987, Bunzl 1991, Petritsch 1987, Rathkolb 1994, Karmasin 1987, and Marboe 1984.

15. See, for example, *Time*, 16 March 1970.

16. In 1973 Arab terrorists kidnapped Soviet Jewish emigrants on the Austrian-Czech border and demanded the closure of the Schönau transit camp. Kreisky apparently gave in to the demands but provided other facilities for emigrants instead.

controversy over this notorious handshake (*New York Times*, 25 January, 28 January, and 30 January 1985; Pauley 1992). Karmasin (1987: 105) noted in a study on Austria's image abroad that even before the Waldheim affair, Austria's problematic past was more present in the American media than in the media of other countries such as Germany.

The Waldheim Shock

The Waldheim affair differed not only in its scope but also because all of Austria became identified with its elected president. The "defiant, xenophobic" (Deming and Seward 1986) reaction of Austria's public to the charges from abroad contributed to this perception. But more important were domestic developments in the United States itself, namely, the increased awareness and presence of the Holocaust in the public consciousness. Together, these intensified the impact of the affair and contributed to the unprecedented decline and radical shift in Austria's image in the United States. Some questioned the legitimacy of the Moscow Declaration, which in addition to assigning coresponsibility to Austria for the war also declared Austria to be a victim of Nazi aggression.[17] Many compared Waldheim unfavorably with German President Weizsäcker and reversed the post-1945 images of Austria and Germany. While Germany had traditionally been associated with its Nazi past, it was now lauded for how it was dealing with this terrible heritage (see, for example, *New York Times* 1986). This theme was repeated in commentary during commemorations in Austria of the fiftieth anniversary of the Anschluss. These observers accused the Allies of allowing Austrians to get away with their refusal to accept common responsibility with their German partners in Nazi crimes. While Germans became pariahs, Austrians appeared as aristocratic anti-Nazis. One writer noted that "for every person who knows something of the reality of recent Austrian history a million have seen *The Sound of Music*" (Wheatcroft 1988). He claimed that Austrian identity was "artificial" and could be shaken by an eventual German reunification and increasing German hegemony in Europe.

The Jewish-American Dimension

Holocaust awareness proved more central, of course, for Jewish Americans than for the general public. While there might have been differences of opinion between the WJC and other organizations (Avineri 1987), the Waldheim affair became a rallying point for the entire Jewish community in the United

17. See, for example, Lewis 1986 and Craig 1986.

States. It is important to understand that Waldheim, and to a lesser extent all of Austria, soon became symbols that developed a dynamic of their own. The visit of Pope John Paul II to San Francisco in 1987 provides a case in point. Waldheim was in no way directly involved with this event, but his recent meeting with the pope in Rome caused a major argument in the context of the latter's San Francisco visit (Hertzberg 1987). At stake was nothing less than the role of Christianity in the history of antisemitism, including the Holocaust; as a result, it became a key event for defining Christian-Jewish relations. The Jewish community in San Francisco hotly debated whether one of its representatives should meet the pope. Within this debate the reception of Waldheim in the Vatican acquired a highly symbolic significance:

> In Jewish eyes Waldheim represented the quintessential unrepentant Nazi who denied his role in the greatest crime in human history and contended that he "only did his duty". By receiving and appearing to condone him, the Pope conjured up associations for Jews of the perceived silence of Pope Pius XII during World War II toward Nazi war crimes. In brief then, the Waldheim affair seemed to many Jews to be a *symbolic reenactment* of events nearly half a century ago. (Biale and Rosenbaum 1990: 261; emphasis added)

Why did a European event of half a century ago acquire such topicality in the United States at this time? The issue is, of course, complicated and can be dealt with only briefly here. Several factors seem to have been at play. As traditional religious elements of Jewish identity had lost much of their significance and the integrity of Israel as a state seemed to be less threatened, the Holocaust remained the single most emotional issue touching American Jews. In the growing climate of ethnic militancy in the United States, the past suffering of Jews in the Holocaust became a powerful motive for mobilizing Jews; central to this were notions of victimization. Because of the social, cultural, and political status of the Jewish community in the United States, Jewish concerns became Americanized and the Holocaust became a national issue. This found expression in increased efforts to investigate alleged Nazi criminals residing in the United States and the promulgation of special laws for this purpose; in public remembrances, museums, exhibitions; in films like *Schindler's List* on the Holocaust theme; and in efforts to politicize the Holocaust by exploiting Holocaust-related sentiments. It is in this context that the election of Kurt Waldheim as Austrian president was transformed into an emotionally heated international affair.

After Waldheim

The transformations in Central and Eastern Europe, including the unification of Germany, eventually overtook the Waldheim affair. The amount of attention devoted to it and perspectives on Austria changed accordingly. The heavy focus on Waldheim and Austria had been due to developments in the United States and to the extraordinary prominence of the former UN secretary general and his election in Austria, which proved to be a unique combination of circumstances.

Not surprisingly, traditional clichés about Austria returned (Koppensteiner 1991; Prader 1995). Yet Austria's image did not remain unaffected by the events of 1989, especially the unification of Germany. German reunification was supported by the Bush administration, but the public at large and especially the American media were less enthusiastic (Jarausch 1994; James and Stone 1992). Even some former public officials like Alexander Haig (1990) found it appropriate to warn of a new "Reich": "No one fears the Germany of good times, the Germany of Helmut Kohl. It is the Germany of bad times ... that rattles the skeletons of history." *Time* ran a story entitled "The New Germany Flexes Its Muscles" (Jackson 1992). With regard to the former Yugoslavia and negotiations for enlarging the EU, reports used terms such as "forcing," "elbowing," and "muscling" to describe German behavior (Schölgen 1992). In promoting Austrian entry into the EU, "German diplomats twisted arms mercilessly" (Jakobson 1994). In a word, the "resurgence of Teutonic arrogance" occupied sections of the American media. In part, this discourse may have reflected the disappearance of the traditional Soviet enemy and the search for substitutes. Perhaps understandably, those chosen—Germany and Japan—represented the enemies of half a century ago. Nazism proved to be a useful counterimage to the American dream, a role that is now being filled by the Islamic world. Xenophobic outrages in Germany fit well into this scenario and offered an occasion to contrast the German ethnic concept of nation with the American model (Pfaff 1992; Rosenthal 1992).

The implications of German reunification for Austria did not constitute a major preoccupation for American observers, but some remarks deserve to be mentioned. Michael Z. Wise (1990) noted that the transformations in Eastern Europe would decrease the significance of Austria's neutrality. He argued that German reunification elicited "little response" in Austria and its long-term ramification need not cause concern because neutrality had contributed to "Austria's postwar sense of separateness from Germany." Only a few public officials discussed Austria in the context of German unification. Senator Claiborne Pell, chairman of the Senate Foreign Relations Committee, thought that in talking about the unity of the German people "one could include Austria"; consequently, "one should examine very carefully what Germans mean by 'German re-unification'" (Federal News Service, 11 December 1989; see also Ferraud 1990).

Several commentators were of the opinion that Austria's entry into the European Union would "augment German clout in Europe" (Kaplan 1990) because of "Austria's strong trade and cultural ties to Germany" ("Cold War's End Leaves Austria Seeking a Role in the New Europe" 1990). Although he recognized that most Austrians did not identify with or as Germans, Wise (1992) predicted an identity crisis. Of greater concern seemed to be the emergence of ethnic concepts of nation associated with the German tradition. Thus *Time* worried that the German concept of *Sprachraum* (the German-speaking world) would "include more than a hundred million people in Germany and potential EC-member states Austria and Switzerland plus millions more in Eastern Europe whose main second language is German" (Jackson 1992). Other observers such as William Pfaff (1993a,b) contrasted the "German," "ethnic" concept of nation with the multinational tradition of the Habsburg monarchy: "To be Austrian in the past was not a nationality but citizenship.... The essential point is that nationality is cultural but that citizenship has to be secular, unconnected to real or imagined ethnic identity."

These and similar comments are very much influenced by values within American society, which can be seen especially in commentary on xenophobia in Central Europe. Austria's anti-immigrant attitudes are mostly associated with the right-wing Freedom Party (FPÖ) led by Jörg Haider. What makes this association particularly interesting is the German national tradition of Haider's movement. Marc Fisher (1990) observed that "Haider preaches cultural Germanism, talking of Austrians as a part of the greater German Volk." Another commentator (Tempest 1990) noted that antiforeigner agitation in Austria was specifically directed against "non-germanic newcomers."

The Future

The rise of Jörg Haider within the Austrian political landscape h some reaction in the American media. Official American support i trian independence and recognition of the country's vital role in Cen. Europe, especially with respect to the former Yugoslavia, seem assured.[18] B a few comments in the American media allude to the end of political stabi ity in Austria for the first time in half a century. This concern is usuall linked to the rise of Haider as "a far-right nationalist who has run on a anti-foreigner, anti-Europe and 'pro-German culture' platform ... [and wh is considered] ... Europe's strongest far-right leader" (Dornberg 1995; see also Kirschbaum 1995).

18. See, for example, the visits of President Klestil (October 1995) and Chancellor Vranitzky (November 1995) to the United States. For a critical American view of Austrian policies in the former Yugoslavia, see Lewis 1995.

It is highly questionable whether the rise of this leader to an official position of power (a goal he set for himself to happen by 1998) would cause similar consequences for American-Austrian relations as the election of Waldheim as president. The former secretary general of the UN was a well-known figure in the United States, while it is not likely that many people have heard about Haider, in spite of his attempts to contact and imitate former Speaker of the House Newt Gingrich (Janncsy 1995; Seifert 1995). Still, Haider's ascent to power would be enough to cause some irritation and some reconsideration of American policies toward Austria.

References

Albrich, T. 1994. "'Es gibt keine jüdische Frage'. Zur Aufrechterhaltung des österreichischen Opfermythos." In *Der Umgang mit dem Holocaust. Europa – USA – Israel*, ed. R. Steininger, 147–66. Vienna.

Avineri, S. 1987. "The Waldheim Affair: How the WJC Blew It." *Present Tense*, May–June.

Bailey, T. A. 1946. *Diplomatic History of the American People.* New York.

Beer, S. 1992. "Exile between Assimilation and Re-identification: The Austrian Political Immigration to the USA, 1938–1945." In *The European Immigrant Experience in the USA*, ed. W. Hölbling and R. Wagnleitner, 39–50. Tübingen.

Biale, D., and F. Rosenbaum. 1990. "The Pope Comes to San Francisco: An Anatomy of Jewish Communal Response to a Political Crisis." In *American Pluralism and the Jewish Community*, ed. S. M. Lipset, 234–62. New Brunswick.

Bischof, G. 1990. "Between Responsibility and Rehabilitation: Austria in International Politics, 1940–1950." Ph.D. diss., Harvard University.

_____. 1992. "The Western Powers and Austrian Neutrality, 1953–1955." *Mitteilungen des österreichischen Staatsarchivs* 42:368–93

_____. 1993. "Die Instrumentalisierung der Moskauer Erklärung nach dem Zweiten Weltkrieg." *Zeitgeschichte* 20, no. 11/12:345–66.

Bunzl, J. 1991. *Gewalt ohne Grenzen. Nahostterror und Österreich.* Vienna.

Clough, N. P. 1933. *Beiträge zur Beurteilung der österreichischen Anschlußfrage in der öffentlichen Meinung der Vereinigten Staaten von Nordamerika.* Heidelberg.

"Cold War's End Leaves Austria Seeking a Role in the New Europe." 1990. *New York Times*, 11 August.

Craig, G. A. 1986. "The Waldheim File." *New York Review of Books*, 9 October.

Cronin, A. K. 1986. *Great Power Politics and the Struggle over Austria, 1945–1955.* Ithaca.

Deming, A., and D. Seward. 1986. "Austria's Show of Support: Defiant Voters Rally to Waldheim's Defense." *Newsweek*, 14 April.

Dornberg, J. 1995. "Coalition Collapse Signals New Order: Far-Right Freedom Party Emerges as Real Winner in Big Upheaval." *International Herald Tribune*, 25 October.

Eppel, P. 1992. "Exiled Austrians in the USA, 1938–1945: Immigration, Exile, Re-emigration, No Invitation to Return." In *The European Immigrant Experience in the USA*, ed. W. Hölbling and R. Wagnleitner, 25–37. Tübingen.

Fellner, F. 1972. "Die außenpolitische und völkerrechtliche Situation Österreichs 1938. Österreichs Wiederherstellung als Kriegsziel der Alliierten." In *Österreich. Die Zweite Republik*, vol. 1, ed. E. Weinzierl and K. Skalnik, 53–90. Graz.

Ferraud, P. 1990. "The Dubious Drive toward German Reunification …" *Chicago Tribune*, 23 February.

Fisher, M. 1990. "Europe's Upheaval Prompts Austria to Reassess Neutrality and Lean to West." *Washington Post*, 13 July.

Goldner, F. 1977. *Die österreichische Emigration 1938–1945*. Vienna.

Haig, A. M. 1990. "An Alliance for All Europe." *New York Times*, 18 January.

Hausmann, A. 1972. *Die amerikanische Außenpolitik und die Entstehung der österreichischen Republik 1917–1919*. Ph.D. diss., University of Vienna.

Hertzberg, A. 1987. "Waldheim's Vatican Visit: Jews Feel 'Burning Outrage.'" *International Herald Tribune*, 23 June.

Herz, M. F. 1984. *Understanding Austria: The Political Reports and Analyses of Martin F. Herz, Political Officer of the US Legation in Vienna, 1945–1948*. Ed. R. Wagnleitner. Salzburg.

Hofer, S. 1931. *Die Anschlußfrage und die internationale Presse*. Vienna.

Jackson, J. O. 1992. "The New Germany Flexes Its Muscles." *Time*, 13 April.

Jakobson, M. 1994. "Join Germany's Effort to Widen Europe." *International Herald Tribune*, 24 May.

James, H., and M. Stone. 1992. *When the Wall Came Down: Reactions to German Reunification*. London.

Janncsy, I. 1995. "Ein kleiner Österreicher. F-Obmann Jörg Haider auf großer Aufklärungsfahrt in Amerika." *Profil*, 22 May.

Jarausch, K. H. 1994. *The Rush to German Unity*. New York.

Jones, M. A. 1960. *American Immigration*. Chicago.

Junker, D. 1988. *Kampf um die Weltmacht. Die USA und das Dritte Reich 1933–1945*. Düsseldorf.

Kaplan, R. D. 1990. "Austria—Second Try: Austria has Faced—and Overcome—Many of the Challenges that Now Face Eastern Europe." *Atlantic Monthly*, September.

Karmasin, F. 1987. *Das Bild Österreichs in ausländischen Medien 1965–1986*. Vienna.

Keyserlingk, R. H. 1988. *Austria in World War II: An Anglo-American Dilemma*. Kingston.

Kirschbaum, E. 1995. "Haider Eyes Pinnacle of Power." *International Herald Tribune*, 25 October.

Knight, R. 1986. *Kalter Krieg, Entnazifizierung und Österreich*. In *Verdrängte Schuld, verfehlte Sühne. Entnazifizierung in Österreich 1945–1955*, ed. S. Meissl, K.-D. Mulley, and O. Rathkolb, 37–51. Vienna.

_____. 1988. "Ich bin dafür, die Sache in die Länge zu ziehen." *Wortprotokolle der österreichischen Bundesregierung von 1945–1952 über die Entschädigung der Juden.* Frankfurt.

_____. 1991. "Restitution and Legitimacy in Post-war Austria, 1945–1953." *Year Book* (Leo Baeck Institute) 36:413–41.

Koppensteiner, J. 1976. "Das Bild Österreichs in amerikanischen Nachrichten-magazinen." *Zeitgeschichte* 2:129–39.

_____. 1991. "'Wohlwollende Klischees': Das Österreichbild amerikanischer Deutschlehrer/innen." *Zielsprache Deutsch* 22, no. 3:168–75.

Leidenfrost, J. 1986. "Die amerikanische Besatzungsmacht und der Wiederbeginn des politischen Lebens in Österreich 1944–1947." Ph.D. diss., University of Vienna.

Lewis, F. 1986. "Austrians Will Choose an Image." *International Herald Tribune,* 25 April.

_____. 1995. "Austria: Its Role in Europe and the Balkan War." *International Herald Tribune,* 16 June.

Low, A. D. 1985. *The Anschluss Movement 1931–1938 and the Great Powers.* New York.

Luchak, J. M. 1987. "Die amerikanisch-österreichischen Beziehungen von 1955–1985. Neutralität und Ost-West-Konflikt." Ph.D. diss., University of Vienna.

Mamatey, V. S. 1957. *The US and East Central Europe, 1914–1918.* Princeton.

Marboe, P. 1984. "Kreisky, Ghadafi und die Mozartkugeln. Österreichs Bild im Spiegel amerikanischer Medien." *Die Presse,* 26–27 August.

Matsch, E. 1990. *Wien – Washington. Ein Journal diplomatischer Beziehungen 1838–1917.* Vienna.

McClelland, C. E. 1987. "President Wilson and the Austro-Hungarian Monar-chy." In *From Wilson to Waldheim,* ed. P. Pabisch, 33–51. Riverside, Calif.

Meysels, L. O. 1960. "Die politischen Beziehungen zwischen den Vereinigten Staaten und Österreich 1933–1938." Ph.D. diss., University of Vienna.

Mikovits, M. 1992. *Die jüdische Emigration von Österreich nach Amerika zwischen März 1938 und September 1939.* Master's thesis, University of Vienna.

Mitten, R. 1993. "The Eyes of the Beholder: Allied Wartime Attitudes and the Delimiting of the 'Jewish Question' for Post-War Austria." Vienna. Manuscript.

New York Times. 1986. "President of Austria." Editorial, 11 June.

"Österreich-USA. Zuviel Schmuserei?" 1983. *Profil,* 31 January.

Pauley, B. F. 1992. "The USA and the Jewish Question in Austria." *Year Book* (Leo Baeck Institute) 37:481–96.

Petritsch, W. 1987. "Die österreichisch-amerikanischen Beziehungen in der Ära Kreisky (1970–1983)." In *From Wilson to Waldheim,* ed. P. Pabisch, 239–56. Riverside, Calif.

Pfaff, W. 1992. "The German Question Poses a European Question." *International Herald Tribune,* 3 September.

_____. 1993a. "Not All News from Central Europe Is Bleak." *International Herald Tribune,* 30–31 January.

_____. 1993b. "Revive Secular Citizenship above 'Ethnic' Nationality." *International Herald Tribune,* 20 July.

Prader, J. 1995. "The Image of Austria." In *The Sound of Austria. Österreichpolitik und öffentliche Meinung in den USA*, ed. J. Bunzl, W. Hircy, and J. Vansant, 99–110 (Vienna). First published in *Austrian Information* 45, no. 10 (1992):3–6.

Pucher, W. 1980. "Die Beziehungen Österreichs zu den USA 1918–1932." Ph.D. diss., University of Vienna.

Rathkolb, O. 1984. "US-Entnazifizierung in Österreich zwischen kontrollierter Revolution und Elitenrestauration (1945–1949)." *Zeitgeschichte* 12, no. 9/10:302–25.

_____. 1986. "NS-Problem und politische Restauration: Vorgeschichte und Etablierung." In *Verdrängte Schuld, verfehlte Sühne. Entnazifizierung in Österreich 1945–1955*, ed. S. Meissl, K.-D. Mulley, and O. Rathkolb, 73–99. Vienna.

_____. 1988. "Von der Besatzung zur Neutralität." In *Die bevormundete Nation: Österreich und die Alliierten 1945–1949*, ed. G. Bischof and J. Leidenfrost, 371–405. Innsbruck.

_____. 1990. "Historische Bewährungsproben des Neutralitätsgesetzes 1955. Am Beispiel der US-amerikanischen Österreich-Politik 1955–1959." In *Verfassung. Juristisch- politische und sozialwissenschaftliche Beiträge anläßlich des 70-Jahr-Jubiläums des Bundesverfassungsgesetzes*, ed. N. Dimmel and A.-J. Noll, 122–41. Vienna.

_____. 1994. "Bruno Kreisky: Perspectives of Top Level US Foreign Policy Makers, 1959–1983." In *The Kreisky Era in Austria*, ed. G. Bischof and A. Pelinka, 130–51. New Brunswick.

Rauchensteiner, M. 1979. *Der Sonderfall. Die Besatzungszeit in Österreich 1945–1955*. Graz.

Rosenthal, A. M. 1992. "Germany Is Everyone's Business." *International Herald Tribune*, 23 September.

Schmid, G. E. 1968. "Die amerikanische Österreich-Politik zur Zeit der Pariser Friedenskonferenz." Ph.D. diss., University of Salzburg.

Schölgen, G. 1992. "Deutschlands neue Lage. Die USA, die BRD und die Zukunft des westlichen Bündnisses." *Europa Archiv Folge* 2:125–32.

Schwegel, H. 1904. "Die Einwanderung in die Vereinigten Staaten von Amerika mit besonderer Rücksicht auf die österreichisch-ungarische Auswanderung." *Zeitschrift für Volkswirtschaft, Sozialpolitik und Verwaltung* 13:161–207.

Seifert, T. 1995. "Lehrbub Haider." *Falter*, 31 May.

Slosson, P. W. 1930. "America and the Anschluss Question." In *Die Anschlußfrage*, ed. F. Kleinwächter and H. von Paller, 194–97. Vienna.

Spaulding, E. W. 1968. *The Quiet Invaders: The Story of the Austrian Impact upon America*. Vienna.

Stiefel, D. 1981. *Entnazifizierung in Österreich*. Vienna.

Stourzh, G. 1985. *Geschichte des Staatsvertrages 1945–1955. Österreichs Weg zur Neutralität*. Vienna.

Tempest, R. 1990. "What, Vienna Becoming Chicago? Crime, Foreigners Are Voter Issues." *Los Angeles Times*, 4 October.

Wagnleitner, R. 1991. *Coca-Colonisation und Kalter Krieg. Die Kulturmission der USA in Österreich nach dem Zweiten Weltkrieg.* Vienna.

Wechsberg, J. 1973. "Letter from Vienna." *New Yorker,* 10 December.

Wheatcroft, G. 1988. "Absurd Reich." *New Republic,* 28 March.

Wimmer, A. 1992. "'Expelled and Banished', The Exile Experience of Austrian 'Anschluss' Victims in Personal Histories and Literary Documents." In *The European Immigrant Experience in the USA,* ed. W. Hölbling and R. Wagnleitner, 51–72. Tübingen.

Wise, M. Z. 1990. "Austria at a Crossroad amid East Bloc Upheaval. Neutral State Long Viewed as Bridge between East and West, Faces Calls to Redefine Role." *Washington Post,* 6 March.

_____. 1992. "Austria's Identity Crisis: Country Battles Cultural 'Colonization' by Germany." *Washington Post,* 26 February.

Wittke, C. 1952. *Refugees of Revolution: The German Forty-Eighters in America.* Philadelphia.

Zelter, R. 1961. "Die Politik des Präsidenten Wilson im Spiegel der österreichischen diplomatischen Berichte 1912–1917." Ph.D. diss., University of Vienna.

Chapter 2

BRUNO KREISKY'S PERCEPTIONS OF THE UNITED STATES

Oliver Rathkolb

Strongly pro-Western in sentiment … not entirely uncritical …

— *John W. Fisher (1959: 7–8) on Bruno Kreisky*

Introduction

Immediately after Bruno Kreisky became Austrian foreign minister in 1959, the first secretary of the U.S. Embassy in Austria, John W. Fisher, produced a ten-page biographical report focusing on the ambivalence of Kreisky as both a "convinced anti-Communist" and a person "not always sympathetic with American policies to cope with that threat" (Fisher 1959: 8–9). My chapter provides a deeper analysis of Fisher's view of Kreisky that stands in contrast not only to overtly polemical views (Khol 1993: 6–11) but also to the interpretations of historians who neglect more subtle evaluations and sum up Kreisky's foreign policy as "anti-Americanism."[1]

---

1. For example, Michael Gehler (1995: 238) focuses on the allegedly anti-American Middle East policies of Chancellor Kreisky. I have countered this by analyzing the political relationship of the Austrian chancellor with American presidents from Nixon to Reagan in Rathkolb 1994. For a broad introduction to the subject of Kreisky and American-Austrian relations, see Mussi 1983. General biographical details in English can be found in Secher 1993.

The Ideological Roots

As a young socialist, Bruno Kreisky certainly was influenced by Austro-Marxism and especially Otto Bauer's ideological views, although he seemed to lean more toward the kind of political pragmatism advocated by Karl Renner and the right wing of the Social Democratic Party (see Kreisky 1991 and 1986: 149–60, 220–32). Together with Max Adler this "school of socialist theoreticians tried to apply Marxist methods to dominant and urgent problems of the time" and produced the ideological framework used by Kreisky in the interwar period (Kreisky 1986: 149). Even as a pragmatic but visionary chancellor in the 1970s and early 1980s he formulated domestic policies through these ideological perceptions. From the very beginning he was a strict anticommunist and tried to agitate against communist youth functionaries by using the writings of Lenin and other communist theoreticians as arguments against Stalinism.

Reading always played an important role in his political work and certainly shaped part of his perceptions of the United States. When Kreisky was imprisoned during the Schuschnigg dictatorship, he kept a prison diary, which reflected his impressions from his readings at the time (Kreisky 1935–36). Like many of his Social Democratic "comrades," Kreisky was impressed by the sociocritical works of Sinclair Lewis (especially *Babbitt*), John Dos Passos, Jack London, and Upton Sinclair (especially *Jimmy Higgins*) (Kreisky 1986: 76–77; Pfoser 1980: 155–58). He was also fascinated by Agnes Smedley's novel *Daughter of Earth*, which focused on the story of an American woman, the daughter of a farmer, who fought for the civil rights of women from a socialist point of view. Kreisky did not mention authors and titles in his prison diary since he feared that the "revolutionary" book might be confiscated. His diary perfectly expresses many of his political ideas that were suppressed by the state and provides evidence for the reduced role of intellectuals within the workers' movement.

After Kreisky was imprisoned again in 1938 and forced by the Nazi secret police to leave Austria, he moved to Sweden. As an émigré activist and later as president of the Austrian Association in Sweden, he held numerous meetings with American officials from the embassy in Stockholm. In 1941, he even thought about emigrating to the United States but stayed in Sweden primarily because he did not have the papers he needed to obtain a visa.[2] Swedish friends and Swedish books about America, like Gunnar Myrdal's *An American Dilemma* and Alva Myrdal's *Kontakt mit Amerika*, both published in 1944, shaped his views.

Kreisky was well informed about the social and racial conflicts within American society. At the same time, he was convinced that the inner strength

2. For more details, including American documents, see Rathkolb and Etzersdorfer 1985.

of American democratic institutions and society would overcome these conflicts. He was very impressed that the United States lifted the restrictive quotas on immigration to take in refugees from Europe fleeing the Nazi terror and that these refugees were integrated into American society and accepted as full citizens.

Containment, the Marshall Plan, and the Limits of the Cold War

Due to a restrictive military policy that did not permit remigration, Kreisky was forced to use a French connection to travel to Vienna in 1946. Yet he was already convinced by that time that the United States was the only power capable of defending Europe against communism. In his numerous talks with Americans, he emphasized that the policy of containment (as advocated by President Harry S. Truman, George F. Kennan, and Dean Acheson) was "extremely successful despite its defensive character" (Kreisky 1985: 5) and that the Marshall Plan fostered the economic revival of Western Europe and limited the political influence of communist parties in France and Italy (Kreisky 1984).

Like many other Austrian Social Democrats and trade-union leaders, Kreisky believed that the most convincing pro-American argument was to point to the success of the European Recovery Program (ERP). In his opinion, the Marshall Plan not only saved Western Europe after 1947 and hindered further communist take-overs but also served as the perfect model for large-scale economic solidarity programs with developing countries. As early as 1958, he referred in a speech at a congress of the Socialist Party of Austria to the "grandiose act of international solidarity in the form of the Marshall Plan and I want to state that we will soon have to be prepared for an even bigger act of grandiose international solidarity" (quoted in Haselbach 1981: 3).

Apparently Kreisky did not take part in the debate within the ideological left wing of the Socialist Party on a "third way" between Soviet-style communism and Anglo-American capitalism (see Gärtner 1985). He referred to Otto Bauer's proposals for large-scale assistance to overcome the economic depression in 1931 by granting Germany international loans for industrial infrastructure to emphasize the theoretical high standing of the Marshall Plan even within Austro-Marxism (Kreisky 1980a: 55). When Kreisky returned to Austria in 1950, his closest political friend was the important trade-union leader Franz Olah, who also represented this new pro-American stream within the party and the trade-union movement. Whereas Olah tried to strengthen his personal power base by establishing an undercover guerrilla army with CIA money (Konrad and Lechner 1992; Svoboda 1990; Olah 1995), Kreisky did not leave the democratic track.

The First Signs of an Austrian *Ostpolitik* and Small-Scale Détente Efforts

Kreisky's first major disagreement with American foreign policy reflected his general views as the undersecretary of state for foreign affairs after the death of Stalin in 1953. Kreisky believed that the Soviet leadership was prepared to take action on certain disputed East-West issues, including solving the Austrian problem and bringing an end to the Allied administration of Austria. But U.S. Secretary of State John Foster Dulles, like Soviet Foreign Minister Molotov, blocked an Austrian solution at a conference in Berlin in 1954.[3] Kreisky tried to convince Dulles that the concept of Swiss neutrality articulated by the secretary of state as a model for an Austrian solution was much narrower in terms of Western integration than the Austrian proposals concerning *Koalitions- oder Allianzfreiheit* (freedom from coalitions and alliances).

> Dr. Kreisky intervened to say that Switzerland is more neutral than Austria should be, as Austria wishes to join the UN, Council of Europe, and other such organizations. The Secretary said that Article 4 bis may prove the most important bargaining point and should be saved for the end if it is to be taken up at all. (U.S. Department of State 1986: 1132)

Kreisky remained adamant and tried to persuade Dulles to accept a binding neutrality declaration in exchange for a Soviet troop withdrawal:

> The Secretary suggested that if that unlikely point is reached, Dr. Figl should ask for a recess to permit consultation with the three powers, in accordance with his instructions. He went on to point out the dangers and disadvantages for Austria in staying out of collective security arrangements and becoming a vacuum, stressing the importance of raising an Austrian Army. He noted that Austria could become an inviting invasion route to the South comparable to Belgium in 1914. He reiterated that the US would not wish to stand in the way of an Austrian policy in favor of military neutrality, but said that the cost to Austria would be heavier and that the Western Powers and, he supposed, the Austrian Government would not wish to leave a vacuum in Austria. (U.S. Department of State 1986: 1133)

During these meetings with John Foster Dulles in Berlin, Kreisky developed Austrian-centered ideas of limited détente in the East-West relationship. These included liberalizing Western "economic warfare" against the

---

3. For details concerning Molotov's opposition to Khrushchev's and Malenkov's efforts to solve the Austrian question, see Zubok 1996.

Eastern bloc, which involved compiling special lists to prevent technology and strategic transfers into the communist orbit. Dulles immediately rejected these proposals.

Despite these differences on how far Austria should open up toward the Soviet Union, American diplomats considered Kreisky to be a reliable pro-Western politician of high caliber. Especially in March and April 1955, when Molotov had invited a high-level Austrian delegation to fly to Moscow and hold negotiations on a direct, bilateral level concerning the Austrian State Treaty, the channel of communication between U.S. Ambassador Llewellyn Thompson and Kreisky became important for the United States:

> Kreisky is probably most intelligent member of Austrian Govt concerned in foreign affairs and is completely pro-Western. He has been influenced however by his long service in Sweden (he has a Swedish wife) and he naturally has a strong interest in securing Austria's independence and is naturally intrigued by possibility of protecting Austria from being squeezed to death in a great power struggle. He will of course inform Schaerf of gist of this conversation and I was perhaps indiscreet in going so far but it seemed most dangerous to me in view of his increasing influence to let him go to Moscow with serious misconceptions regarding our point of view. Incidentally Kreisky states Schaerf completely sceptical possibility anything constructive be accomplished in Moscow. (Thompson 1955b: 25)

Like Adolf Schärf, Kreisky was considered the "Western" component in the Austrian delegation in Moscow even though he feared rumors that the American military was more interested in keeping Austria under occupation than was the Soviet Union. Thompson tried to counter this argument since "we were far more interested, so far as Austria was concerned, in cold war than in a hot war, particularly in these days of atomic bombs and modern communications" (Thompson 1955b: 25).

Between the 1930s and the late 1950s, Kreisky's cultural views concerning the United States were dominated by a very strong pro-British sentiment, which seemed to weaken appreciably during the 1960s, when Kreisky spent considerable time in America giving lectures and meeting politicians (Thalberg 1984: 288–89). Very early on, he used public-relations techniques typical of American politics, and as foreign minister, he hired a PR man, Carleton Smith. Smith organized highly successful lecture tours. Former President Truman attended one of Kreisky's lectures, and his 1963 tour ended in a special appointment with President Kennedy.

Kreisky's pro-American sentiments, however, vanished immediately whenever Austrian national interests were endangered. He had been the only politician opposed to the carte blanche signing of the so-called Vienna memorandum, which in the final phase of the Austrian State Treaty negotiations accepted all restitution claims of American and British oil firms despite their questionable legality. American diplomats reported that Kreisky was "slightly annoyed with the West" (Thompson 1955a: 1). Later in the decade, the issue of extensive "oil claims" continued to be a major problem for the then Foreign Minister Kreisky because the United States had blocked billions of schillings from the Counterpart Funds left over from the Marshall Plan in order to pressure the Austrians to give in on them (Bundesministerium für Auswärtige Angelegenheiten 1959: 2ff.). Kreisky even accused the American government of pursuing "gunboat diplomacy in Central Europe" (quoted in Fuchs 1959).

The Policy of Flexible Anticommunism Advocating Détente and Ideological Confrontation

It became obvious after 1955 that Kreisky had accepted the major role of the United States in the policy of containment and in the Marshall Plan, which aimed at limiting communist influence in Europe. Yet contrary to the general foreign-policy goals of the Eisenhower administration and the view of Secretary of State Dulles, Kreisky believed that "the policy of détente ... came into existence" as "the attempt of Khrushchev ... not only to revise the Stalinist domestic policy, but the foreign policy as well" (Kreisky 1985: 5).

After the mid-1950s, Kreisky continued to believe in the possibility of increasing détente through confidence-building measures and permanent negotiations without, however, ignoring overarching ideological differences and conflicts. Kreisky's geopolitical stance was a central pillar of Austria's foreign policy as a small state between the two superpower blocs. Neither Dulles nor the State Department considered it appropriate for Austria to play such a role. The "Austrian example," which involved the peaceful deescalation of a limited East-West conflict, was not to be copied again. Kreisky was not successful in convincing top-ranking members of the State Department to join in the policy of establishing good relations with the small states in the Eastern bloc, especially with Austria's immediate neighbors such as Hungary (Bundesministerium für Auswärtige Angelegenheiten 1959: 10–11). From Washington's perspective, the Eastern bloc, with the exception of Yugoslavia, was monolithic and tightly controlled by the Soviet Union. Today we know that this simplistic view of cold-war geopolitics did not correspond with reality, although it is true that many communist hard-liners were to be found in the satellite countries, as the case of East Germany demonstrates very well.

The ambiguity of Kreisky's pro-Western, strictly anticommunist stance and his efforts in mediating the East-West conflict surfaced especially on the occasion of the Seventh World Youth Festival for Peace and Friendship in early 1959. In May 1958, after Chancellor Julius Raab had agreed to organize the Youth Festival in Vienna, Kreisky developed a plan for a counterfestival that would demonstrate the pro-Western ideological orientation of Austria. Dominated by communist youth organizations, the youth festival was to bring fifteen thousand young people to Austria (Rauchensteiner 1987: 410). Raab wanted to demonstrate goodwill vis-à-vis Moscow, but Kreisky thought that in the absence of public opposition the festival would be perceived as another sign that Austria was drifting toward procommunist nonalignment rather than neutrality. Klaus Dohrn, a conservative journalist of German origin, transmitted Kreisky's views to C. D. Jackson, a prominent journalist with high-level access to the Eisenhower administration, including the president himself:

> For obvious reasons my friend cannot well make approaches or, so to speak, go on the open market with his suggestions. They should on the contrary be handled with the utmost discretion but also with the utmost speed....
>
> Now it is Kreisky's point that since it was not possible to prevent the festival from being held in Vienna, the best should be made of it. At the last festival in Moscow already certain chances of contamination (the other way) became apparent. They would undoubtedly be multiplied in Vienna, but they should be systematically prepared and organised. Kreisky has a point when he feels that the Austrian Socialists are particularly well placed to act in this sense. Of course he is thinking of a united effort with other groups (such as Catholic youth groups etc.) but he feels the Socialists should take the lead. He sees great opportunities in organising personal contacts, inviting participants to workers' apartments, scheduling attractive events (with speakers who cannot easily be dismissed as "reactionary") whenever the festival's schedule leaves a free moment, seeing to it that at any public demonstrations the streets are not lined with Communist fellow-travellers but with Socialist youth and workers groups carrying appropriate signs and slogans, distributing leaflets, perhaps even a regular festival daily paper in several languages etc. He also thinks that some kind of surveillance and intelligence squads should be prepared. They could possibly profit from official records available to the Austrian police on the basis of participant registration. These are only some hints. The possibilities are obvious....
>
> Personally I have complete trust in K.'s intelligence and integrity and think he deserves credit for offering such a unique chance for "indirect action" and propaganda by proxy. (Dohrn 1958)

Indeed this "special project" was put into effect with considerable American financial assistance, obviously financed by the CIA through Jackson. Kreisky's strategy shows how deeply he was opposed to communism, especially where Austrian domestic issues were involved. Yet at this time, Kreisky actively pursued détente by trying to establish a direct channel of communication between Willy Brandt, his friend during exile in Sweden and then mayor of Berlin, and Khrushchev.[4]

4. For more details, see Rathkolb 1995: 141–42.

The "Kennedyization" of America's Image in Europe

In his speeches, Kreisky often cited Franklin Delano Roosevelt, whom he called "the greatest liberal bourgeois statesman," usually along with Winston Churchill, whom he called the "greatest conservative bourgeois statesman" (Kreisky 1980b: 732). He also cited Truman in the context of his efforts in containing communism, but he never cited Dwight D. Eisenhower, although Kreisky had presented an Austrian medal of honor to him after Eisenhower left office.

Kreisky kept pictures of all American presidents from Truman to Jimmy Carter in his living room but favored, above all, the picture of John F. Kennedy. Kennedy seemed to embody the perfect young modern type of politician who was able to move not only a whole society but also the world community on specific issues. Kennedy's inaugural speech was published on the front page of almost all Austrian newspapers, and the way he presented his policies mesmerized a whole generation of Austrians. For the first time ever, the Austrian press covered not only American foreign policy but also issues relating to internal American problems like racial conflict. The Kennedy myth also affected Kreisky; he regarded the young President as "a fascinating personality with very similar political ideas" (quoted in Rathkolb 1986: 79).

In the fall of 1956 and 1957, Kreisky visited the United States as a member of the Austrian delegation to sessions of the UN General Assembly in New York. During the latter visit, he had very brief discussions with senior officers in the State Department. He reported being "greatly impressed with the United States and with the vigour and activity of its life" (quoted in Bennett 1957: 1). In New York, he met with leading American labor and business officials but was unable to conduct any substantial conversations with State Department officials.

He had easy access to high-level officers in the diplomatic service before 1959 even though there seemed to be little interest in his specific viewpoints. With the change of administration in 1961, Kreisky believed that for the first time there was interest in his geopolitical analysis and in discussing his policy stances, even at the highest decision-making levels.

Kreisky studied policy making in America very carefully and paid special attention to the influence and power of the media. He realized very early on the importance of using the media to cultivate a political personality in public. After a lecture tour in 1963, Kreisky had gained in stature, and the White House staff decided to organize a personal meeting with President Kennedy, whom Kreisky had already met during a state visit of Austrian Chancellor Alfons Gorbach. In a memo to Kennedy, the historian and Kennedy staff member Arthur Schlesinger, Jr., took special interest in this young politician. He wrote to Kennedy that Kreisky was a lively and engaging man. He has been touring around the country giving a talk entitled "The New Image of America in Europe." ... When he gave the talk the other day in Kansas City, President Truman, who was chairing the meeting, seized the microphone after Kreisky had finished and said, "That is the best damned talk I have heard in years."

The Kreisky speech was, in fact, excellent propaganda for a Democratic foreign policy. Kreisky defended Roosevelt's foreign policy, credited European economic revival to the Marshall Plan, praised the Alliance for Progress and the civil rights effort, etc.

Kreisky is an old Socialist whose roots go back to the Second International. The Austrian Socialist Party was, of course, one of the strongest of the European Socialist Parties. Kreisky has close fraternal ties with the other European Socialist leaders.

I am sure he would appreciate it if you would ask him his impression of political and intellectual currents in Europe, especially among young people. (Schlesinger 1963)

The American president was, however, not interested in polishing his image as a young and gifted modern democratic leader but focused exclusively on East-West issues. He wanted to hear Kreisky's views of Khrushchev and his perceptions of the United States in Europe. Here again Kreisky tried to sell his *Ostpolitik* and even predicted a new German *Ostpolitik* carried out by Willy Brandt.

Although Kennedy was certainly skeptical about Kreisky's ideas on having a permanent and intensive dialogue with the Soviet leadership, he accepted this Austrian-centered policy, in contrast to Eisenhower, and did not interpret it as an effort to lead the "Western alliance into the direction of 'neutrality'" (Tyler 1962). Kreisky's recognition of the People's Republic of China did not prevent Austria from being classified by the State Department as pro-Western, even pro-American with respect to foreign-policy issues, although neutral in a narrow military sense.

Heated periods of conflict with George W. Ball, the key Europeanist in the Kennedy administration, over the efforts of the three neutrals—Sweden, Switzerland, and Austria—to join the European Economic Community as associate members did not change this perception. The White House staff proposed to the president the following strategy during a visit of Chancellor Alfons Gorbach and Foreign Minister Kreisky:

From our point of view this visit can be turned to most useful account by making it the vehicle to move the Austrians away from their position of solidarity with the Swiss and Swedes in the "association" question and towards a constructive position on their relations with the Common Market.

Specially, we would wish that Austria might:

1. Move away from the insistence on institutional "association" with the Common Market;

2. After MFN [Most Favored Nation] negotiations under our Trade Expansion Act, seek special bilateral solutions to its residual problem, which we believe the Common Market countries would accept and to which we would take a sympathetic attitude;
3. Strengthen its ties with the Atlantic nations by more intensive participation in the OECD, whose non-political character would protect Austria from Soviet interference. (Tyler 1962)

Despite the State Department thesis that Kreisky was responsible for the coordinated negotiating strategy of the three neutrals, Ball blamed mainly Switzerland and to a lesser extent Sweden because Austria seemed to have been subjected to greater economic and geopolitical pressures. Later Ball and Kreisky became good friends and in the 1980s both opposed Reagan's "Star Wars" program and the strict pro-Israeli stance in American foreign policy. In the 1960s, Ball did not agree with Kreisky on the issue of the neutrals because he believed that including them in the European Economic Community would have destroyed the trend toward political and military union.

Avoiding "Vietnam" by Concentrating on Détente and Peaceful Coexistence in Europe

The American military engagement in Vietnam was criticized all over Europe and in Kreisky's own party. Young Austrian socialists (among them his own son Peter) protested against American policy in Asia, but Kreisky did not join in the criticism. This seems strange because already in Sweden he had become very interested in Asian problems and even wrote about them (Rathkolb and Etzersdorfer 1985: 207–24). A clue to Kreisky's position can be found in his speeches in 1965, when he pleaded against a "preoccupation with Asia," since "we tend to forget that not too long ago South-East Europe, the Danubian area, has been the scene of similar tensions and, in equal measure, a threat to the peace of the world" (Kreisky 1965: 3). Apparently, Kreisky feared that Washington would lose interest in détente in Europe in view of the growing military disaster in Southeast Asia. At the same time, he argued that a gradual internal evolution inside the Eastern bloc might lead to more liberal state systems. Believing that economic warfare could no longer trigger regime transformations, he thought Western Europe and the United States should assist this evolutionary process by fostering economic relations with the East.

Kreisky continued to press for economic cooperation with the Soviet bloc, which in the 1980s caused major difficulties because of the shift in American policy in the late Carter years and especially during the Reagan administration. He was convinced that Europe could not stand a new economic war against the Soviet Union and Eastern Europe and that economic pressure could not change the character of the communist regimes. According to Kreisky, technological change inside the Eastern bloc was strong enough to overcome Western blockades of technology. This was demonstrated by the Soviet development of the atomic bomb and the launching of *Sputnik* and by the increased energy dependence of Western Europe on the Soviet bloc. Kreisky considered both the aggressive reactions of the Carter administration after the Soviet intervention in Afghanistan and the establishment of military dictatorship as political overkill that might endanger peaceful coexistence in Europe.

His stand on these issues did not mean that he had abandoned his original position as a confirmed anticommunist. He was the only Western leader during the Conference for Security and Cooperation in Europe (CSCE) to plead for continuing the ideological struggle against communism and to ask explicitly that human rights be respected in Eastern Europe and the Soviet Union along the lines of the CSCE Agreement. As a result, Kreisky's reputation in this sense was quite negative in communist countries like Czechoslovakia, where the regime pursued an extreme course against opposition movements. He ran into direct conflicts with Soviet leaders, too, when he tried to intervene in favor of political prisoners like Sakharov during state visits in Moscow. But Kreisky's main priority continued to be permanent détente and cooperation between the East and West, which brought him into a natural conflict with the Reagan administration.

The New Agenda: The Middle East

As Austrian foreign minister, Kreisky maintained close relations with Egypt and in 1964 paid a visit to President Nasser, who at that time was considered an outcast by the West. In his first meetings with President Nixon, Kreisky focused on his new foreign-policy goal, and in 1969 he even tried to place the Middle East conflict on the agenda in the planning phase of the Conference for Security and Cooperation in Europe. He was not able to convince the American and Europeans that the region was of direct security interest to Europe, but the first oil price shock of 1974 brought a reversal, and the Middle East once again became of vital interest to European states such as Great Britain and France.

Kreisky's basic approach to a peaceful solution in the Middle East at the time contrasted sharply with the official pro-Israeli foreign policy of the United States, although both Nixon and Henry Kissinger had already tried to reverse this traditional course and conferred several times with Kreisky on this very issue. The Austrian chancellor believed, especially after an intensive series of fact-finding missions to the Middle East, that only official recognition of the PLO as representative of the Palestinian people and endorsement of the creation of a Palestinian state could solve this issue. The United States, however, was initially prepared to follow only some of Kreisky's ideas for integrating Egypt into the Western orbit. Here, too, Kreisky was very much interested in bringing President Sadat into the Western camp, but at the same time he wanted to go much further by integrating the Palestinians into the negotiations. For this reason, he thought that the Camp David agreement between Israel, Egypt, and the United States had only very limited impact on the roots of the conflict because the Palestinian problem was excluded from the agreement.

President Carter received considerable information from Kreisky on the PLO and the movement for a formal political institution under Yassir Arafat, but for domestic policy reasons he could not be convinced to take the decisive step. Apparently Carter feared that he would lose powerful segments within the Jewish community in the United States, which traditionally tended to vote for candidates from the Democratic Party.

Despite deep ideological differences with the Reagan administration over détente, the armaments race, and technology transfer into the communist orbit, Kreisky was impressed by its Middle East approach in 1982 and continued to back the Reagan plan until 1984. He was convinced that for the first time the PLO could be included in the negotiations and that both the Reagan plan and the Arab Fez plan could become the basis for solving the conflict (Rathkolb 1994: 142–44).[5]

Conclusion

Kreisky's perceptions of the United States are perhaps best summed up at the end of a speech commemorating the bicentennial anniversary of the Declaration of Independence in 1976: "Austria is a neutral country, is a non-committed country in a purely military sense, but it is deeply committed to the basic ideas of democracy, which are the same ideas created 200 years ago in the Declaration of Independence" (Kreisky 1980b: 615). In February 1977, an Austrian national committee decided to bestow on the United States a special bicentennial gift from the Austrian people as a visible manifestation of these perceptions. The purpose of the gift was "to establish a Center for Austrian Studies at the University of Minnesota and to endow it with one million dollars raised through individual donations from the Austrian public"

5 . The argument that Kreisky's Middle East and détente policies caused the World Jewish Congress to attack former UN Secretary General Kurt Waldheim is not supported by the evidence and served only domestic political purposes in Austria. See Rathkolb 1994: 145.

(Kreisky 1977: 1). Fifteen American institutions of higher learning expressed interest in such an endowed center, but the heavy lobbying of Kreisky by Vice President Walter Mondale and Senator Hubert H. Humphrey and Minnesota's existing strength in Austrian studies decided the "contest." As part of the same project, a chair for research on Austria was established at Stanford University. Together, the Center for Austrian Studies and the chair at Stanford are symbolic of the close political and cultural ties between the United States and Austria in the mid-1970s.

Bruno Kreisky was impressed until the end of his life with American anticommunist interventionism as represented by the early policy of containment and by economic assistance through the ERP. His foreign-policy views were shaped by Austria's geopolitical situation. Two Eastern bloc countries bordered Austria. Also, the Soviet Union had liberated eastern Austria and occupied the region until 1955, and it remained on the scene as signatory power of the Austrian State Treaty. As a consequence, Kreisky very early on developed a grassroots notion of peaceful coexistence with the neighboring communist countries and advocated increasing communication and negotiation between the two superpowers on the key issues of détente and disarmament. His ideas were accepted in the 1960s but came under attack during the Reagan years by conservatives in the United States. In this sense, Kreisky's oft-cited philosophical picture based on Schopenhauer's fable seemed to be obsolete:

> On a cold wintry day a company of porcupines moved closer to each other to find protection against the frost by seeking each other's warmth. Soon, however, they felt each other's quills, which made them pull apart again. Whenever the need for warmth brought them together, the other ill repeated itself. So they moved back and forth from one pain to the other until they found the appropriate distance that each could tolerate. (Kreisky 1985: 10)

Some politicians from the Austrian People's Party and some journalists portrayed Kreisky as "anti-American" and his policies as harsh, the effect of Austria's exclusion from the Atlantic coalition. But many high-level American politicians, diplomats, and respected journalists recognized the deeply pro-American character of Kreisky's policies, even though they challenged mainstream American concepts. Kreisky was never at odds with the democratic foundations and traditions of the United States and the American people. Yet, as James Reston (1983), the grand old man of American journalism, noted in his tribute to Kreisky, "he insists on negotiation, on talking across the Iron Curtain and other barriers, not only in Europe but in the Middle East: with his Jewish comrades, with their Arab neighbors and enemies, always insisting on the possibility of reconciliation." But as Reston observed, "Washington listened to the old man's faith, but was not really convinced."

References

Bennett, W. T. 1957. Memo of conversation, 10 December. RG 59. File 511.633/12-1757. National Archives, Washington, D.C.

Bundesministerium für Auswärtige Angelegenheiten (Ministry of Foreign Affairs). 1959. Memo of conversation, Kreisky-Herter, 23 September. Foreign Ministry. USA folder. Stiftung Bruno Kreisky Archiv (Kreisky Archives), Vienna.

Dohrn, K. 1958. Dohrn to Jackson, 21 July. C. D. Jackson Papers. Box 95. Dwight D. Eisenhower Library, Abilene, Kansas.

Fisher, J. W. 1959. "Biographic Report," 28 August. RG 59. File 763.521/8-2859. National Archives, Washington, D.C.

Fuchs, M. 1959. Diaries of Martin Fuchs, 29 Sept. Fuchs Collection. Austrian Institute for Contemporary History, Vienna.

Gärtner, H., ed. 1985. *Ein dritter Weg zwischen den Blöcken? Die Weltmächte, Europa und der Eurokommunismus.* Vienna.

Gehler, M. 1995. "Kontinuität und Wandel. Fakten und Überlegungen zu einer politischen Geschichte Österreichs von den Sechzigern bis zu den Neunzigern. Teil 1." *Geschichte und Gesellschaft* 14:203–38.

Haselbach, A. 1981. "Bruno Kreisky's Drive for a Large-Scale Economic Solidarity Programme with Developing Countries."Occasional paper 1981/3, Vienna Institute for Development, Vienna.

Khol, A. 1993. Introduction to *Neue Außenpolitik in einer neuen Welt,* ed. A. Khol, 5–16. Vienna.

Konrad, H., and M. Lechner. 1992. *Millionenverwechselung. Franz Olah-Die Kronenzeitung-Geheimdienste.* Vienna.

Kreisky, B. 1935–36. "Gefängnistagebuch." Collection from the interwar period. Stiftung Bruno Kreisky Archiv (Kreisky Archives), Vienna.

_____. 1965. "Is the Cold War in Europe Over? Changes in the Danubian Area. Speeches, Yale University, 14 October. Stiftung Bruno Kreisky Archiv (Kreisky Archives), Vienna.

_____. 1977. Kreisky to Hubert H. Humphrey, 8 February. USA Collection. Folder: 200 Years USA. Stiftung Bruno Kreisky Archiv (Kreisky Archives), Vienna.

_____. 1980a. *Reden I.* Vienna.

_____. 1980b. *Reden II.* Vienna.

_____. 1984. "America and Europe: Conditions for a Democratic Partnership." Speeches, 9 July. Stiftung Bruno Kreisky Archiv (Kreisky Archives), Vienna.

_____. 1985. *Is There a Chance for a New and Global Détente?* Ed. International Institute for Applied Systems Analysis. Laxenburg, Austria.

_____. 1986. *Zwischen den Zeiten. Erinnerungen aus fünf Jahrzehnten.* Berlin.

_____. 1991. Introduction to *Austromarxismus und Staat. Politiktheorie und Praxis der österreichischen Sozialdemokratie zwischen den beiden Weltkriegen,* by C. Butterwegge, 9–18. Marburg, Germany.

Mussi. I. 1983. "Bruno Kreisky und der schöpferische Dialog mit den Vereinigten Staaten." In *Ära Kreisky,* ed. E. Bielka, P. Jankowitsch, and H. Thalberg, 117–42. Vienna.

Olah, F. 1995. *Die Erinnerungen.* Vienna.

Pfoser, A. 1980. *Literatur und Austromarxismus.* Vienna.

Rathkolb, O. 1986. "The U.S. Presidency: An Austrian Perspective." In *The American Presidency: Perspectives from Abroad,* ed. K. W. Thompson, 75–90. Lanham, Md.

_____. 1994. "Bruno Kreisky: Perspectives of Top Level U.S. Foreign Policy Decision Makers, 1959–1983." *Contemporary Austrian Studies* 2:130–51.

_____. 1995. "Austria's 'Ostpolitik' in the 1950s and 1960s: Honest Broker or Double Agent?" *Austrian History Yearbook* 26:129–45.

Rathkolb, O., and I. Etzersdorfer, ed. 1985. *Der junge Kreisky. Schriften, Reden, Dokumente 1932–1945.* Vienna.

Rauchensteiner, M. 1987. *Die Zwei. Die Große Koalition in Österreich 1945–1966.* Vienna.

Reston, J. 1983. "An Old Man's Faith." *New York Times,* 6 February.

Schlesinger, A. 1963. Memorandum for the president, 11 October. Papers of President Kennedy. President's Office Files. Box 111. John F. Kennedy Library, Boston.

Secher, H. P. 1993. *Bruno Kreisky, Chancellor of Austria: A Political Biography.* Pittsburgh.

Svoboda, W. 1990. *Franz Olah. Eine Spurensicherung.* Vienna.

Thalberg, H. 1984. *Von der Kunst, Österreicher zu sein. Erinnerungen und Tagebuchnotizen.* Vienna.

Thompson, L. 1955a. Memo of conversation, Thompson-Raab-Schärf-Figl-Kreisky, 10 May. RG 59. Lot 58 D223. Box 8. National Archives, Washington, D.C.

_____. 1955b. Thompson to secretary of state, 4 April. RG 59. File 663.001/4-455. National Archives, Washington, D.C.

Tyler, W. 1962. Briefing paper for president's meeting with Austrian chancellor, 26 April. Vice Presidential Papers, 1961–1963. Subject file: Austria. Lyndon B. Johnson Library, Austin.

U.S. Department of State. 1986. *Foreign Relations of the United States, 1952–1954.* Vol. 3, pt. 1, *Germany and Austria.* Washington, D.C.

Zubok, V. M. 1996. *Inside the Kremlin's Cold War: From Stalin to Khrushchev.* Cambridge, Mass.

Chapter 3

BITBURG, WALDHEIM, AND THE POLITICS OF REMEMBERING AND FORGETTING

Richard Mitten

Bitburg and Waldheim: An Overview

In 1986, Menachem Rosensaft, head of the Association of Families of Holocaust Survivors, recalled that in 1985 Kurt Waldheim had "publicly endorsed the ill-conceived visit of President Reagan and West German Chancellor Helmut Kohl to the Bitburg cemetery. Small wonder. As we now know," Rosensaft continued, "Waldheim has a great deal in common with the 49 members of the Waffen-SS who lie buried there. Presumably, he considered a formal tribute to the memory of dead Nazi soldiers to be no worse than electing a retired Nazi officer to serve as the chief executive of the United Nations." Barely a year later, Waldheim, by then the front-runner in the campaign for the Austrian presidency, had been "unmasked as a proven liar and an alleged war criminal who, for almost forty-one years, had concealed the fact that throughout the Second World War he had been at best, an obedient and enthusiastic servant of Adolf Hitler and the Nazi regime. Nonetheless," Rosensaft lamented, "in an interview broadcast on the Austrian state radio on April 26, 1986, Kohl, in effect, endorsed his 'old personal friend' Waldheim as 'a great patriot'" (quoted in Levkov 1987: 728).[1] The disdain

---

1. The Bitburg controversy has been well documented in two books in English: Levkov 1987 and Hartman 1986. The Levkov volume contains primarily original contemporary documents relating to the controversy (newspaper articles, speeches, resolutions of the U.S. Congress and the West German Bundestag, etc.). It is more comprehensive than the Hartman

Kohl expressed in this interview in 1986 for what he described as "the arrogance of the late-born" who were criticizing Waldheim did cause a few eyebrows to be raised at the time, but Rosensaft was one of only a few who spoke explicitly of a "Waldheim-Kohl-Bitburg Axis" (quoted in Levkov 1987: 728).

Shortly before he left office in 1992, President Waldheim was invited by his friend Kohl to visit Munich. The uniformly hostile editorial reaction in the United States to the visit demonstrated anew that Waldheim's pariah status had remained unchanged, even if not unchallenged: six years into his term as Austrian president, Waldheim still elicited condemnation as an archetypical traducer of the historical memory of the victims of Nazism. Helmut Kohl's invitation to Waldheim and the pope's awarding Waldheim the Ordine Piano, a papal "knighthood" (James 1994), both breached recognized standards of international etiquette and met with near universal disapproval. However, the ritualized nature and selective application of this criticism (the public-relations bonanza that Václav Havel and Richard von Weizsäcker had handed Waldheim by their visit to the Salzburg festival in 1990, for example, curiously did not seem to vitiate their putative moral credentials in the eyes of their adoring publics) suggest that Waldheim had by then become a symbol not entirely commensurate with either his importance or his shortcomings.

In part, this is because the kind of past that gave rise in Austria to what has been ironically referred to as "Waldheimer's disease" has a thoroughly European dimension: "Most of occupied Europe," Judt argues (1992: 85), "either collaborated with the occupying German forces (a minority) or accepted with resignation or equanimity the presence and activities of the German forces (a majority)."

At the same time, the Waldheim affair also provided the occasion—particularly in the United States—for reaffirming faith in the values believed to be enshrined in the Allied victory over Nazi Germany. The occasion was convenient because claiming the moral high ground against Waldheim enabled many to pursue vicariously a struggle against Nazism in the 1980s that the contingencies of history had denied them in fact. This carried no real political price and helped becloud discomfiting details about the role of the Western democracies in abetting official Austria's postwar self-portrayal as exclusively Hitler's victim and their obliging accommodation of the silent reintegration of high-ranking Wehrmacht officers into the Federal Republic after the war. In a little-noticed remark made on 25 April 1985 to the West German Bundestag in the midst of the Bitburg controversy, Chancellor Kohl put the point in a way worthy of the party of Konrad Adenauer: "Does

---

collection, although the latter contains a number of important original essays on various aspects of the controversy not found in Levkov. German documents relating to the Bitburg controversy are collected in Sprenger 1985 and Presse- und Informationsamt 1985.

it truly fall to us," Kohl asked rhetorically, referring to the Waffen-SS soldiers buried at Bitburg, "to judge people who were involved in that injustice and lost their lives, while we respect others who were perhaps no less involved, but survived and have since then rightly made use of the opportunities that life has afforded them, who have served the cause of freedom and our republic by participating in the political parties?" (quoted in Levkov 1987: 108)

Kohl had hit on something profound, but also profoundly disturbing, about the vulnerability of the presumed moral imperative of Holocaust memory, which suggests why the reaffirmation of faith in "the values of Nuremberg" during the Waldheim affair appeared slightly desperate. In my view, the vehemence of the Bitburg and Waldheim controversies indicates the conviction of the postwar generation that vigorously propagating the unassailable moral stature of memory with respect to National Socialist crimes will in some way combat the legacy of accommodation toward postwar Germany and Austria bequeathed by the practitioners of postwar Western realpolitik. In addition, it points to the anxiety that came from sensing it was all a bit of a bluff. For if the controversy surrounding Ronald Reagan's visit to the Kolmeshöhe military cemetery near Bitburg in 1985 demonstrates anything, it is that gestures of commemorative vigilance about the Nazi abomination and its victims are hopelessly at peril when they conflict with the perceived needs of Western realpolitik.

Of course, the Bitburg controversy also demonstrated a great deal more, especially when viewed from a post-Waldheim perspective. Together these two events exemplify the inadequacy of categories like memory, history, morality, and historical responsibility in meeting the demands placed upon them, namely, to ensure reverence for the suffering of Nazism's victims and to maintain vigilance against the possible recurrence of such deeds, while offering a contrite post-Nazi democratic West German society a bridge back to the community of civilized nations.

The Bitburg affair turned on the issue of how to commemorate the German war dead without reviling the memories of the victims. "The evil world of Nazism," Reagan stated on 5 May 1985 in his speech at the American military base in Bitburg, "turned all values upside down. Nevertheless, we can mourn the German war dead today as human beings, crushed by a vicious ideology" (quoted in Levkov 1987: 169). Given the terms of the debate, in particular the notion of "historical responsibility," I question whether it would ever be possible to honor the German war dead from World War II at any cemetery, at any time, without doing injustice to the memory of Holocaust victims. Asked by *Der Spiegel* to explain the circumstances under which he might "acknowledge the President's claim that young German soldiers could also be considered 'victims of fascism,'" Elie

Wiesel responded, "Under no circumstances whatsoever, never, and even the exceptions, which there certainly were, change nothing about that" (quoted in "Bitburg hat schweren Schaden angerichtet" 1985). The Waldheim affair, coming a year after Bitburg, underscored even more than the Bitburg debate the inherent difficulties in devising and applying any concept of historical responsibility to present-day Austria and Germany, where questions of guilt and responsibility elide and get subsumed under the rather more diffuse notion of memory.

I cannot deal here with all the implications of the questions I have raised, much less propose an elaborated conceptual framework for thinking about history and memory. My more modest objective is to broach some of the conceptual difficulties suggested by the Bitburg and Waldheim controversies. I cannot resolve address the debate on how to preserve the memory of the Holocaust, who has authority to speak about the past, and what the contents of that memory ought to be because I believe that there is a dilemma at the heart of such debates that is insoluble within our current discursive framework. Instead, I offer some critical insights to help us pose questions more rigorously and be skeptical of pat answers, and I suggest why the idea of "historical responsibility" has become, in Nietzsche's famous phrase, "of advantage for life."

Metaphor, Memory, and History

That scholars, writers, or politicians should adopt metaphors or coin concepts to order their thoughts about Auschwitz and its significance in Western culture, and especially German-speaking Central European culture, is neither new nor surprising. In the 1980s, the proper historiographical buzzword was *Vergangenheitsbewältigung,* or "coming to terms with the past." Over the last several years *Vergangenheitsbewältigung* has fallen into disfavor (Mitten 1995). The current buzzword is centered on the idea of "memory." Although I believe that in principle it is possible to understand how the past is constructed without adopting either anachronistic retroactive moralizing or morally insensate historicism, I remain skeptical that the term "memory" really holds the key.

Nor are prevailing psychological analogies terribly helpful. Part of the difficulty is agreeing on the definition of terms. Even if there were a consensus on what terms like "repression" and "sublimation" might actually mean, the whole conceptual edifice, and any historical explanations that make use of it, could be sustained only as long as there were a prior agreement on the validity of psychoanalytic theory, the source of most such concepts. And while the reigning consensus on psychoanalytic theory has not yet been seriously challenged among historians,[2] the controversy in the United States surrounding the notion of "recovered memory"—together with Frederick Crews's sustained assaults on certain Freudian assumptions—suggests the advisability of a bit more skepticism.[3]

In short, if we are to use metaphors in history, especially those taken from individual psychology, we should take the concepts themselves seriously. This applies especially to the idea of memory. Historians might well remember a few points about individual memory when they employ the term to describe social collectives.[4] One of the most important is that past events are not stored in a special part of the brain as a kind of video-taped record that can be picked up with near-perfect recall. Memory is inherently sketchy and reconstructive, and it decays drastically over time, though periodical "rehearsal" of past experiences will to some extent counteract this decay. However, memory is easily corrupted in both subtle and less subtle ways. A therapist can unwittingly adulterate memory as much as can an experimenter by deliberate intervention. Moreover, an unavoidable "retrospective bias" serves to accommodate one's sense of the past to one's present values. Perceptions, then, are actively constructed rather than passively registered. Individual memory is a complex intermingling of fantasy and of events accurately recalled.

If the most significant feature of individual memory is that it is actively constructed, then this must hold all the more for the metaphor of public memory. As a specific appropriation of the past, a given memory, like the narrative of the past that informs it, is embedded in specific discourses on what the past is and which categories of experience are meaningful. Though there are competing memories, these are linked by shared assumptions and are imbricated with other histories. Thus, if we wish the concept of individual memory to serve as an metaphor for understanding a collective appropriation of the past, we must not raise explanatory expectations for the metaphor that individual memory itself cannot fulfill. For if the past itself "is not just another country," as Judt (1992: 100) has argued, "but a positive archipelago of vulnerable historical territories," what then of a national memory, the site of a congeries of competing values: a political society's founding myths, a governing elite's view of a state's geopolitical imperatives,

2. See, for example, Wollheim 1994 and Robinson 1994. One of the most informed and eloquently sympathetic accounts of the value of psychoanalytic theory for history is Loewenberg 1995.

3. See Crews 1995, which collects long review essays published in the *New York Review of Books*. See also the exchanges in the letters column and Crews's reply in the *New York Review of Books*, 3 February 1994.

4. Here I am broadly following the argument in Crews 1995. Although I would not endorse Crews's ultimate, quite severe, verdict on Freudian theory as a whole, his polemic against certain psychoanalytic assumptions is of great value as a general cautionary heuristic device for historians inclined to utilize these terms.

and individual and group self-understanding, each boasting a grounding historical narrative that is itself ultimately grounded by nothing less, but nothing more, than linguistic conventions?[5]

The Bitburg and Waldheim "affairs" each involved the American government and a Western country that had formerly been a part of the Third Reich in a controversy directly relating to the memory of the Holocaust. For the dynamics of the disputes, it is certainly relevant that the Waffen-SS culprits in the Bitburg cemetery were long since dead, while Waldheim was very much alive. Both incidents were the subjects of lively media interest in the United States, Germany, and Austria. Although the opposition to Reagan's visit and criticism of Waldheim extended to wide sections of the public, the principal adversaries of the American policy with respect to Bitburg and the main lobby advocating action by the American government in the Waldheim affair were prominent Jewish individuals or organizations. In the end, both controversies involved a government action, though each was of very divergent significance. However controversial was Ronald Reagan's official visit to the Bitburg cemetery, the event, if not the debate surrounding it, ended after his visit. In contrast, the Waldheim affair dragged on over months, even years, and involved a major policy decision by the American government: the unprecedented act of placing the sitting president of a friendly country on the "watch list" of undesirable aliens under the terms of the 1981 Holtzman amendment.

Comparing the two affairs can help illuminate to what extent official American gestures of condemnation of (or indifference to) the National Socialist legacy are conditioned by their perceived foreign-policy implications weighed against their possible negative domestic political and media fallout. Comparing Reagan's visit to Bitburg with the American government's handling of the watch-list decision might also provide insights into how two different countries—the small state of Austria and the much larger and more powerful Federal Republic of Germany, which was also a military ally—tried to utilize their respective geopolitical importance to finesse difficulties arising from essentially symbolic issues that had a significant domestic political salience in the United States.

The Bitburg Affair

The Bitburg controversy had its origins in a meeting in Washington in November 1984 during which Chancellor Kohl obtained President Reagan's agreement to pay a special visit to the Federal Republic while he was in

---

5. On the more general problem involving the past and its appropriation, see Mitten 1995 and 1992: 249–56.

Europe to attend the world economic summit in Bonn (5–8 May 1985). Kohl initially suggested three options for this gesture of reconciliation, which was also to serve as a sign of German-American friendship: visits to Cologne cathedral on V-E Day, the Dachau concentration camp memorial, and a military cemetery (Smith 1988: 371).[6] Kohl hoped to pay honor to the victims of National Socialism and to the German war dead, "to achieve peace and reconciliation across the graves," as he later told the German Bundestag (quoted in Levkov 1987: 106). The visit to a military cemetery proposed by Kohl at the November 1984 meeting was intended to replicate a ceremony at Verdun in September 1984. At that ceremony, held at a military cemetery near a World War I battlefield, Kohl and French President François Mitterand joined hands to emphasize the overcoming of French-German hostility. One difficulty with this Verdun "model" was that there are no American soldiers buried on German soil. Moreover, the commemoration of the dead from World War I had conveniently enabled Kohl and Mitterrand to skirt the more politically charged issues of National Socialism and Vichy. Reagan's decision to visit a German military cemetery meant that he would be honoring only German war dead, chiefly from World War II (Smith 1988: 371–72).

In January 1985, the White House announced that President Reagan would commemorate the fortieth anniversary of V-E Day with Chancellor Kohl but gave no details. Even before this announcement, however, Reagan had begun having second thoughts about his visit to Dachau. There is some dispute as to how and why the visit was dropped from the itinerary. According to journalist Hedrick Smith, Reagan's change of heart was heavily influenced by his wife Nancy. *Der Spiegel,* and later the White House and other writers, suggested that the Kohl government backed away from the original plan.[7] Whatever the reason, on 21 March 1985 Reagan announced at a

6. Compare "Eine eigenartige geistige Gymnastik" 1985 and "Auf Kohls Rat hören wir nicht wieder" 1985.

7. Smith (1988: 371) writes that Nancy Reagan had reacted to an article that appeared in the West German news weekly *Der Spiegel* on 19 January 1985 suggesting that Reagan was considering a visit to Dachau. Levkov, on the other hand, refers to a *Der Spiegel* article from 20 January 1985 as evidence for his assertion that Reagan's visit to Dachau was against Kohl's wishes. In fact, *Der Spiegel* appeared on neither the nineteenth nor the twentieth, but on Monday (the day it normally appears) the twenty-first. Moreover, I was not able to find any reference in that week's issue of *Der Spiegel* to Reagan's planned visit to Dachau or to Kohl's opposition. See *Der Spiegel,* 21 January 1985. In its 22 April issue, *Der Spiegel* quoted an internal document of the West German Foreign Ministry that argued strongly against having Reagan visit any concentration camp site because "An event with the American President in a concentration camp would, however, presumably represent the event of the presidential visit that stands out most, especially in the American press. We cannot be interested in such a one-sided view of a visit, [a view] that alludes to the extermination of the Jews" ("Eine eigenartige geistige Gymnastik" 1985). This evidence, however, does not disprove the claim that Kohl had originally suggested

news conference that his stay in Germany would not coincide with V-E Day celebrations after all and that he would not visit a concentration camp, as this "would reawaken the memories ... and the passions of the time.... [S]ince the German people have very few alive that remember even the war, and certainly none of them who were adults and participating in any way" but do have "a guilt feeling that's been imposed upon them," Reagan felt that they "should be recognized for the democracy that they've created and the democratic principles they now espouse" (quoted in Levkov 1987: 34).

If Kohl and Reagan had hoped that the trip could serve as a sign of the Federal Republic's definitive acceptance as a full-fledged member of Western democratic nations and in this way offset, or at least attenuate, the ignominy of Germany's Nazi past by focusing on its proven democratic virtues and reliable support for the Western alliance, they miscalculated badly. Critics in the United States, at first mainly veterans and Jewish organizations, initially objected to Reagan's decision to visit a military cemetery containing German war dead but not a concentration camp or an Allied military cemetery. Elie Wiesel, for example, could not believe that Reagan, whom he had "seen crying at a Holocaust remembrance ceremony," could do such a thing. Wiesel suspected a conspiracy: for such "a sensitive man" to "show such insensitivity" must have been due to the baneful influence of his advisers. "I do not know who they are or what their motives are," Wiesel stated, "but I am sure that it is the wrong advice" (quoted in Levkov 1987: 35).

On 11 April the White House announced that Kolmeshöhe cemetery near Bitburg would be the site of the planned wreath-laying ceremony. The cemetery had been chosen because of its proximity to an American military base and because Reagan's advance team, led by Michael Deaver, had been assured by their German counterparts that there were "no painful surprises" in the Bitburg cemetery. The pain threshold is apparently somewhat higher in Germany than in the United States, for news reports soon revealed that members of the Waffen-SS were also buried at Bitburg (*New York Times*, 15 April 1985; *Der Spiegel*, 29 April 1985).

Discussion now focused on this revelation. Reagan's announcement on 16 April that he would be visiting a concentration camp in addition to the military cemetery did not stem the tide of criticism. On the contrary, Reagan poured oil on the flames at a question-and-answer session held for broadcasters and editors on 18 April when he defended his decision in a way that seemed to equate the victims of the Holocaust with their persecutors. "Those young men" buried at Bitburg, Reagan said, making no distinction

---

the visit to the concentration camp, a claim repeated by Kohl government spokespeople. Levkov suggests that Kohl's change of mind might have been due to his wish not to have to share the spotlight with Franz Josef Strauss, which a visit to Dachau near Munich would have entailed (Levkov 1987: 23).

between the Waffen-SS and the Wehrmacht, "are victims of Nazism also, even though they were fighting in the German uniform, drafted into service to carry out the hateful wishes of the Nazis. They were victims, just as surely as the victims in the concentration camps" (quoted in Levkov 1987: 39).

On 19 April, in a White House ceremony at which he received the Congressional Gold Medal of Achievement, Elie Wiesel, in an oft-quoted speech, reacted to Reagan's remarks the previous day and implored the president "to do something else, to find a way, to find another way, another site. That place, Mr. President, is not your place. Your place is with the victims of the SS" (quoted in Levkov 1987: 44; "Bitburg hat schweren Schaden angerichtet" 1985). Reagan's continued refusal to call off his visit to Bitburg, especially in light of his remarks on the "victims" buried there, engendered criticism from several sides and increasingly urgent attempts to pressure him to change his mind. The inaugural meeting of the Association of Families of Holocaust Survivors condemned Reagan's decision, as did the American Legion, the associations of Catholic and Jewish war veterans, and numerous American newspapers. Members of the Senate and House, as individuals and in groups, appealed in speeches, letters, and petitions to Reagan to cancel his trip to Bitburg and to Kohl to withdraw his invitation.[8] By then, Reagan had altered his plans to spend V-E Day in Germany with Kohl but pressed ahead with his scheduled visits to Bergen-Belsen and Bitburg. At Bergen-Belsen, Reagan gave what was viewed as a moving speech, appropriate to the occasion, even as his itinerary continued to be criticized.[9]

Both visits were accompanied by protests. Menachem Rosensaft attempted to lead a protest during Reagan's appearance at Bergen-Belsen but was prevented from doing so by West German police acting at Reagan's request. His group "reconsecrated" the site at Bergen-Belsen after Reagan had gone. Jewish leaders and many prominent members of the German Social Democratic Party and the Greens refused to attend either Bergen-Belsen or Bitburg.[10]

The ceremony at Kolmeshöhe cemetery on 5 May was as short as tolerable, with Reagan seemingly hiding behind General Matthew Ridgway, whose distinguished career included commanding the XVIII Airborne Corps during the Battle of the Bulge, the campaign in which many buried at the cemetery had been killed. It was left to Ridgway to shake hands with Lt. General Johannes Steinhoff of the West German Bundeswehr; there was

8. See documents in Levkov 1987: 42–92.

9. An editorial in the *New York Times* (1985), although harshly critical of the visit, referred to Reagan's "eloquent words" at Bergen-Belsen.

10. See the speech of Menachem Z. Rosensaft at Bergen-Belsen, "A Jew At Bergen-Belsen" (Levkov 1987: 136–38), and his article, "A Journey to Bergen-Belsen" (Levkov 1987: 152–65); the *New York Times,* 6 May 1985; and Walter Ruby, "Protesters in Bergen-Belsen: More Than Just Grandstanding" (Levkov 1987: 141–51).

no Kohl-Reagan clasping of hands across the graves (Smith 1985). The wreath-laying ceremony at Kolmeshöhe was followed by the more upbeat, congenially Reaganesque visit to the soldiers based at Bitburg, where in his famous "I am a Jew" speech he invoked a letter from a young Jewish girl to legitimize the visit he had just made to the military cemetery.[11]

The axes of the Bitburg controversy, as well as the formulation of the specific issues, were generally different in Germany and the United States, even though they tended to be symbiotic. In the United States, Reagan was criticized for dropping his visit to Dachau and for what appeared to be the insensitivity involved in his one-sided commemoration of former enemy soldiers of the United States but not their victims. However, the controversy really heated up only after it was reported in mid-April that the cemetery contained graves of the Waffen-SS. From that point, the debate over Reagan's visit to Bitburg centered on this issue and transcended any notions of mere tastelessness and imbalance. There were five main arguments advanced on both sides, many of which overlapped.

1. After searching desperately for an alternate cemetery that contained no graves of the Waffen-SS (Smith 1988: 372; *Der Spiegel*, 29 April 1985), the Reagan administration, supported by the Kohl government in Bonn, attempted to diminish the significance of the forty-nine Waffen-SS soldiers buried at Bitburg, citing their young age, the fact that many had been conscripted into the Waffen-SS without their knowledge, etc.[12] Some commentators, such as Jody Powell, former press secretary to President Jimmy Carter, and conservative writer William F. Buckley, defended the decision despite the presence of SS graves. Buckley, for example, found Reagan's statement that the soldiers buried at Bitburg "were victims just as surely as the victims in the concentration camps" "quite right," "in terms entirely logical," and advised Eli Wiesel to "applaud Mr. Reagan for continuing the struggle to keep us conscious of holocausts, major and minor, that continue their grisly course, as in Cambodia, as in Nicaragua, as in Afghanistan" (quoted in Levkov 1987: 453–54). Powell encouraged Reagan not to cancel his visit, not only because to do so would "be a nasty rebuff to West German Chancellor Kohl and to his people" but also because

11. "One of the many who wrote about this visit was a young woman who had recently been bar [*sic*] mitzvahed. She urged me to lay the wreath at Bitburg cemetery in honor of the future of Germany, and that is what we have done. On this 40th anniversary of World War Two, we mark the day when the hate, the evil and the obscenities ended and we commemorate the rekindling of the democratic spirit in Germany" (quoted in Levkov 1987: 171).

12. See Helmut Kohl's statement to the Bundestag on 25 April 1985 (Levkov 1987: 105–9) and Reagan's remarks made during a question-and-answer session to broadcasters and editors on 19 April 1995 (Levkov 1987: 38–39).

Reagan's decision "was right and proper on its own merits." Reagan's visit "can, if we let it," Powell argued, "express our ability to understand and sympathize with the grief of the widow and the orphan, however abhorrent we find the cause for which the husband and father died" (quoted in Levkov 1987: 441).

2. This sentiment was echoed in commentary by most German newspapers. Despite considerable disagreements on the Bitburg visit, virtually every German newspaper agreed with the liberal *Süddeutsche Zeitung* that "every fallen soldier, in whichever uniform [he fought],… deserves a worthy commemoration" (quoted in Bergmann 1994: 419).[13]

3. In Germany, moreover, some press commentaries attempted to combat what American historian Robert Arthur Gelwick has called the "prevailing myths about the Waffen SS" and to introduce the idea that, as historian George Stein, author of a history of the Waffen-SS, has written,"the SS was actually far more differentiated and complex than the monolithic organization of criminals who stood trial at the International Military Tribunal" (quoted in Höhne 1985).

4. In the United States, newspapers investigated the units of soldiers buried at Bitburg and found links to specific atrocities committed during the war. The *New York Times*, for example, revealed on 28 April that among the graves were soldiers from the Second SS Panzer Division, "Das Reich," which had been responsible for the massacre of 642 villagers in Oradour-sur-Glane, France, in June 1942.

5. Apart from isolated commentaries like those of Powell and Buckley, the media, for the most part, stressed that there were graves of Waffen-SS soldiers at Bitburg and that the SS (including the Waffen-SS) had been recognized as a criminal organization by the Nuremberg tribunal. The press argued that visiting a cemetery containing graves of those whom Reagan had called merely "villains" would, in effect, undermine the consensus unconditionally condemning the role of the SS in implementing the genocidal policies of the Nazis, one of the most self-evident aspects of Holocaust memory and an essential component of the consensus "Nuremberg values." The importance of the SS graves continued to dominate the debate until the very end. Reagan's "somber path through the Kolmeshöhe cemetery," wrote Hedrick Smith (1985), "took him within three feet of some SS graves, but he did not glance at them."

Those who attempted to downplay the significance of the SS graves at Bitburg and make it into just another military cemetery and those who most fervidly opposed Reagan's visit shared an assumption about the Holocaust: that

13. Compare "Die Kriegstoten" 1985.

one could morally distinguish between the SS, the "villains" who did the dirty work of the war, and the morally "upright" (*anständig*) Wehrmacht, which merely did its duty on the front. Indeed, the Bitburg controversy is virtually incomprehensible without this assumption. This belief about the morally upright Wehrmacht, which has been one of the most resilient features of postwar politics and military scholarship, is a myth. The criminal role of the Wehrmacht, or at least of the high command, in preparing for and waging "aggressive war" and in offering logistical support to the SS in carrying out the "final solution" is well known.[14] The criminal orders of the Wehrmacht issued to pursue the "ideologically driven war" (*Weltanschauungskrieg*) are less familiar, or at least less emphasized. These ranged from the "commissar order" issued by Wilhelm Keitel, which provided that all captured Soviet military commissars (that is, soldiers in uniform who were also charged with political responsibilities) should be shot, to the directives issued by Field Marshall von Brauchitsch "that the battle of race against race must be waged, and with the necessary severity," to the orders of Field Marshall von Reichenau, which appealed to the soldiers to steel themselves and understand "the necessity of the severe retribution against Jewry [*Sühne am Judentum*]" (quoted in Manoschek 1995: 5–8).[15]

Official commemorations of historical events in all Western-style democratic states attempt to articulate a public consensus on the past that is also capable of suggesting a moral that appears meaningful within the prevailing value system.[16] Historians have been working to define the precise role of the Wehrmacht in the crimes that are conventionally described as the Holocaust. The task requires, among other things, periodizing the German army's initial broad observance and abrupt abandonment of the laws of war; specifying the

14. Most notably in Hilberg 1985 but also in Friedman 1972a, 1972b.

15. Raul Hilberg (Hartman 1986: 15–26) has conveniently summarized the evidence: (1) The German army in the east established many Jewish ghettos. (2) The German army gave logistic support to the Einsatzgruppen of Heydrich's Reich Security Main Office. (3) Intelligence units helped locate Jews for shooting. (4) Military governments in Belgium, France, Serbia, and Greece issued anti-Jewish regulations in the economic sphere, including "Aryanizations" of Jewish property and taxes in the form of "fines." (5) Armament officers administered contracts with German firms employing Jewish slave labor. The German army itself made use of such labor in its own installations. (6) Transport officers in France, Greece, Italy, and elsewhere were involved in the dispatch of trains to death camps. (7) German troops stood by to deal with Jewish resistance. An artillery unit fought in the Warsaw ghetto battle. A battalion of security troops was alerted for the suppression of the revolt in the Sobibor death camp. The military was available to frustrate any large-scale breakouts from Auschwitz. (8) The German army transferred Jewish Soviet prisoners of war to the SS to be shot. (9) It engaged in killings of its own, shooting the Jewish men in Serbia and wiping out a population of ten thousand Jews in the Blebokie region of Poland. See also Bartov 1991, Messerschmidt 1969, and Streit 1991.

16. On this point, see Wodak et al. 1994: 9–38.

criminal activities of individual officers, units, and soldiers; and, more generally, ascribing individual agency within the power structure of the Wehrmacht.[17] The moral issue, however, seems rather straightforward, at least as portrayed in the Bitburg controversy, because the debate on the members of the Waffen-SS buried in the Bitburg cemetery turned less on their individual roles than on the known facts about the Waffen-SS as an organization (wholly in keeping with the precedent set at Nuremberg).[18]

The available evidence on the Wehrmacht's criminal complicity in the Holocaust vitiates any grounds for morally differentiating it from the SS, even assuming that in its overall activities the degree of the Wehrmacht's criminal complicity was proportionately smaller than that of the SS. But if there are no grounds for drawing a moral distinction between German soldiers in the Wehrmacht and the Waffen-SS, the highly moralistic terms used to debate the Holocaust memory make it seem conceptually impossible to commemorate any German war dead without sullying the memory of the Holocaust. There are simply no overarching values that can bridge these differences.

The inability to reconcile these competing imperatives thus seems to deprive contemporary German society of any moral legitimacy in honoring fallen German soldiers, a concern that was voiced by the press in Germany but was scarcely acknowledged in the United States. Holding to this moral stance consistently, however, seems to reinforce the idea of certain German politicians (and Waldheim supporters in Austria) that keeping the memory of the Holocaust alive is tantamount to criminalizing an entire generation of soldiers.[19] But unless one ascribes to German soldiers a kind of involuntary mass dementia during World War II, then their complicity in a criminal

17. The most authoritative work on this issue to date is the excellent collection of essays in Heer and Naumann 1995.

18. This was true even when the opposition to the Waffen-SS did not directly allude to the murder of the Jews. Thus American Legion National Commander Clarence M. Bacon writes in *USA Today*: "Bitburg cemetery contains the remains of not only German soldiers, but also at least 30 elite Waffen SS troops. The cemetery is on the site of a Battle of the Bulge staging area used by the Panzer Army under the command of SS General Josef 'Sepp' Dietrich. And, Waffen SS troops were responsible for the summary execution of more than 75 unarmed US prisoners at Malmedy, just 30 miles from Bitburg. Are these the same SS troops buried beneath the stones of Bitburg?" (quoted in Levkov 1987: 66).

19. In his letter (19 April 1985) to Senator Howard Metzenbaum (who had written a letter to President Reagan dated 15 April 1985, cosigned by fifty-two additional U.S. senators, urging him to cancel his visit to Bitburg), Alfred Dregger, the head of the Christlich-Demokratische Union/Christlichsoziale Union faction in the West German Bundestag wrote: "My only brother, Wolfgang, died in the Kurland pocket on the Eastern front in 1944, I do not know how. He was a decent young man, as were the overwhelming majority of my comrades.... If you call upon your President to refrain from the noble gesture he plans to make at the military cemetery in Bitburg I must consider this to be an insult to my brother and my comrades who were killed in action" (quoted in Levkov 1987: 95).

enterprise, if not in what Menachem Rosensaft (1986) has called an "absolute evil," is beyond doubt. In that case, to what "worthy commemoration" (*Süddeutsche Zeitung*) could they conceivably be morally entitled?

Conflicts between the putative moral injunctions of Holocaust memory and the requirements of Western geopolitics and West German domestic politics have ordinarily been resolved by making pragmatic compromises that have etiolated these perceived moral principles, while maintaining at best a strategic silence and at worst a collusive deception about the compromise made. For the most part, the demands for justice on the part of a post-Nazi generation have been met with a combination of exemplary punishments of selected individuals at Nuremberg, a largely administrative and exceedingly generous denazification, and the gradual acceptance of the penitent German notion of historical responsibility.[20] This response was always a fudge of sorts, but one reason it became the preferred mode of engagement seems to have been that the Manichaean moral imperatives of post-1945 Holocaust remembrance were incompatible with the realpolitik imperatives of the cold war and the tenets of Western democratic societies in general. The willingness of the postwar West German political elite to assume the burdens of historical responsibility as the Western occupying powers and later military allies had defined them meant that the vulnerability of the entire conceptual edifice went largely unnoticed, or at least unchallenged.

Postwar Austria followed a very different path. In the Moscow Declaration, issued on 1 November 1943, Allied foreign ministers declared Austria "the first free country to fall a victim to Hitlerite aggression," at the same time warning her of "a responsibility which she cannot evade, for participation in the war on the side of Hitlerite Germany" (United States 1963). In part to bury definitively the idea of a possible future anschluss between Austria and Germany, the Allies, particularly the United States, were exceedingly indulgent after the war of Austrian leaders' clear self-interest in promoting the "victim" passage while failing to acknowledge "responsibility" of any kind for the Nazi abomination. Indeed, Austrian negotiators were even able to have the reference to Austria's responsibility for the war removed from the draft text of the 1955 Austrian State Treaty that reestablished Austria's independence (Stourzh 1985). Thus, far from being coerced or enticed to acknowledge a historical responsibility for the Holocaust, the Allies had sanctioned Austria's self-declared status as Hitler's first victim. All that changed with the Waldheim affair. In the absence of clear notions about memory and historical responsibility, but with growing public awareness of postwar Western indulgence toward many former Nazis, the American government in 1987 defused a potential political controversy by recourse to the administrative watch-list decision that appeared to have

---

20. On denazification in Germany, see Niethammer 1972 and Stern 1992.

solid judicial grounding and demonstrated the Reagan government's anti-Nazi moral resolve. But precisely because the remedy was administrative and the judicial trappings deceptive, this solution failed to bring the conceptual clarity, much less the moral consistency, that the memory of the Holocaust seems to demand. Indeed, Austria's lack of geopolitical importance is a key reason why Kurt Waldheim today remains an undesirable alien.

The Waldheim Affair

The Waldheim affair[21] arose from the disclosure of the previously unknown past of Kurt Waldheim, former secretary general of the United Nations, which became known during his campaign for the Austrian presidency in 1986.[22] The affair not only focused international attention on Waldheim personally but also raised broader questions relating to the history of anti-semitism in Austria and the role played by Austrians in the Nazi dictatorship and the final solution. The Waldheim affair also witnessed the reemergence in contemporary Austrian political culture of antisemitic appeals with political ends. Employing a coded idiom more appropriate to "post-Auschwitz" political debate, the Waldheim camp (principally the Austrian People's Party that had nominated him) helped construct a hostile image of Jews (*Feindbild*) that deflected criticism of Waldheim's credibility and explained the international "campaign" against him. The key assumption of this *Feindbild* was that Waldheim and Austria were under attack from an international Jewish conspiracy (Mitten 1992). However, it is the international dimension that is more significant here because the way the debate on Waldheim "played" in the United States is more, though of course not exclusively, relevant to the issues of memory, commemoration, and historical responsibility.

The Waldheim affair itself began on 3 March 1986, when the Austrian weekly *Profil* first published documents revealing details of Waldheim's unknown past. *Profil*'s disclosures were followed on 4 March by nearly identical revelations by the World Jewish Congress (WJC) and the *New York Times*. In both his public statements and in the relevant passages in his memoirs, Waldheim had always denied any affiliation with the Nazis and had claimed that his military service had ended in the winter of 1941–42, with his being wounded

21. The evidence for most of the claims made in this section is to be found in Mitten 1992, which cites the relevant sources.

22. The details of the election campaign are of only marginal importance here. Waldheim's opponents in the first round of the presidential election were Kurt Steyrer, the candidate of the Socialist Party (SPÖ), Freda Meissner-Blau, the candidate of the Greens, and Otto Scrinzi, who ran as an independent candidate of the German nationalist far Right. See Mitten 1992: 42–50.

on the eastern front. The evidence made public by *Profil*, the WJC, and the *New York Times* suggested that on the contrary the former secretary general had been a member of the Nazi Student Union and that he had also belonged to a mounted riding unit of the Sturmabteilung, or SA, while attending the Consular Academy in Vienna between 1937 and 1939. Other documents revealed that Waldheim had returned to duty in the spring of 1942, after his wound had healed. At the end of March, Waldheim had been assigned to Army High Command 12 (which became Army Group E in January 1943), then based in Thessaloniki, and remained attached to it until the war's end. Army Group E, commanded by Alexander Löhr, was involved in the deportations of Jews from Greece and noted for the savagery of its military operations against Yugoslav partisans and their suspected civilian supporters.

The WJC, based in New York, was the principal source of documents relating to Waldheim's past and his most vocal critic. The WJC's primary activities involve defending threatened Jewish communities throughout the world and lobbying for what it perceives as the common interests of Jews. Its press releases and disclosures of documents (twenty-four between 4 March and 8 July, the date of the second round of the Austrian presidential election) largely set the pace and the terms of the debate on Waldheim in the United States. In the early phase of the controversy, the WJC published evidence relating to Waldheim's membership in the SA and in the Nazi Student Union, which it believed amounted to proof of his Nazi past. The material first presented by the WJC was patchy and inconclusive, but over the next several months it made public dozens of additional documents that helped complete the picture of Waldheim's various duties in the Balkans.

A major turn in the affair came on 22 March 1986, when the WJC published a copy of the Central Registry of War Criminals and Security Suspects (CROWCASS), a list compiled by the U.S. Army containing persons suspected of war crimes that showed that Waldheim had been sought by Yugoslavia after the war for, among other things, murder. The basis for CROWCASS was a file of the United Nations War Crimes Commission (UNWCC), and this latter file was in turn based on a dossier that the Yugoslav authorities had prepared and submitted to the UNWCC shortly before the latter concluded its deliberations in 1948. With the publication of the Yugoslav file, known as the *Odluka,* or "decision," the debate on Waldheim's past acquired a far more serious dimension: allegations of war crimes had been leveled against Waldheim by the Yugoslav War Crimes Commission, and these had been reviewed and endorsed by the UNWCC. The WJC's subsequent disclosures and the public debate on Waldheim's past in general were heavily influenced by this new discovery.

The WJC continued to offer documents it believed corroborated the findings in the *Odluka* and urged U.S. Attorney General Edwin Meese to place Waldheim's name on the so-called watch list of undesirable aliens, effectively barring him from entering the United States. In the international media, calls for publishing Waldheim's UN file were coupled with more intensive efforts to find a "smoking gun."

In response to the initial disclosures in Austria and the United States, Waldheim continued to deny membership in both Nazi organizations and offered evidence suggesting his ideological hostility to Nazism. He conceded having served in Army Group E, but he denied participation of any kind in atrocities committed by units under Löhr's command and claimed to have known nothing of the deportation of the Jews of Thessaloniki. As the controversy grew, Waldheim and his supporters pursued a strategy of branding the disclosures as part of a "defamation campaign" initiated by socialists, led by the WJC, and promoted by the international press, particularly the *New York Times*. Waldheim disputed having knowledge of any Jewish deportations or having participated in any way in other atrocities. Waldheim also attempted to identify his own fate with that of his generation and country by claiming that he, like thousands of other Austrians, had merely done his "duty" during World War II. If, Waldheim argued, he were to be blamed for such things, then truly every Wehrmacht soldier would also come under suspicion, an appeal that struck a responsive note among many Austrian voters. Waldheim polled 49.7 percent of the votes in the first round of the election, just short of the required absolute majority, but won the second round handily with 53.9 percent.

The Symbolism of the Waldheim Affair

The enduring symbolic importance of the Waldheim affair has its origins in the initial dynamics of the discussion itself. Several factors exacerbated the difficulties of reaching a sober judgment: the piecemeal nature of the gathering and disclosure of the relevant documents, the inherent difficulties of reconciling the desire to provide authoritative interpretations of documents with the exigencies of contemporary investigative journalism, the faulty or inadequate background knowledge that would have provided a more comprehensive context for interpreting disparate bits of information, and the well-known unreliability of Waldheim's own statements about his past. Left largely to their own devices, journalists or other writers covering the Waldheim affair would necessarily filter the information through assumptions about National Socialism, World War II, and the Nuremberg tribunal that derive from the narratives constituting public memory. Moreover, the extent of Waldheim's proven disingenuousness was in a sense seen to be proportionate to the heinousness of the activities he had concealed. Even the best media accounts relating to the two substantive allegations about Waldheim's past that emerged during the course of the controversy—whether he had been a Nazi and the extent of his knowledge of and involvement in atrocities and war crimes—were hampered by structural impediments in news gathering and by the ideological and political filters through which the news passed. These limitations held all the more for politicians and the wider public, whose perceptions of the issues depended on media accounts that were often undependable and always inconclusive. I offer two examples to illustrate the point.

First, there is little doubt that Waldheim belonged both to the Nazi Student Union and to an equestrian unit of the SA while he attended the consular academy. However, the evidence strongly suggests that Waldheim's Nazi affiliations owed less to conviction than to a cloying opportunism aimed at advancing his career opportunities. Neither of these memberships would have fallen within the purview of the "denazification" laws passed after the war. According to the linguistic conventions of postwar Austria, only those who had been in one of the denazification categories (a group that had not included Waldheim) were described as former Nazis. In the United States, such distinctions were seldom, if ever, drawn or even understood, and their relevance for any debate on an individual's role in Nazi Germany went unnoticed. Waldheim had been, quite simply, a Nazi,[23] from which a great deal was believed to follow.[24] The possibilities for inferring something exaggeratedly opprobrious about Waldheim's service in the Wehrmacht from his previously concealed "Nazi past" were thus legion, though not necessarily warranted (Mitten 1992: 62–69).

Second, the publication of CROWCASS, the UNWCC file, and the *Odluka* transformed vague intimations about Waldheim's possible knowledge of or involvement in the atrocities committed by units under the command of Army Group E into concrete suspicions of complicity in war crimes. Yet the dubious way the *Odluka* was compiled, which became known only much later, seriously undermined, if not vitiated, the charges made in it (Herzstein 1988: 192–211). In addition, the issue of Waldheim's possible war criminality was complicated by ignorance of or disregard for standard practice in the Nuremberg tribunal. Much of what the Wehrmacht did to Yugoslav Partisans was—according to the judgments in Case 7, which dealt with crimes in the Balkan theater—thoroughly gruesome but entirely "legal." Equally important, these same judgments narrowly circumscribed the conditions under which an officer of Waldheim's rank and position

23. This could range from the WJC's perfunctory references to Waldheim as "a former Nazi and a liar" (quoted in Sichrovsky 1986) to *New York Times* columnist William Safire's assertion (1986) that Waldheim was a "secret follower" of Adolf Hitler.

24. See, for example, Ryan 1986.

could even incur criminal liability (Mitten 1992: 69–118). For these reasons, several authoritative studies have concluded convincingly that Waldheim's activities as a Wehrmacht lieutenant in the Balkans did not imply criminal complicity (Born 1987; Czernin 1987–88; Collins et al. 1988; United Kingdom 1989; Thames Television/Home Box Office 1988).

Nonetheless, the odium of an ill-defined real or symbolic culpability for the Holocaust that emerged in the debate in 1986 continues to attach itself to Waldheim. Not unsurprisingly, Edgar Bronfman, president of the WJC in 1986, described Waldheim's election as Austrian president as a "symbolic amnesty for the Holocaust" (Bronfman 1986). But it is perhaps less evident why in 1994 Waldheim remained for *Washington Post* columnist Richard Cohen "the personification of the nonentity without whom the Holocaust, not to mention the massacres of other peoples, would have been impossible" (Cohen 1994). For many, especially in the United States, Waldheim had become a symbol of the Austrians' failure to acknowledge their historical responsibility (unlike the Germans), of Western leniency toward former Nazis (exemplified by Waldheim's career advancement), and of the inherent difficulties of maintaining Western vigilance toward renewed signs that the Holocaust was being trivialized.

Waldheim and the "Watch List"

The symbolic role of Waldheim has been due in no small part to the decision by the Justice Department in 1987 to place him on the "watch list" under the terms of the so-called Holtzman amendment to the Immigration and Nationality Act.[25] A close look at the Justice Department's justification of this highly political decision demonstrates the same conceptual imprecision found in the Bitburg affair, where categories of guilt, complicity, and responsibility elide.

The U.S. attorney general's office first requested documents relating to Waldheim from the WJC on 26 March 1986 in response to the WJC's demand that Waldheim be entered on the watch list.[26] At the end of April, the Office of Special Investigation (OSI), which has as its chief purpose the enforcement of the Holtzman amendment, completed a report recommending that Waldheim be barred from entering the United States. Attorney General Edwin Meese initially refused to follow the recommendation and ordered the OSI to undertake a more thorough investigation. In April

25. For the allegations levied in the file prepared by the OSI against Waldheim in support of the decision to refuse him an entry visa, see the *New York Times*, 28 April 1987, and *Profil*, 18 May 1987.
26. The following section is based on Mitten 1992: 134–37; 1987.

1987, on the basis of this new report, the Justice Department announced that Waldheim was indeed to be placed on the list.

The Immigration and Nationality Act, which controls who may enter the country, contains the paragraph affecting Waldheim, the so-called Holtzman amendment. Like similar laws elsewhere, the act gives the attorney general wide discretionary powers in determining a person's eligibility for an entry visa. Moreover, the rules of evidence in immigration procedures are substantially less stringent than in criminal court proceedings: under American law, a prima facie case suffices to deny someone an entry visa. If the attorney general determines that the evidence justifies placing a person on the watch list, then the person must be barred, unless the attorney general can be dissuaded or another ground for exemption can be found.

Section 1182 of this act covers "General Classes of Aliens Ineligible to Receive Visas and Excluded from Admission," as well as "Waivers of Inadmissibility." The provision relevant to Waldheim is Subsection (a), Paragraph (33) of Section 1182. This paragraph excludes:

> Any alien who during the period beginning on March 23, 1933, and ending on May 8, 1945, under the direction of, or in association with—(A) the Nazi government of Germany, (B) any government in any area occupied by the military forces of the Nazi government of Germany, (C) any government established with the assistance or cooperation of the Nazi government of Germany, or (D) any government which was an ally of the Nazi government of Germany, ordered, incited, assisted, or otherwise participated in the persecution of any person because of race, religion, national origin, or political opinion. (United States 1980: 38–39)

Depending on how the words "assisted" and "participated" are defined, this passage, if interpreted tendentiously, could encompass anything from paper shuffling to the gassings at Auschwitz. When announcing their conclusions, Justice Department representatives even stated that mere knowledge of such events constitutes involvement in persecution. A decision need not, and in Waldheim's case certainly did not, rest on a determination of an alien's complicity in the commission of war crimes. The prima facie finding that Waldheim had "assisted or otherwise participated in the persecution of any person because of race, religion, national origin, or political opinion" rests on a far more elastic formulation that certainly subsumes not only all war crimes and crimes against humanity but also many other lesser deeds.

Kurt Waldheim was placed on the watch list because the activities he performed while stationed in the Balkans fell under the terms of the Holtzman amendment, not because these were found to be criminal under American law. No judicial authority has tried, much less convicted, Waldheim of criminal conduct, yet several independent bodies and some well-informed legal bodies, most notably the international historians commission, the panel of judges involved in the Thames-HBO *Commission of Inquiry*, and the British Ministry of Defence, have all examined the question of Waldheim's criminality. None found evidence to suggest that there was a criminal case for Waldheim to answer. The depth and thoroughness of these investigations, together with a devastating point-by-point refutation of the OSI's assertions by Austrian journalist Hubertus Czernin, have cast serious doubts on the assumptions and reasoning underlying the OSI's deliberations.[27] Yet even on the purely hypothetical assumption that a court in the United States had the jurisdiction and the evidence to acquit Waldheim of all substantive allegations of criminal complicity, he would still be excludable under the provisions of the Holtzman amendment, with all the ignominy this entails, not the least of which is the continuing popular belief that he is a war criminal.[28]

Although its allegations have not been and were not required to be scrutinized by a court of law to determine whether they would be sufficient to indict Waldheim, much less convict him for criminal behavior, the OSI has made extensive claims for its findings. It purports to have evidence of Waldheim's involvement in the delivery of civilians to the SS, the dissemination of antisemitic propaganda, the deportation of civilians to concentration and death camps, reprisal measures taken against hostages and the civilian population, the deportation of Jews from Greek islands, and the mistreatment of Allied prisoners of war. Mere knowledge of such events amounts to participation in the eyes of the OSI, so any one of these points would have sufficed to place Waldheim's name on the watch list (Department of Justice 1987; WJCCHCN 1988; *New York Times,* 28 April 1987; *Profil,* 18 May 1987).

Because other recent prominent cases handled by the OSI, for example Karl Linneas, John Demjanjuk, and Andrija Artukovic, had led to the deportation of persons suspected of direct involvement in especially serious war crimes, the watch-list decision seems to have encouraged the suspicion

27. For the best discussion of weaknesses in the OSI allegations, see Czernin 1987–88 and *Profil,* 18 May 1987.

28. Just how widespread this belief continues to be may be indicated by a recent issue of the newsletter of the Bougainville Freedom Movement. The Bougainville Freedom Movement is leading a struggle for independence of Bougainville—a part of the Solomon Islands—from Papua New Guinea. In an article published in *Garamut,* the movement's newsletter, author Max Watts asks what "Kurt Waldheim, Macbeth, Hamlet's uncle, the king of Denmark and 'Australian Foreign Minister' Senator Owens in Robert Cockburn's play *Hotel Hibiscus* have in common?" The answer: "All have had trouble with a ghost. The ghost of their crimes. There they went, successful, powerful. Unsuspected. Murderers. Condoning, commissioning, committing crimes." "But their victims," he continues, "the Balkan Jews, Bosnians and Greeks, who Kurt Waldheim had hung and gassed during his Nazi army days ... are, after all, all dead. Gone." "Of course," Watts avers, "neither Nazi Lieutenant Kurt Waldheim in the Balkans nor Australian Senator Owens in Canberra killed anyone personally. They had this done for them.... Lt. Waldheim during the war by his Wermacht [*sic*] soldiers ..." (Watts 1995: 3).

of Waldheim's complicity. Descriptions in the press of the OSI and the background to its decisions have reinforced this belief. Yet none of this justifies drawing any inferences about Waldheim's criminal behavior from the watch-list decision alone.

Unfortunately, most reporters covering the decision, especially those writing for widely respected newspapers in the United States, have uncritically accepted both the OSI's description of itself and its role, and all the allegations made in its report, even though these allegations have never been subjected to either judicial or critical public review in the United States. *New York Times* reporter Elaine Sciolino (1986), for example, described the role of the OSI as being "to track down, investigate and deport Nazi war criminals." Sciolino's interpretation obscured significant evidentiary distinctions and assumed a trial procedure by a recognized judicial authority that led to a conviction based on suspected crimes. Yet Kurt Waldheim has been tried by no judicial authority and was placed on the watch list because the OSI had determined that his activities in the Balkans amounted to assistance or participation as defined in the Holtzman amendment, not because he was a "war criminal," as implied in Sciolino's wording. Philip Shenon (1986), also of the *New York Times*, similarly described the OSI as being "responsible for tracking down and deporting Nazi war criminals." Shenon also described one of the OSI's functions as deporting war criminals, which had absolutely no bearing on Waldheim, who was simply barred from entering the United States. If, as both articles stated, the task of the OSI was indeed to track down "Nazi war criminals," did it not follow that the OSI had in the case of Kurt Waldheim "tracked down" a "Nazi war criminal"?

The obfuscation regarding this point in newspaper accounts shows no signs of abating. Even in mid-1994, for example, *International Herald Tribune* journalist Barry James (1994) described the "damning report on Waldheim's war record" that had been prepared by the OSI. He noted, correctly, that in the report the then Austrian president had been accused "of expediting and probably ordering a series of atrocities" but added, erroneously, that Waldheim had been "barred from the United States since 1987 *as a suspected war criminal*" (emphasis added).

The watch-list decision, the Justice Department's justification for it, and its presentation in the media together illustrate how ambiguities in a "language of guilt" might be manipulated for political purposes in response to an issue involving the memory of the Holocaust. Waldheim's ineptly mendacious handling of the allegations made against him seemed to confirm the worst suspicions about him personally, while the perceived unwillingness of the Austrians to act out the role expected of them in this Western morality play appeared to vindicate Waldheim's claim to be *homo austriacus*. Evidence showed that the former United Nations secretary general had been a member of two Nazi organizations, had served for three years in various units attached to Army Group E, had been accused by the UN War Crimes Commission of murder, and had lied about most of this past. The OSI, whose ostensible mission is to hunt down "Nazi war criminals," prepared a report strongly implying Waldheim's personal complicity in a range of criminal or (merely) reprehensible activities and recommended that his name be entered on the watch list, the only legal measure open to it. By acting on the OSI's recommendation, the Reagan administration in a sense made amends politically for its Bitburg embarrassment and validated its anti-Nazi credentials without paying any appreciable political price. By having elected such a man president and then failing to exert sufficient pressure for him to resign, Austria demonstrated its failure to confront its National Socialist past and accept its historical responsibility. It was thus only fitting that Waldheim, despite being the head of a friendly state, was barred from entering the United States; to do otherwise would imply a kind of symbolic amnesty by the Reagan administration for those involved in perpetrating the Holocaust. For the American government, moreover, it was the path of least resistance: Austria was not such an important and powerful ally, and its constitutional structure allowed the chancellor to assume most of the representative functions the Austrian president would normally be expected to perform. Thus, Waldheim's being on the watch list, although unprecedented, did not encumber foreign relations sufficiently to deter the Justice Department under Reagan from placing him on it and from reaffirming the decision under both the Bush and Clinton administrations.

Historical Responsibility and Public Memory

I have argued that the watch-list decision provided a way for the American government to show vigilance against disparagements of Holocaust memory. But it may offer only short-term emotional succor because it is a concrete measure against an identifiable culprit, which in the end must be considered unreliable. American geopolitical interests are subject to change, which may leave what once seemed like moral fervor looking more like a commemorative velleity. Also, the specific targets are not always as clear, nor as easy, as Kurt Waldheim and the Austrian state. Where ambiguities exist or interests collide, government leaders will reaffirm the rhetorical obligation of preserving memory, but they are unlikely to be able to define the substance of this memory or to specify precisely who is entitled to uphold memory and on whose behalf it should be upheld.

The Bitburg controversy suggests that reconciling the moral imperatives following from the Holocaust with universally recognized commemorative rituals of military honor is extremely difficult. The Waldheim affair shows that in such debates assumptions about individual criminal complicity and collective historical (moral) responsibility are frequently unwittingly confused or willfully conflated. But if a range of issues in Holocaust memory remains hotly contested, one important arena of the contest has received less attention: identifying what historical responsibility is, who is obliged to acknowledge it, and how. There have been few efforts to devise an explicit, generally applicable definition of historical responsibility, which is probably not accidental. Discussions of the issue illustrate the elasticity, if not elusiveness, of the concept and underline the need to rethink the overall approach to memory and commemorative vigilance.

Largely because of Western prodding, but also due increasingly to enlightened political self-interest, West Germany became the archetypical case of a state whose leaders accepted "historical responsibility" and offered moral and political arguments to buttress it. In the wake of the Waldheim affair, Austrian politicians have attempted to articulate an apposite version of historical responsibility. In both Germany and Austria, references to historical responsibility are uttered for the most part during or in connection with specific commemorative occasions.

In his address delivered at the fortieth anniversary of the liberation of the Bergen-Belsen concentration camp on 21 April 1985, Helmut Kohl logically embedded his view of Germany's historical responsibility in a decidedly "intentionalist" interpretation of power under National Socialism and of how individual morality failed in the face of it. "This darkest chapter of our history" must be remembered

> not because of the question of why those who risked their lives in opposing terror ultimately failed in their efforts. The decisive question is, instead, why so many people remained apathetic, did not listen properly, closed their eyes to the realities when the despots-to-be sought support for their inhumane program, first in back rooms and then openly, out in the streets. The intentions of the National Socialists were apparent well before November 9, 1938, when 35,000 Jews were abducted to concentration camps.
>
> We ask ourselves today why it was not possible to take action when the signs of National Socialist tyranny could no longer be overlooked—when books regarded as great cultural works of this century were burned, when synagogues were set on fire, when Jewish shops were demolished, when Jewish citizens were denied a seat on park benches. Those were warnings. Even though Auschwitz was beyond anything that man could imagine, the pitiless brutality of the Nazis had been clearly discernible. (quoted in Levkov 1987: 97–98)

"Germany bears historical responsibility for the crimes of the Nazi tyranny," Kohl argued later. "This responsibility is reflected not least in never-ending shame" (quoted in Levkov 1987: 99).

Three days after President Reagan and Chancellor Kohl had visited Bergen-Belsen and Bitburg, the West German Bundestag held a ceremony commemorating the fortieth anniversary of the end of World War II in Europe. The speech delivered by President Richard von Weizsäcker to the Bundestag has come to be seen as something of a benchmark for commemorative rhetoric and was often used as the standard against which the statements and speeches of Kurt Waldheim were found wanting.[29] This praise is in many respects well deserved, for in this speech Weizsäcker addressed poignantly the themes of shame, German sins of omission, the nature of the war, and the need for tolerance and civic courage in the present in ways consonant with the "philosemitic" inflection given to rhetoric about the past in postwar West Germany's political culture (Stern 1992). For example, the West German president described 8 May as the day that "liberated [the Germans] from the inhumanity and tyranny of the National Socialist regime," and he clearly stated that "the initiative for the war" had come "from Germany, not the Soviet Union," that the "genocide of the Jews" was a crime "unparalleled in history," and that though the destruction itself "was concealed from the eyes of the public … every German was able to experience what his Jewish compatriots had to suffer, ranging from plain apathy and hidden intolerance to outright hatred."[30] Yet one passage not only seems to conflict with the speech's overall compunctious tone but has surprisingly (especially in light of the Bitburg controversy) passed without criticism. In it, Weizsäcker first urged his listeners to recall "an occurrence honestly and undistortedly so that it becomes a part of our very beings" and then invited them to "mourn all the dead of the war and the tyranny." He continued:

> In particular we commemorate the six million Jews who were murdered in German concentration camps. We commemorate all nations who suffered in the war, especially the countless citizens of the Soviet Union and Poland who lost their lives. As Germans, we mourn our own compatriots who perished as soldiers, during air raids at home, in captivity or during expulsion. We commemorate the Sinti and Romany gypsies, the homosexuals and the mentally ill who were killed, as well as the people who had to die for their religious or political convictions.

Apart from the inaccurate and potentially explosive claim that six million Jews were killed in concentration camps,[31] this passage recalls the deaths of German

29. See, for example, Lewis 1986, *New York Times* 1986, and Maier 1988: 11.

30. Quoted in Hartman 1986: 263–73. All quoted passages are taken from this text.

31. It is fairly common knowledge that hundreds of thousands of Jews were murdered by the Einsatzgruppen operating behind the front lines during the campaign against the Soviet Union. Though it is common to refer to the conditions of the murder of the Jews in this shorthand way, Weizsäcker's imprecision seems nonetheless peculiar, given the attempts by deniers of the Holocaust to pick up on such inaccuracies to contest the extent, or even the fact, of National Socialist extermination policies.

soldiers alongside those of the Jews, Romany and Sinti gypsies, captured Soviet soldiers, resistance fighters, etc. Not only does Weizsäcker suggest a kind of moral equivalence of the suffering, but the German "compatriots" who "perished as soldiers" most assuredly included members of the Waffen-SS. Perhaps because the speech as a whole, described by *New York Times* columnist Anthony Lewis (1986) as "one of the great speeches of our time," was so moving and so explicit about moral responsibility, such comments might have seemed merely captious. Still, Weizsäcker's remarks on mourning were the rhetorical equivalent of the Kohl-Reagan Bitburg visit.

Of more immediate relevance are Weizsäcker's comments on guilt and responsibility. "There is no such thing as the guilt or innocence of an entire nation," he stated. "Guilt is, like innocence, not collective, but personal." But though "no discerning person can expect [the vast majority of today's population] to wear a penitential robe simply because they are Germans," he argued, "their forefathers have left them a grave legacy. All of us, whether guilty or not, whether old or young, must accept the past. We are all affected by its consequences and liable for it" (quoted in Hartman 1986: 265).

Although they are less practiced in commemorative pronouncements than their German counterparts, Austrian political leaders, in particular Chancellor Franz Vranitzky and President Thomas Klestil during their respective official visits to Israel, have articulated notions of historical moral responsibility along the lines of Kohl and Weizsäcker. On 9 June 1993, for example, when he received an honorary doctorate at the Hebrew University of Jerusalem, Chancellor Vranitzky rejected, as had Weizsäcker and later did Klestil, "collective guilt" but acknowledged the Austrians' "collective responsibility," which he defined as "the responsibility of each and every one of us to remember and to seek justice." This shared "moral responsibility," according to Vranitzky, derived from the fact that "many Austrians welcomed the 'Anschluss,' supported the Nazi regime and helped it to function." Vranitzky dismissed the idea that Austria as a political entity could had been responsible for the suffering imposed by the Nazi regime—"the state," he argued, "no longer existed"—but conceded that "some of her citizens inflicted" suffering "on other people." "We [Austrians]," Vranitzky noted, "admit to all that has happened in our history and to the deeds of all Austrians, be they good or bad. Just as we claim credit for our good deeds, we must beg forgiveness for the evil ones: the forgiveness of those who survived and of the descendants of those who perished" (Vranitzky 1993: 4–5).

Austrian President Thomas Klestil's state visit to Israel in November 1994 took on an added symbolic dimension because his predecessor was Kurt Waldheim. Klestil's remarks echoed themes addressed by Vranitzky in 1993, in particular the ritual rejection of "collective guilt," but in certain respects they went beyond them. Historical truth, the "entire truth," Klestil stated, "is complex. The thin line that ran between perpetrators and victims at that time ran right through the people, through their families, and often enough through one and the same heart. The seed of foment and the tragic blend of force and fascination gave rise to the Jewish tragedy in Austria. For too long," he added, "it has inhibited a critical reappraisal of the past and proved such a burden for a frank and open dialogue of trust between our two peoples." In the most memorable passage of the speech, Klestil remarked that "all too often we have only spoken of Austria as the first state to have lost its freedom and independence to National Socialism—and far too seldom of the fact that many of the worst henchmen in the Nazi dictatorship were Austrians." Rising to and simultaneously eschewing the expectations circulating in the Israeli press that he would apologize in the name of the Austrian people, Klestil stated bluntly that "no word of apology can ever expunge the agony of the Holocaust. On behalf of the Republic of Austria, I bow my head, with deep respect and profound emotion in front of the victims" (Klestil 1994: 3–4).

Both German and Austrian politicians who presume to speak in their citizens' name must choose words that are forceful enough to meet the demands of the immediate audience yet not too contrite to offend their domestic constituencies. Whether it resides primarily in "shame," in seeking forgiveness for evil deeds done by one's unnamed forebears, or for admitting the "whole truth" about the country's past, the historical or collective responsibility acknowledged by Weizsäcker, Kohl, Vranitzky, and Klestil when called upon to perform acts of official commemoration has had to satisfy parties with divergent moral priorities and political agendas.

Writers who reflect in public on the notion of historical responsibility do not suffer under the constraints faced by politicians, who ordinarily can discharge their duties by merely uttering words like historical responsibility. These writers perhaps ought to be somewhat more systematic in drawing out the implications of their arguments, but two examples show that they tend to advance us no further than speeches by Helmut Kohl or Franz Vranitzky on a good day.

Menachem Rosensaft has been among the most vocal and most prolific of those working to keep the memory of the Holocaust alive by underlining the importance of historical responsibility. In response to Ronald Reagan's claim that no one still living in West Germany had been "adults and participating in any way" in the Holocaust, Rosensaft at the height of the Bitburg debate wrote:

> But Nazi war criminals are not the only Germans who were adults between 1940 and 1945. West Germany's president, Richard von Weizsäcker, is 65 years old; the Bavarian prime Minister, Franz Josef Strauss, is only 70. They, together with all the surviving veterans of Hitler's armed forces and storm troopers, bear at least

a share of responsibility—if not personal guilt—for the Holocaust. (quoted in
Levkov 1987: 69)

In this article, Rosensaft formally distinguishes between personal guilt and
the vague, but clearly less reprehensible, category of responsibility. Yet his
usage is confusing; when he states that no one born after 1945 "should be
held personally responsible for the Holocaust" (quoted in Levkov 1987:
69), he seems to be conflating notions of guilt and responsibility. He goes on
to argue that this postwar generation, especially leaders like Weizsäcker and
Strauss, shares "responsibility" in the weaker sense because the extermination of the Jews "was planned and implemented by the German government
in the name of the German people" and "a nation's identity is the totality of
its past, the bad as well a the good" (quoted in Levkov 1987: 69). But this
presumes several very strong claims about the legitimacy of the Nazi regime,
its continuity with the Federal Republic, and, more generally, about the
possibilities of independent political action and the nature of political obligation in a regime devoid of democratic procedures. Despite the qualifica-
tions he offers, Rosensaft seems to be suggesting that having lived in Nazi
Germany, or even living in the post-Nazi Federal Republic, saddles one with
responsibility for policies under the Nazi regime because it claimed to have
acted "in the name of the German people."

Just before the second round of the Austrian presidential election in
1986, Rosensaft (1986) elaborated his views on personal guilt and responsibility. Kurt Waldheim, Rosensaft argued, "may or may not in fact have
been a war criminal. But that hardly exonerates him of guilt for his participation in the absolute evil of the Hitler era." According to Rosensaft, Waldheim should share the same obloquy as Eichmann and Mengele because of
the acts he committed and because failing to protest all the atrocities he
knew about was tantamount to endorsing them. Lest one imagine that such
rigorous standards were reserved merely for "Nazi soldiers" like Waldheim,
Rosensaft then explained that "the threads of direct and indirect responsibility reach far beyond those who were actually present on the scene."
Although he did not define what constituted "participat[ion] in the Nazi
movement," Rosensaft declared that all who did so endorsed the "central,
reprehensible goal" of the Nazis, namely, "the absolute domination of
mankind by the Aryan race," and hence "participated in [the] absolute evil"
of Nazism. But his phrase "who participated in any way in implementing
the Nazi ideology," which seems to suggest that volition ought to play some
role in determining who was "collectively responsible" for the Holocaust, is
mitigated by his earlier claim that failure to protest acts implied endorsing
them. In the end, moreover, such distinctions were irrelevant, for he argues
that "in matters of historical responsibility, no one is only a little bit guilty."

Rosensaft's judgments against Waldheim, against those who lived under the Nazi regime, and even against those born after 1945 are severe, and the responsibility he assigns them is metaphysical. Indeed, Rosensaft dissolves the boundaries between guilt and responsibility, and he is explicitly unwilling to acknowledge the category of "opportunist." This stance makes it slightly more comprehensible why German and Austrian leaders feel invariably obliged preemptively to rebut the allegation of "collective guilt."[32]

Less stringent, and far more systematic, is Charles Maier's discussion (1988) of these issues in his detailed account of the so-called *Historikerstreit,* the public debate in Germany in the mid-1980s on National Socialism and its relationship to German history as a whole. In the book's opening chapter, Maier discusses how the "Bitburg history" makes it difficult "to pin down any notions of collective responsibility." At issue, Maier acutely observes, is

> the degree to which West Germany as a national society accepts responsibility for the Nazi past, and for how long it must acknowledge such responsibility. In what sense does collective responsibility exist?... [I]nsofar as a collection of people wishes to claim existence as a society or nation, it must thereby accept existence as a community through time, hence must acknowledge that acts committed by earlier agents still bind or burden the contemporary community.... Insofar as past acts are acknowledged as injurious, whatever reparation is still possible must be attempted. West German leaders have accepted that responsibility, not with consistently good grace but to a major degree. Nor does this responsibility have a time limit. Responsibility for a burdened past can justifiably become less preoccupying as other experiences are added to the national legacy. The more remote descendants of these original victims have a more diluted claim to compensation. But like the half-life of radioactive material, there is no point at which responsibility simply goes away.

Bitburg history, he suggests, "comes perilously close to arguing that by now further efforts to encourage collective memory are obsessive" (Maier 1988: 14–15).

Maier's argument hinges on his conception of German national society. So long as the German "nation" wishes to remain the German nation, or at least wishes to consider itself the German nation, it must take responsibility for acts of others who have laid claim to the same mantle: if contemporary Germans want to retain Goethe, Schiller, and Hegel in their national pantheon,

---

32. In his talk at the Hebrew University, Vranitzky (1993: 4) stated that "the connotation of 'collective guilt' does not apply to Austria," while Klestil (1994: 3) emphasized to the Knesset that "no people should be blamed with collective guilt." The present essay was written before the appearance of Daniel Jonah Goldhagen's *Hitler's Willing Executioners,* but the arguments advanced there, and the very sympathetic popular response to Goldhagen's book, only strengthen my point.

they are obliged, Maier seems to suggest, to accept Hitler, Goering, and Himmler as well. This seems a simple enough point, not dissimilar to Weizsäcker's injunction to "reflect on the course taken by our history" (quoted in Hartman 1986: 262). On closer examination, however, Maier's argument begs a number of questions.

Maier nowhere explicitly explains what defines any nation, and in particular the German nation, but he suggests that it is "a collection of people [that] wishes to claim existence" as such. Because the idea of the nation is historical and the time when inhabitants of what later became Germany claimed to be a nation can scarcely be said to predate the nineteenth century, Maier's definition would seem to exclude the prior period from any German national tradition. While this would have no bearing on the period between 1933 and 1945, it would severely circumscribe the broad view of German "national" history and would diverge markedly from conventional historical writing. More significantly, if all national communities and indeed all communities are "imagined," as Benedict Anderson (1983) has argued, then the "imagination" of the "national community" need not and cannot remain static or immutable. If that is so, then what would prevent the West German Federal Republic from renouncing the National Socialist conception of "Germanness" as illegitimate, or at least otiose? On Maier's terms alone, there seem to be no grounds for him, as a nonmember of this "collection of people," to claim that this temporally more inclusive "German" nation exists, much less to offer compelling arguments that West German democratic leaders are this nation's legitimate heirs. Maier (1988: 15) seems to acknowledge this when he attests that West German leaders, as the heirs of the German "nation," have themselves accepted the "responsibility for a burdened past."

In Maier's terms, however, short of a contrived racial theory of nationhood, no compelling grounds exist for contemporary German leaders to assume the mantle of "national" legatee of the Nazis and thus become the bearers of the responsibility to which Maier alludes. West German leaders' assumption of this responsibility was based originally principally on strategic political considerations. It involved employing a vocabulary of contrition that not only was believed to correspond to the expectations of both Western political leaders and the international (Jewish) community but also could simultaneously justify this responsibility and the reparation measures it implied to the non-Jewish German public. Over the years, West German leaders seem to have internalized the arguments "grounding" this notion of historical responsibility. In my view, what might be seen as a ritualization of a "historically responsible" philosemitic political culture in West Germany explains both why gestures such as Willy Brandt's kneeling at the memorial to the Warsaw Ghetto or Richard von Weizsäcker's eloquent speech at the fortieth anniversary of the end of World War II were even possible and the widespread praise these gestures elicited.[33]

This reading of postwar German "memory" also helps explain not only why, prior to the Waldheim affair, leaders of the Second Austrian Republic did not feel constrained to accept any historical responsibility for Nazi crimes and were reluctant to acknowledge restitution claims but also why the years since then (especially in 1988, the fiftieth anniversary of both the Anschluss and the *Reichskristallnacht*) have witnessed a surfeit of attempts to "come to terms" with Austria's National Socialist past and, in comparison with West Germany, belated public acknowledgments by Chancellor Vranitzky and President Klestil of an ambiguous Austrian version of historical responsibility (Wodak et al. 1994; Uhl 1992).

The Politics of Memory

"Oh, we know there are political and strategic reasons, but this issue, as all issues related to that awesome event, transcends politics and diplomacy" (quoted in Levkov 1987: 44). Elie Wiesel's words, spoken in his futile attempt to dissuade Ronald Reagan from visiting the military cemetery in Bitburg, forcefully state the conflict between politics and morality at the heart of every issue involving Holocaust memory. If Reagan's visit to Kolmeshöhe cemetery in 1985 was seen to violate the moral dictates of Holocaust memory as Wiesel and others understand them, the U.S. Department of Justice's decisions to place and retain Kurt Waldheim on the watch list offered the Reagan administration the chance to restore the putative convergence between morality and politics that Reagan's Bitburg visit had sundered. Yet the language of morality is protean and malleable. As we have seen in the case of Bitburg, the moral injunction to combat trivialization of the Holocaust was impossible to reconcile with the competing moral claim not to hold people responsible for acts they did not commit. In the Waldheim affair, at least as it played out in Austria, both calling someone to account for trivializing German atrocities and defending someone against alleged slanders (in Waldheim's case somewhat precariously) can be defended as moral conventions. Perceptions about the morality of the one or the other stance depended on the assumptions underlying the perceptions.

33. I am not arguing that the pragmatic nature of these public gestures and speeches suggests that the individuals who made them did not in reality abhor Nazi crimes or feel sadness and remorse for their victims. I do argue, however, that the categories that determine an individual's response to the Holocaust are not necessarily applicable to these individuals in their role as political leaders.

Political decisions are regularly accorded moral status and are defended (or attacked) by adducing moral claims, but not all issues can be posed in such absolutist terms. Pace Wiesel, there is no "transcendent" authority for judging or choosing between such lesser conflicting moral claims: in these cases, the "moral" position is the one that becomes conventionally accepted as such. Thus, both the Waldheim and Bitburg affairs offer strong evidence that when moral issues, including those related to the Holocaust, assume public character, they will be adjudicated politically.

They also show that in attempting to maintain vigilance against those intent on forgetting, historicizing, or trivializing the Holocaust, we should neither suspend intellectual rigor about the imprecision of the moral categories nor forget the contingency of the moral language we employ. Perhaps this is ultimately a trivial point, but my discussion of responsibility shows how frequently it is ignored or denied. In the end, our ability to counter a repeat of Nazi-type racial policies, wherever they occur and in whatever guise, will depend less on the consistency or even merits of our moral arguments than on our willingness to act and our ability to exert sufficient political pressure on those whose power really counts.

References

Anderson, B. 1983. *Imagined Communities: Reflections on the Origin and Spread of Nationalism.* London.

"Auf Kohls Rat hören wir nicht wieder." 1985. *Der Spiegel,* 29 April.

Bartov, O. 1991. *Hitler's Army: Soldiers, Nazis and War in the Third Reich.* New York.

Bergmann, W. 1994. "Die Bitburg-Affäre in der deutschen Presse. Rechtskonservative und linksliberale Interpretationen." In *Schwieriges Erbe. Der Umgang mit Nationalsozialismus und Antisemitismus in Österreich, der DDR und der Bundesrepublik Deutschland,* ed. Werner Bergmann, R. Erb, and A. Lichtblau, 418–19. Frankfurt.

"Bitburg hat schweren Schaden angerichtet." 1985. *Der Spiegel,* 29 April.

Born, H. 1987. *Für die Richtigkeit. Kurt Waldheim.* Munich.

Bronfman, E. 1986. "Shame on Austria." *New York Times,* 10 June.

Cohen, R. 1994. "Now It's Waldheim the Knight, Courtesy of a Forgetful Vatican." *International Herald Tribune,* 30–31 July.

Collins, J. L., Jr., H. Fleischer, G. Fleming, H. R. Kurz, M. Messerschmidt, J. Vanwelkenhuyzen, and J. L. Wallach. 1988. "Der Bericht der internationalen Historikerkommission." Supplement to *Profil,* 15 February, Vienna.

Crews, F. 1995. *The Memory Wars: Freud's Legacy in Dispute.* New York.

Czernin, H. 1987–88. "Waldheims Balkanjahre." Parts 1–7. *Profil,* 7 December–
25 January.

Department of Justice. 1987. Press release, 27 April.

"Eine eigenartige geistige Gymnastik." 1985. *Der Spiegel,* 22 April.

Friedman, L., ed. 1972a. "The Nuremberg Judgment." In *The Laws of War: A
Documentary History,* vol. 2, 923–1026. New York.

_____. 1972b. "Opinion and Judgement of United States Military Tribunal at
Nuremberg in United States vs. Wilhelm von Leeb et al." In *The Laws of War:
A Documentary History,* vol. 2, 1421–70. New York.

Hartman, G., ed. 1986. *Bitburg in Moral and Political Perspective.* Bloomington.

Heer, H., and K. Naumann, eds. 1995. *Vernichtungskrieg. Verbrechen der
Wehrmacht.* Hamburg.

Herzstein, R. 1988. *Waldheim: The Missing Years.* London.

Hilberg, R. 1985. *The Destruction of the European Jews.* Revised and definitive edition. New York.

Höhne, H. 1985. "Das ist die Mentalität eines Schlächters." *Der Spiegel,* 29 April.

James, B. 1994. "Pope Offends Jews by Granting Waldheim a Knighthood." *International Herald Tribune,* 29 July.

Judt, T. 1992. "The Past is Another Country: Myth and Memory in Postwar
Europe." *Daedelus* 121, no. 4 (fall):83–118.

Klestil, T. 1994. "Address of the Federal President of the Republic of Austria, Dr.
Thomas Klestil, to the Knesset in Jerusalem on Tuesday, November 15, 1994."
Jerusalem. Typescript.

"Die Kriegstoten." 1985. *Frankfurter Allgemeine Zeitung,* 26 April.

Levkov, I., ed. 1987. *Bitburg and Beyond: Encounters in American, German and
Jewish History.* New York.

Lewis, A. 1986. "The Need to Remember." *New York Times,* 5 May.

Loewenberg, P. 1995. *Fantasy and Reality in History.* Oxford.

Maier, C. 1988. *The Unmasterable Past: History, Holocaust, and German National
Identity.* Cambridge, Mass.

Manoschek, W. 1995. "Es gibt nur eines für das Judentum: Vernichtung." Introduction to *Das Judenbild in deutschen Soldatenbriefen 1939–1944,* ed. W.
Manoschek, 5–8. Hamburg.

Messerschmidt, M. 1969. *Die Wehrmacht im NS-Staat. Zeit der Indoktrination.* Hamburg.

Mitten, R. 1987. "Ohne KURToisie." *Profil,* 11 May.

_____. 1992. *The Politics of Antisemitic Prejudice: The Waldheim Phenomenon in
Austria.* Boulder.

_____. 1995. "Was bedeutet: Aufarbeitung der Vergangenheitsbewältigung?" In
Totalitäre Sprache – Langue de Bois – The Language of Dictatorship, ed. R. Wodak
and P. Kirsch, 21–39. Vienna.

New York Times. 1985. Editorial, "Conceal Not the Blood," 6 May.

_____. 1986. Editorial, "Dutiful in Austria," 6 June.

Niethammer, L. 1972. *Die Mitläuferfabrik. Säuberung und Rehabilitierung unter
amerikanischer Besatzung.* Frankfurt.

Presse- und Informationsamt, ed. 1985. *Erinnerung, Trauer und Versöhnung.
Ansprachen und Erklärungen zum vierzigsten Jahrestag des Kriegsendes.* Bonn.

Robinson, P. 1994. *Freud and His Critics*. Berkeley.

Rosensaft, M. 1986. "He Can't Be Exonerated of His Guilt." *New York Times*, 6 June.

Ryan, A. 1986. "Waldheim May Be Innocent, but Why Is He Acting like So Many Nazi War Criminals Have?" *Washington Post*, 27 April.

Safire, W. 1986. "Waldheim's Secret Life." *New York Times*, 21 April.

Sciolino, E. 1986. "U.S. to Request Access to U.N. File on Waldheim." *New York Times*, 9 April.

Shenon, P. 1986. "Justice Department Official Urges Waldheim Be Barred from U.S." *New York Times*, 25 April.

Sichrovsky, P. 1986. "'Soll ein ehemaliger Nazi und Lügner Vertreter Österreichs sein?'" *Profil*, 24 March.

Smith, H. 1985. "Delicate Reagan Path." *New York Times*, 6 May.

———. 1988. *The Power Game: How Washington Works*. New York.

Sprenger, H. 1985. "'Bitburg über alles' Versöhnung oder psychologische Nachrüstung?" *Vorgänge* 4:31–44.

Stern, F. 1992. *The Whitewashing of the Yellow Badge: Antisemitism and Philosemitism in Postwar Germany*. Oxford.

Stourzh, G. 1985. *Geschichte des Staatsvertrages 1945–1955. Österreichs Weg zur Neutralität*. Graz.

Streit, C. 1991. *Keine Kameraden. Die Wehrmacht und die sowjetischen Kriegsgefangenen 1941–1945*. Bonn.

Thames Television/Home Box Office. 1988. *Kurt Waldheim: A Case to Answer?* Television broadcast, June.

Uhl, H. 1992. *Zwischen Versöhnung und Verstörung. Eine Krontroverse um Österreichs historische Identität fünfzig Jahre nach dem Anschluß*. Vienna.

United Kingdom. Ministry of Defence. 1989. "Review of the Results of Investigations Carried Out by the Ministry of Defence in 1986 into the Fate of British Servicemen Captured in Greece and the Greek Islands between October 1943 and the Involvement, If Any, of the Then Lieutenant Waldheim." London.

United States. Department of State. 1963. *Foreign Relations of the United States, Diplomatic Papers 1943*. Vol. 1. Washington, D.C.

———. 1980. *Immigration and Nationality Act, with Amendments and Notes on Related Laws: Committee Print for the Use of the Committee on the Judiciary, House of Representatives, United States*. 7th ed. Washington, D.C.

Vranitzky, F. 1993. "Address of the Federal Chancellor of Austria Dr. Franz Vranitzky on the occasion of the Special Convocation of the Hebrew University of Jerusalem." Jerusalem. Typescript.

Watts, M. 1995. "Waldheim's Ghost." *Garamut: Bougainville Freedom Movement Newsletter*, September.

Wodak, R., F. Menz, R. Mitten, and F. Stern. 1994. *Die Sprachen der Vergangenheiten*. Frankfurt.

Wollheim, R. 1994. *The Mind and Its Depth*. Cambridge, Mass.

World Jewish Congress Commission on the Holocaust and Crimes of the Nazis (WJCCHCN). 1988. "Waldheim's Nazi Past: The Dossier." Manuscript.

Part Two

THE AUSTRIAN IMPACT ON AMERICAN CULTURE

Chapter 4

MASS EMIGRATION AND INTELLECTUAL EXILE FROM NATIONAL SOCIALISM

The Austrian Case

Egon Schwarz

History is made up of continuities and discontinuities. To do it justice it is necessary to take both of these ordering principles into account. Exile and banishment have always existed—mass expulsions and mass deportations have been recorded since Nebuchadnezzar's rule in the sixth century B.C. (see Tägil 1990). But because of their power of expression and criticism, writers, intellectuals, and artists have been favorite targets for tyrants' wrath, and for those same reasons writers and intellectuals are the prime witnesses of the exile experience. Ovid's elegiac lament, Dante's bitter pride, Heine's poisoned homesickness, and Unamuno's scornful hatred are famous manifestations of the exile's state of mind.

In modern times the nature of exile has changed. In former epochs, individuals or defeated ethnic and religious groups were forced to leave their homelands. This form of expulsion continues to exist, as exemplified by the fate of Russian, East German, African, and South American writers. But in the age of large social upheavals like the French and Russian revolutions, entire social classes became outlawed and homeless. This proscription

This chapter is a slightly revised version of an article by the same title that first appeared in the *Austrian History Yearbook* 27 (1996):1–20, which in turn is based on the Kann Lecture, delivered at the University of Minnesota on 3 November 1994.

affected mainly the privileged of the old order. It was different during the National Socialist dictatorship. No longer were the ruling circles the ones persecuted; instead, in accordance with the irrational party ideology, a motley array of communists, Social Democrats, and racial undesirables were deprived of their basic human rights, such as the right to have possessions and to live, much less to live in liberty. People of the most heterogeneous origins—rich and poor, above all Jews, but also out-of-favor non-Jews, members of religious sects, gypsies, and artists whose styles were deemed decadent by the fine connoisseurs of art that the Nazis were—lost their livelihoods, residences, friends, safety, and citizenship. Many were thrown into charnel houses called concentration camps, never again to reemerge. Others were released on condition of emigrating. No wonder hundreds of thousands tried to leave this dangerous country—among them some who had little to fear, who left from loyalty to their friends and spouses or simply from disgust of the regime.

Fortunately, before the war broke out many were able to escape the Nazi rage by emigrating. It is sad to say that many more could have been saved if the rest of the world had been more forthcoming with its help, for example, by simply relaxing the tight grip on its frontiers. No country was willing to take in a shipload of refugees who were not allowed to land in Cuba despite their legitimate visas. Eleanor Roosevelt implored her husband in vain to let these people in. They were taken back to Europe to an uncertain fate, or rather a fairly certain one. In the United States not even the legal quotas were filled. The new Holocaust Museum in Washington bluntly cites the reason: antisemitism in the State Department. People were also turned away from the Swiss borders to their destruction. Even in cases of the direst need, Michael Marrus (1990: 54) complains, the Allies failed to "provide a single ship to carry Jewish escapees from Rumania, Turkey or other countries, when such a passage might have saved thousands of lives from the Nazi Holocaust." Contrast this with Francisco Franco, who intervened in the deportation of six thousand Sephardic Jews from Berlin to the annihilation camps: the Nazis relented and sent them to Spain. These are only a few examples of what should not have been done and what could have been done.

In the beginning, state boundaries were not yet hermetically sealed, but the situation deteriorated rapidly. The fear of provoking Hitler, a desire for peace at any price, latent and often overt antisemitism, a bad economy and local unemployment, the growth of indigenous fascist movements, the hope of using Hitler's Germany as a bulwark against Bolshevik Russia—all these causes made obtaining legal immigration permits increasingly difficult. Those who had money and connections abroad, the mobile young and unattached, the early pessimists, and, of course, the lucky ones escaped; the others perished.

The purpose of my essay is to examine how the phenomenon of emigration from Nazi persecution played itself out specifically in Austria. I am certainly no Ovid or Unamuno, but over these writers I have the advantage of being able to piece together a story, significant portions of which I have personally lived through, which I hope will imbue it with the flavor of authenticity.

As a heuristic device I distinguish five phases of the so-called exile phenomenon. The first demands an understanding of the conditions that make emigration necessary or highly desirable—an examination of the when and how of Nazi persecution, the attitudes of the general population, and so on. Phase two requires insight into how a change of venue is effected. While some émigrés reached a final destination swiftly, beginning to settle down from day one, many were homeless migrants for months and years, changing, in Bertolt Brecht's phrase, countries more often than shirts. This phase involved endless battles with border guards, immigration authorities, and the police; deportations; and sometimes prison and concentration camps. The third phase is characterized by the obtainment of a visa or other entry permit, escape from the arenas of turmoil mostly to overseas locations, arrival in a foreign country, and the first mental and physical stocktaking of the new environment, which is sometimes harsh and exotic, rarely welcoming and accommodating. The fourth phase encompasses the changes that make an immigrant out of an emigrant: the search for and finding of a steady livelihood, often the struggle with and eventual mastery of a new language, the adjustment to a new environment (meteorological, social, and economic), adaptation to and acceptance by a new population, new mores —in short, a new culture. Finally, there is phase five, the end of exile, either in the shape of the refugees' total absorption into the host country or in their return to their places of origin, once livable conditions have been restored there. This can take the form of an attempted and failed return, with all the symptoms of a second exile and the realization that one cannot go home again, but it can also entail the long process of reconciliation, successfully coming to terms with the past. Please note that I am using the expressions "émigré," "refugee," and "exile" interchangeably, since the boundaries between them are much too fluid for artificially rigid distinctions to help our understanding.

It has never been easy, even at the time of the Habsburg monarchy, to say with confidence what is Austrian. But especially in the twentieth century, when focusing on some Austrian event, process, movement, or other phenomenon, a large obstacle is likely to intrude on the analysis: Germany. Whether it is the Austrian economy, literature, newspapers, or, above all, national identity that one wishes to illuminate, Austria's big neighbor to the north casts a large shadow on the problem. Austrians tend to define themselves with a view to the Germans. Much depends on the way Austrians perceive them or think they are perceived by them and on the degree to which they do or do not think of themselves as Germans. Because of their common language and intersecting history, this dependence is especially observable in cultural matters, so the critic needs to disentangle the phenomenon in question from its German ramifications. I could cite numerous cases to corroborate this contention but will be satisfied with one. Speaking of movie history, Georg Schmid (1983: 709–10) asks, "Is it at all possible to draw a precise dividing line between Austrian and German film?" He also refuses to blame economic factors during the First Republic for Austria's lack of international film success and asserts that this failure "no doubt is due to Austria's traditional and chronic dependence on Germany."

Since at the time of which I speak the small Austrian republic had been annexed to the German Reich and had ceased to exist as an independent entity, the plight of the persecuted population groups resembled in fundamental respects that of their German counterparts. But there were also some very marked differences. Despite many similarities, phases one and two of the exile syndrome, forcible uprooting and flight, can be narrated with reference to specific Austrian conditions. In phases three and four, reaching a safe haven and resettlement, the fate of the Austrian refugees blends more with that of other victims of Nazism, but even here traces of their national origin can be found to color their experiences. In phase five, denouement, the peculiar vicissitudes of postwar Austria, in contrast to those of the two Germanys, again play a significant role. One must not, however, forget that the flight from political oppression inherently transcends national origins and boundaries in many respects, and I examine the events of half a century ago in part to illuminate the plight of the millions driven from their homes today. Each of these expulsions is of course sui generis, but the distinctive features can only be perceived by comparing them. Historians are trained to bring out the individual features of events, while sociologists tend to concentrate on similarities: I shall try to adopt a sociohistorical stance to keep an eye on both.

When Hitler became chancellor of the German Reich in January 1933, the people whose lives were immediately threatened and had to flee forthwith were activists who had enraged the Nazis by word or deed in the political struggles preceding the take-over. Others, uncomfortable as they may have been, adopted a wait-and-see attitude. But as the Nazis consolidated their power, more and more people, above all Jews, felt the pressure to emigrate. The persecutions following the Reichstag fire, the book burnings of May 1933, the boycott of Jewish stores, the dismissal of Jews and Socialists from their teaching jobs and other public positions, the Nuremburg racial laws of 1935, and the gradual imposition of ever more restrictive measures drove thousands to the consulates and into emigration. In the earlier years it was still possible to take some personal possessions along. Of equal importance was the willingness of some countries to accept refugees from Germany as long as there was only a trickle. In other words, from 1933 to 1938 the affected Germans had five years of warning, which they could heed at several political junctures or ignore at their risk. They had some time to get mentally accustomed to their situation and to realize that this was not another dubious government of the Weimar Republic, one that would fade away like its predecessors, but a lasting deadly threat. They had time to seek contacts abroad, to wind up their affairs, to apply for visas, or to explore other possibilities of escape.

Their Austrian counterparts had no such luxuries. I am not claiming that the Austrian anti-Nazis had no warning: the Nazi take-over in neighboring Germany, the bloody suppression of the Social Democrats in 1934, the murder of Dollfuss by the Nazis in the same year, the undemocratic regime of the Austrofascists, their ambivalence toward the Jews and drift toward accommodation with Germany, and Mussolini's abandonment of Austria were severe warnings. But the clear and present danger to life and limb came only on 11 March 1938. With the inexorable swiftness of a guillotine, the accumulated laws and hardened attitudes cut the Austrian anti-Nazis loose from yesterday, converting them into outcasts and outlaws overnight, so to speak. The strong Jewish presence in Vienna, approximately 10 percent of the population, was another distinguishing factor of the utmost gravity. With one blow the number of asylum seekers had almost doubled. Large segments of the Austrian population were also fiercely antisemitic, a phenomenon that to some extent still distinguishes the Second Republic from the Federal Republic of Germany. It dates back to the religious indoctrination of the Middle Ages and the Counter Reformation, as well as to Habsburg days when Jews were ubiquitous in the monarchy, the only minority without a fixed territory, who were distrusted or even hated by all others.

In this context it is well to remember that turn-of-the-century Viennese antisemitism profoundly influenced Hitler and that Karl Lueger, the city's antisemitic mayor, became young Hitler's admired and emulated model. Hitler, born in the Austrian city of Braunau, was a typical product of the antisemitic subculture of his time. The Austrian influence on Nazi ideology is incalculable. It is not a mere statistical coincidence that so many torturers in the concentration and annihilation camps were of Austrian origin. Large numbers of illegal Austrian Nazis who had fled to Germany during the Schuschnigg era returned to their homeland in the wake of the German armies, joined forces with the local variety, and unleashed a reign of terror in the streets the likes of which Germany had not seen. I shall cite only one testimony (Schmidl 1987: 233) from an eyewitness: "The extent and the brutality of the 'Nazi terror' in Austria by far exceeded those in Germany. Members of a Jewish family who succeeded in escaping to North Germany were positively astonished at the comparably humane treatment of the Jews in the old Reich."

While the country was still jubilant and the masses were frenetically cheering their Führer, humiliating actions were initiated against those proscribed by the new order. People were dragged from their apartments and, equipped with inadequate tools, forced to remove the symbols and slogans of the campaign for the aborted plebiscite from walls and sidewalks, their tormentors egged on by a derisive and sadistic populace. Today a prominent and controversial monument by the sculptor Hrdlička commemorates these sufferings. Entire streets were cordoned off, and Jews—old or young, strong or feeble—were arrested. Many were ordered to perform knee-bends and other absurd exercises, some were drowned in the Danube, the beards of the pious were set on fire, and others were taken to the hotel Metropol, which had become the dreaded headquarters of the Secret Police. Not until he underwent the agony of waiting for his daughter Anna to return from its torture chambers did Freud, initially reluctant, decide to leave his beloved Vienna. But not everybody was released so quickly, and some never came out again. Tenants were evicted from their apartments or houses and pupils from their schools. Businesses were "Aryanized," which was largely a euphemism for confiscation. Family members did not come home from work or errands because they had been shipped to Dachau. Some showed up again with swollen faces and bruised bodies, afraid to tell what had been done to them. Worse perhaps than the corporeal abuses was the mental agony: the feeling of impotence, the sense of humiliation, the loss of dignity, the lack of recourse, the terror of an unimaginable future.

The arbitrary harassment of persons seeking exit permits increased; long lines formed before the foreign consulates, but the reward for many hours' perseverance was rarely more than application forms to be filled out and handed in, never to be heard about again. A sudden and invariably false rumor that visas were available from some obscure country attracted large crowds to its consulate. The main topic of conversation was emigration; the departure of a family or illegal flight of some courageous person was commented upon and mythologized like a historic event. Owners of visas were admired and envied like the rich and famous of this world. The possession of an American "affidavit," the precondition for entry into the El Dorado of emigration, was worth more than an opulent country estate had been in more pacific times. Parents gave up their offspring because some countries would accept children but not adults. New trades sprang up that had not existed before: agents who obtained documents for the new pariahs and guides that transported the desperate over state borders. People swam across rivers and climbed mountains to escape the Nazi hell—and were often ruthlessly returned. Suicides among the victims abounded. How easy it would have been to save all these people threatened with extinction. But, as today, the world closed its doors to the persecuted and thus is coresponsible for their destruction. In 1938 the international conference of Evian, convened for the purpose of doing something about the refugee problem, brought no relief. One of the reasons advanced for its inaction was that by admitting more asylum seekers, "the processes of appeasement in international relations might be hindered" (Goodwin-Gill 1990: 19). Such blatant yet naive opportunism deservedly elicited the Nazis' scorn. If the world loved the Jews so much, they mocked, why did no one let them in? But the borders remained tight. Like myself, many Austrians were forced to cross them illegally, and therewith began the second phase of emigration.

In personal accounts, novels, and movies—for example, in Erich Maria Remarque's *Flotsam*, Anna Seghers's *Transit*, Georg Stefan Troller's film trilogy *Whereto and Back*, autobiographies such as Lion Feuchtwanger's *Malevolent France* and Alfred Döblin's *Journey of Destiny*, and even comedies such as Franz Werfel's *Jacobowski and the Colonel*—this phase has been described innumerable times.[1] It involves a variety of horrors—hazardous escapes; arrests; deportations; encounters with police, with ruthless immigration services, with the jaded employees of refugee organizations; "protective custody," internment, and even prison; not to mention the need to feed and clothe oneself in the meantime—and a variety of mental torments, for example, those of not being believed and, in general, not being regarded as fully human. In the eyes of the well established, a stigma always adheres to the refugee. Rather than describing such eventualities abstractly, let me relate a couple of episodes that I experienced as a teenager. Mutatis mutandis, they evoke the atmosphere and document the dangers of the political fugitive's life.

Leaving Vienna turned out to be more difficult than entering Czechoslovakia. We were evicted from the only apartment I had ever known in my sixteen years. My father and I had to find living quarters elsewhere. School after the Anschluss was a nightmare, and so was the obtainment of the monstrous *Steuerunbedenklichkeitserklärung* (the declaration of the unobjectionableness of one's tax status), required before leaving the country. I can only guess the agonies my father had to go through while dissolving his business and other affairs. By contrast, crossing the Czechoslovak border was simple: at our approach the ordinarily watchful customs officials turned their backs and pretended not to see us. They had been bribed by our relatives from Bratislava, whom we were going to join. What followed must have been experienced by thousands of refugees. During the next few days we were in

---

1. See Remarque 1941, Seghers 1944, Feuchtwanger 1942, Döblin 1949, and Werfel 1945. The three films in Georg Stefan Troller's trilogy *Wohin und zurück*, which were directed by Axel Corti, are *God Does Not Believe in Us Anymore* (1981), *Santa Fé* (1985), and *Welcome in Vienna* (1985).

high spirits, in a kind of euphoria of freedom and safety. We were asked about the persecutions, the arrests, the concentration camps, the violence in the streets, the cruelty, the glee of bestial oppressors. But soon the routine of everyday living set in again. I observed, much to my astonishment, that once the brief flicker of curiosity had been satisfied, people did not want to hear about Aryanizations, the Gestapo, visas, and passports. Since we had no money, employment, or even a legal residency permit, our movements were severely restricted. We felt superfluous. Moreover, we were rebuked for being overly gloomy. "You'll see, you'll be back in Vienna by fall," we were told again and again by people in a country whose own safety from Hitler was seriously in doubt. Unfortunately, our most pessimistic forecasts were borne out almost immediately. The excellent state of the Czechoslovakian defenses, their pact of friendship with France, the promises of the Allies, and the purported goodwill of the Russians proved impotent in the face of Hitler's evil energy. The Western democracies backed down once more; in the wake of the Sudetenland crisis, the Munich Pact of 29 September 1938 gave the Nazis a free hand. Czechoslovakia was dismembered, and Slovakia became autonomous. With the cleric Tiso at the head of a fascist state, his feared Hlinka guard, a paramilitary troop modeled after the SS, unleashed its terror. One of the new government's first measures was to persecute minorities living in Bratislava; in gratitude to Hitler, the benefactor who had placed them in this enviable position of power, the new authorities devoted themselves to harassing the refugees who had come mainly from adjacent Vienna. Police raids went from house to house, and we eluded them a few times. Eventually, however, we were arrested and deported with a truckload of other unfortunates.

At first we did not know where we were headed. Rumors about prison, forced labor, extradition to Germany, and concentration camps proved wrong. Instead we were brought to the part of the country that, to the disappointment of the Slovaks, had to be ceded to Hungary in accordance with the Munich Pact. We were unloaded in a little town, and from the onlookers we learned its Slovakian name, Dunajska Streda—Dunaszerdahely in Hungarian. A few vehicles had arrived previously, depositing their human cargo in the main square, so that altogether there were about eighty or a hundred of us. Without any order from above—since the Slovak authorities had already left and the Hungarian ones had not yet arrived— the townspeople provided us with tents and food, and we began to arrange ourselves as best we could. But it was clear that camping out in the marketplace of a small Central European town could be only a brief interlude, and indeed as soon as the Hungarians moved in a couple of days later it came to an abrupt end. Again uniformed men appeared, who made us dismantle the tents and collect our belongings. We were marched to the railroad station and loaded into a train that was already standing there pumping steam.

Before long we were heading toward a new obscure destination. At a small village the train halted; we had to descend and march along a rural road until at last we arrived at an abandoned farmstead, where we spent the night herded together like animals. At dawn we were assembled in the courtyard and had to hand over our money and valuables. We started on our way again as on the previous day. Soon our guards faltered, stepped to the side of the road, and indicated to us with vigorous gestures to continue our march. The road became a path, taking us through fields: to the left and right lay tilled land, with piles of hay stacked up high; there was an occasional shrub, but not a tree far and wide, and no human habitation.

Hardly had we advanced two or three hundred feet into this landscape when several bleary-eyed shapes approached us. Their numbers increased, and soon we were surrounded by them. We exchanged questions and answers. Through the din of voices we learned that these were fellow victims who had been brought here a day or two earlier by the Hungarian authorities. We could see the Slovakian border a few hundred meters ahead; behind us a chain of Hungarian soldiers blocked the way back. Between these lay a "demarcation line"—the technical term for a zone that is the object of a change in international border regulations. We were in no-man's-land.

Thus began a strange episode in our lives, different from what any of us had known. Poverty, unemployment, strikes, protests, even the inhumanity with which one person torments the next still belonged to the realm of the imaginable, to the store of past or at least possible experience. But to find expatriates and outlaws struck from the ranks of those who had the right to live—those who were accepted as legal citizens—was still a novelty, something that didn't fit into any category. Yet it happened in peacetime between two Central European states whose leaders were constantly mouthing phrases about morality and Christian values. There were a few hundred of us, a crowd of many languages and backgrounds, with little in common except that we had been swept up by the wave of fascism spreading over Europe.

But life went on. A few clear-headed persons began to organize the group. We had to find provisions. The land stretched out for miles in either direction. Several people were sent to scout for food, and soon potatoes, turnips, corncobs, and whatever had been left over from the last harvest were roasting over small fires. We found water in a pond. It was November; the weather was autumnal, cold, and damp. When a few drops of rain fell, the Orthodox Jews began to pray loudly, raising their voices to heaven, begging for postponement. But hardly anyone else still expected help from that quarter.

I don't know how long we continued this way. I remember one scene that interrupted the monotonous days. A military vehicle suddenly drew up from the Slovakian side, and an apparently high-ranking officer got out, bringing with him a single family: father, mother, and two bluish, half-frozen infants, one of whom actually died a few hours later. These unfortunates had been found on an island on the Danube, where they were hiding from the brutalities of their persecutors. By virtue of our numbers we could still offer them something resembling friendship and protection. But the spectacle we presented was evidently too much for even this hardened soldier. When he saw so many homeless human beings in the middle of the "civilized" world —their obvious misery and battered appearance, the worn faces staring at him in mute entreaty or accusation—he was overcome with pity. He had to cover his eyes and turn away. Sobs shook his body and, touched by his emotion, hundreds of outcasts cried with him.

This touch of human sympathy, however, was to remain a private act, since it could not be translated into official leniency. At the officer's demand, our spokesman, a Viennese doctor, presented him with a list of the things we most needed: food, medicine, and the right to send the pregnant women and the corpses into the nearby town. A few days later the answer arrived. Our requests were refused. Only the dead would be picked up.

In the meantime, however, help had arrived from another source. The Jewish community of Bratislava had had news of our plight and obtained permission to send provisions. From then on our situation improved: the deliveries arrived regularly; there was no lack of things to eat and drink; some money appeared here and there; a kind of fraternization with the border guards began, giving rise to an occasional bit of business; tobacco and cigarettes found their way into the camp; bottles of brandy circulated during the cold nights; and now and then, during the night, someone succeeded in slipping across the border into a temporary and precarious safety.

It was strange to discover years later that my raw and anonymous experience had found its way into the history books. These are the words with which George F. Kennan (1968: 53–54), then secretary of the American Legation in Prague, described this episode:

> The local Slovak authorities routed out 200 or 300 *staatenlos* Jews who were found to be living in Bratislava, and put them across the line on the Hungarian frontier. The Hungarian authorities refused to admit them, and these miserable people, among them over 100 women and children and a number of persons in poor health, were forced to camp out for weeks in the fields between the two lines. Representatives of the Jewish organizations in Bratislava endeavored to provide them with food, clothing, and shelter. But the authorities were not always cooperative and there was evidently considerable real suffering before the Hungarian authorities finally took pity and accepted the refugees.... The fate of two Jewish children, who were found frozen to death in an open truck in the course of these operations, appears finally to have made an impression on the authorities on both sides, and to have led to a greater observance of some of the elementary principles of human decency.

This excerpt is part of a dispatch to the Department of State of 17 February 1939. Much worse was in store for the Jews of Europe, but at this time apparently not everybody was yet completely brutalized, so the treatment of these people was still worth putting in a diplomatic report.

One night my parents and I managed to escape from the camp. I don't know for sure what happened to the others. Later we heard rumors that the camp was dissolved and its inhabitants were interned, which happens to agree with Kennan's understanding. However that may be, given the subsequent fate of the Jews in this area, it is unlikely that many survived. But I am convinced that having been in this camp saved our lives. We made our way to Prague, which was teeming with refugees. Without our recent plight and obvious destitution the tired employees at the Refugee Rescue Organization would scarcely have paid any attention to us, let alone sent our passports to Paris for special consideration. After a couple of months they came back, stamped with Bolivian visas. Since Prague at that point was surrounded by the forces of the Third Reich, ready to pounce on this last outpost of democracy, we had to be flown out to France. There we got our passages to South America, transit visas through Chile—since Bolivia had lost all access to the sea in wars with its neighbors—and eight dollars apiece to start us on our way to a new continent. We reached the port of La Rochelle-Pallice in southern France and embarked on the *Orduña* (crow), a vessel of the Pacific Steam Navigation Company; and therewith begins another sequence, which I wish to describe as characteristic of the third phase of exile.

The boat was a freighter, converted into a passenger ship for use in transporting the refugee masses out of a fascist continent. Soon Europe was nothing more than a streak of gray, hardly to be distinguished from the gray sky and the gray Atlantic, until there was nothing left to see except the ocean's surface, bordered by the horizon. It would be seventeen years before I again saw the continent where I had received decisive impulses that have remained with me for life. During the crossing, which lasted a whole month, I felt the most heterogeneous impressions converge, impressions that ultimately fell into two perceptual categories. The first consisted of the adventurous traversal of two oceans, which I, not yet seventeen, took in with greedy readiness on this exciting self-contained steamer, a tiny molecule of civilization in a hostile element. At first we went through a storm in the Bay of Biscay; then the ocean became smooth and we entered tropical waters. We saw flying fish, after ten days the first land, then the Bahamas, the Panama Canal, and finally the first South American ports.

But the long voyage had another side to it, for it was only too apparent that we were on an emigrant ship. We were traveling third class, of course, and weren't allowed to forget it for a moment. The food was practically inedible and the sleeping quarters, hidden away deep in the hull, became steaming hot as soon as we reached the tropics. The crew treated us with undisguised disdain. According to a rumor, the captain had said he pitied the countries where this human freight was to be unloaded. Apparently the governments at whose ports we stopped felt the same way, because mostly only first- and second-class passengers were allowed to disembark, while the rest had to stay on board. Longingly I stood on deck, baked by the sun, and saw lying before me the white, shimmering "pearl of the tropics," as Latin Americans call Havana, where the exiled beggar was unwelcome. Decades later, when Castro took over the government, this memory sufficed to fill me with satisfaction, for I felt the time of the third class had finally come.

No, at every moment we were reminded that this "crow" was no ordinary passenger liner, but that it transported victims and outcasts. Not just refugees from every corner of Greater Germany populated our ship in thick swarms: there were also Spaniards and Latin Americans who had fought on the side of the republic and, now that the Spanish Civil War had been lost, were either returning home or seeking asylum where their own language was spoken; a motley assortment of people who had been in concentration camps, whose stores had been boycotted by the SA, and whose pianos had been thrown out of the windows onto the street during the Reichskristallnacht; and others who had resisted Francisco Franco in vain under circumstances of incredible sacrifice. There were the Chileans, smoking and speaking unbelievably rapid Spanish; the chess-playing Cubans, each one a miniature Capablanca; and the well-educated Jewish matrons from the ninth and eighteenth districts of Vienna. There were German and Austrian doctors and university professors, who spoke in the polished idiom of intellectuals, and ruffians from the Vienna Prater with a broad dialect who, God knows how, had come into conflict with the Nazis. There were merchants from the Tauentzienstraße, Berlin's Fifth Avenue; Eastern Jews from the Galician shtetl; impoverished Austrian monarchists, clinging to pitiful remnants of elegance; and a whole group that had "been around," that had become acquainted with stables and night asylums, with the Parisian underworld, dirty prisons, and the merciless immigration agents of innumerable countries. And everyone had not one but many tales to tell. This ship was my first university, the first one for years to come and by no means the worst. But the most memorable moment of this lively and instructive crossing occurred on 15 March 1939 as we read the news that was conveyed by telegraph and then posted on a bulletin board. Among a number of trivial, arbitrarily gathered announcements, we read the lapidary sentence: Prague occupied by the Germans. Of the hundreds of thousands for whom this event was equivalent to a death sentence, we had been chosen to survive, without rhyme or reason. So much for a bit of oral history.[2]

2. For a detailed account of these two episodes, see Schwarz 1992: 73–105.

Is there a specifically Austrian dimension in all of this? I believe so. The no-man's-land between Hungary and Slovakia had deep roots in Austrian history, in the unresolved conflicts of the Austro-Hungarian monarchy. And a glance at the map reveals why Bratislava, an hour's train ride from Vienna, received disproportionately many Austrian refugees; in contrast, the German antifascists preferred the Czech city of Prague, far west of Vienna, much closer to Berlin, and almost at the longitude of Munich. The preponderance of Austrians on the ship and later in Bolivia is amenable to similar explanations: the persecutions began relatively late in Austria, and at this historical eleventh hour only the least desirable exile destinations were open to the majority of those seeking safety.

The moment has come to say something about the Austrian intellectuals who had to emigrate. For practical reasons I use the term "intellectuals" to lump together writers, artists, private scholars, scientists, and other university personnel. In many ways they share the multifaceted destinies of ordinary émigrés: the prominent and well connected had no trouble finding havens, while the younger ones who had not yet made names for themselves had to overcome hardships in which many foundered. Sigmund Freud was lionized on his arrival in London. For the first time in his life, he is reported to have said, he realized what it meant to be famous. But fame or the lack of it were not the only criteria that determined success in exile. Timing also played an important role, and in this respect the Austrian intellectuals who left after March 1938 were at a disadvantage as compared with their German confreres who had emigrated earlier. The United States received by far the largest number of these persons, and Lewis Coser, a student of the subject, in part attributes the greater representation of German refugee intellectuals over Austrian ones at American universities to timing. He compares the situation of the Austrians, who came five years after the Germans, to someone who makes a last-minute effort to jump onto a train in motion only to find that all seats are already taken (Coser 1988: 94).[3]

But here, too, countervailing factors interfere with the evidence. The picture is blurred, since the emigration of Austrian natural scientists began in the aftermath of World War I, when opportunities were scarce in a truncated Austria, and many scholars and practitioners of social science emigrated during the clerical fascism of the 1930s. In the universities, discrimination against Jews and thinkers whom we in the United States would call "secular humanists" set in much earlier than 1938. Success in American academia also depended on the discipline the individual represented and its relative affinity with the intellectual culture into which the émigré desired to be absorbed. Austrian economists, for example, who brought along their

---

3. Translations of all sources into English are mine.

neoclassical, mathematically oriented, free-trade traditions fared much better than their German counterparts who, by and large, belonged to the historical school. That most German economists had grown up in lower social spheres than had the Austrians, many of whom belonged to the upper classes, is also supposed to have been influential (Coser 1988: 95).[4] Psychoanalysts met with a friendly reception in both the academic and the private sectors. Other groups found open doors for other reasons: Austrian musicologists because their field was underdeveloped and the members of the Vienna Circle because American and British philosophers were sympathetic to their logical positivism (Coser 1988: 97–98). In contrast, the representatives of Gestalt and cognitive psychology found no jobs in the United States.

In short, the available data do not seem to jell into recognizable patterns. Take as an example the fates of several Austrian writers. Robert Musil died in Swiss exile in restricted economic circumstances, not to say in poverty, while Franz Werfel went from hit to commercial hit in the United States, most notably with his *Song of Bernadette* and his comedy *Jacobowski and the Colonel*. Maybe Musil's situation was due to the esoteric, experimental nature of his great novel *The Man without Qualities*, while Werfel reaped success thanks to his more palatable farce making light of harsh matters and his Catholicizing tale of Lourdes that caters to the masses. But what about Stefan Zweig, the wealthy, world-famous darling of several million readers, who found an enthusiastic reception in Brazil only to succumb to émigré blues and the allure of suicide? Perhaps in the chaotic realm of exile and resettlement, factors such as a strong personality, the right kind of background, age and vitality, being in the right place at the right time—in other words, simple good luck—have a decisive effect. Shedding light on these complex questions requires, as has been said, "the fruitful but difficult combination of scholarship on exile and the history of science and scholarship," an endeavor that has just only started (Stadler 1988a: 31).

A few figures will complement this picture. When large segments of a society's intelligentsia are wiped out as radically as in Austria, the quantitative evidence automatically takes on a qualitative dimension. The exact extent is under dispute, but according to one of my sources, 150,000 to 200,000 persons emigrated in the critical years, starting as early as 1934.[5] Another source (Eppel 1988: 69) speaks of "more than 130,000" whom "the National Socialists drove out between March 1938 and November 1941"—when the borders were closed—"by means of discriminatory edicts, laws

4. Coser makes the point that an unusual number of Austrian economists had the aristocratic "von" in their names: Gottfried von Haberler, Ludwig von Mises, Friedrich von Hayek, and so forth.

5. These figures are largely gleaned from Stadler 1988b.

and open terror."[6] According to this author (Eppel 1988: 69), "Austria indulged" in what was "probably the vastest 'export' of culture, scientific knowledge, practical expertise, and artistic quality in its history."[7] The roster of routed intellectuals, in the words of the mayor of Vienna, reads like the "'Who's Who' of Austrian and European intellectual history."[8] All but three of the Viennese Psychoanalytic Society's fifty members went into exile, and so did fourteen adjunct members. Twenty-nine members (or two-thirds) of Alfred Adler's Movement of Individual Psychology emigrated. All Nobel Prize winners who were active in universities were dismissed and hounded into exile. None of the fourteen who made up the Vienna Circle of philosophy ever returned. Three thousand physicians fled Austria. The renowned Vienna School of Art History was exiled and largely incorporated into the English Warburg Institute. The architectural avant-garde fared no better. About one-fifth of the world-famous Vienna Gemeindebau and half of the Werkbund settlement were driven out partly by the Corporate State and partly by Hitler. Within a few years Austria lost its entire architectural elite (Stadler 1988a: 36). With the Austrofascists' preparatory help, fifty social scientists were driven out forever. After 1945 it was the group around Othmar Spann and not they who were able to reestablish themselves.

Similarly, the popular culture and social reform movements were shunted aside, with fatal results for the unique Viennese workers' culture that was admired all over the world. A comparable development deprived Austria of Hans Kelsen's School of Positivistic Jurisprudence. Natural scientists were wiped out thanks to Hitler's well-known hatred of university-based science: one-third of the empirical and all of the theoretical physicists were dismissed and supplanted by those promoting an insane "Aryan Physics," as its beneficiaries dubbed what they were doing. The brain drain among technicians and engineers, "according to a conservative estimate," amounted to five hundred persons since the beginning of the First Republic. But an accurate assessment of the scientific-technological emigration does not yet exist (Stadler 1988a: 36). It would be possible to continue such stocktaking for every known field—for example, journalism, communications, and media studies—as well as history, whose representatives were understandably loath to study the history of their own discipline: "Most established historians had been in favor of the 'Anschluß' in 1938 and after World War II again determined the socialization of the historical guild—albeit in the guise of an exonerated Austrian ideology" (Stadler 1988a: 35).

6. Adolf Eichmann headed the Center for Jewish Emigration in Vienna. On 2 November 1941, "the last group of emigrants left Vienna for Portugal." Eppel quotes this from DÖW 1984: 200.

7. Quoting Reinhold Knoll (1979: 267).

8. Helmut Zilk, prefatory comments in Stadler 1988b: 23.

Before ending this enumeration I would like to cast one last brief glance at the field of writing. To consider only the Austrian representatives of world literature who were expatriated—Hermann Broch, Elias Canetti, Robert Musil, Joseph Roth, Stefan Zweig, and so on—does not exhaust the subject, because it does not take into account writers like Theodor Kramer, Erich Fried, and Hilde Spiel who either were marginalized while Austrofascism held sway or started to write later. Austrians who were in their teens in 1938 and who reached maturity and prominence only in exile constitute a special category (Stadler 1988a: 36).[9]

The impact of this vast emigration on the host countries' cultural life is immeasurable and has brought forth a literature of its own. The American universities, which attracted and incorporated the majority of the intellectual émigrés—including, for example, the eminent Austrian historian Robert Kann, in whose honor and memory this lecture is named—profited enormously from this influx of new ideas and modes of thinking. That the Austrians among them were a recognizable group with specific problems of integration has already been alluded to. Leaving national origin aside for a moment and focusing on nuclear science alone, one can say that the fugitives from European fascism not only transformed the American university but shaped the course of World War II and indeed that of postwar history. A survey of all the disciplines and their impact on the cultural lives of the various host societies has yet to be made. This would be a different story, anyway, one that I am not called upon to tell today. Despite many individual studies devoted to it, we are still far away from seeing the whole picture. In the meantime, we remain on solid ground when we adopt Stuart Hughes's modest verdict (quoted in Coser 1988: 100) that the refugees succeeded in "deprovincializing American intellectual life."

In short, Austria's loss was other countries' gain. Did Austria recognize the severe depletion of its intellectual resources caused by the exodus of its cultural elites before and especially after the Anschluss? This question leads to an investigation of what happened after the defeat of Hitler's armies in 1945 and again in 1955 after the full restitution of Austria's sovereignty and independence, events that ushered in the fifth and last phase of exile as I have described it, a phase that offers the possibility of remigration. Of course

9. Stadler (1987: 19) credits the author of this essay, together with others who worked abroad, with breaking the monopoly of a nationalistic German literary scholarship: "It was only thanks to the impulses of emigrated literary historians like Heinz Politzer, Joseph Strelka, Egon Schwarz, and Franz Mautner that this domestic domination could be somewhat mitigated." He adds: "To be able to assess the sad extent of this cultural loss and scientific transfer more precisely we must also consider the younger generation of emigrants who did not achieve a university degree until 1938, who had to continue their study in the country of exile because of the rising fascism and had to engage there in science or journalism, for example Kurt Rothschild, Egon Schwarz, or Fritz Kreissler."

Austria does not speak with a single voice. The doctrine that Austria was a victim rather than an agent of Nazism proved highly beneficial in the political sphere but disastrous in the moral one. It obscured the guilt of the masses and the responsibilities of the political class and provided a subterfuge for the most undesirable elements. Nevertheless, many individual Austrians lamented the injustice done to so many of their fellow citizens and deplored the permanent loss of the cultural treasure they represented. But the fact remains that only an infinitesimal fraction of those who had left returned when ostensibly the roads were open again.

Let us examine the reasons. Even though in the case of Austria only seven years had elapsed since Hitler's arrival, many refugees had made sufficiently successful adjustments to their adopted countries and were unwilling to give up their hard-won positions. Many lived in the United States, a traditional immigrant society. They had been absorbed into the economic and professional life of the nation, were deeply grateful for their rescue, had become its citizens, and had developed a new loyalty. A not inconsiderable number who had originally landed in countries where it was more difficult for Europeans to become acclimatized—such as Cuba, the Dominican Republic, other Latin American societies, or Shanghai—had also found their way to the United States, with similar results. Moreover, the bitter memory of the mistreatment to which they, their friends, and their relatives had been subjected still lingered, and there were no assurances that antisemitism and other fascist tendencies had completely subsided. On the contrary, Ruth Wodak et al. (1990), Richard Mitten (1992), and others have irrefutably analyzed the robust persistence of antisemitism in politics, the press, and the population at large. In the Waldheim election this phenomenon became visible to the entire world.

In short, Austria was not alluring. Economically and even physically ravaged, divided into four occupation zones, and with Vienna still partly in ruins, the country lacked any enticement for the émigrés to give up even modest advantages and risk a second uprooting. The cold war that had set in the moment the hot war ended, a war, incidentally, in which sizable numbers of young refugees had fought on the Allied side, cast a pall over the future; and ten years later when the Austrian State Treaty was signed and the foreign armed forces left Austria, the economic situation and social climate had not yet improved sufficiently. It was mainly the political exiles who pressed homeward, and they soon discovered that their reentry into Austrian life was far from smooth and unproblematic. The case of Bruno Kreisky is the exception rather than the rule. The two major parties had made strenuous attempts to break with the past and were embarrassed by what they considered holdovers from unfortunate times. A book with the telling title *"I am in favor of dragging the thing out"* documents the "creeping tactics of prevention" that hampered both the return of the refugees and any program of restitution (Knight 1988).

Austro-Marxism was regarded as "Jewish-tainted," and the return of former Jewish Socialist functionaries was not at all desired. On the contrary, Adolf Schärf and Oskar Helmer, highly placed representatives of the party, "were unanimous in rejecting the integration of these persons after 1945" (Svoboda 1990: 43).[10] In contrast to the Federal Republic of Germany, Austrian refugees were never adequately compensated for their material losses, a result of what has aptly been called "Austria's existential lie," its self-exoneration from all accountability. Austria failed even to do what the leaders of the German Democratic Republic did in the last throes of their regime: admit responsibility for the injustices done to Jewish citizens. Some (Keller 1990: 95) even go so far as to claim that "the proclivity to deny guilt and the tendency to suppress or at least embellish, the disinclination to resolve conflicts, is an Austrian propensity that is older than the Second Republic." Thus it is not putting it too bluntly to say that both the few refugees who returned and the many who kept an eye on Austria from abroad received unmistakable signs that they were not welcome, and this must be regarded as one of the principal reasons why so few thirty-eighters, as I might succinctly call them, found the way back to their former homeland. One who did return (Fabry 1990: 153) has this to report about the reception he got from his former classmates:

10. From those who actually did return we possess contradictory reports. Hilde Zaloscer (1987: 571), an art historian, paints a dismal picture: "Now I live in Vienna, in a spiritual and human desert, I get antisemitic threat letters, I do not know a single person with whom I might talk, in a country stigmatized by the departure of its Jewish intellectual elite, a country that is petty, provincial, and above all so malicious. I was not welcome in Austria. There was no work for me here! 'Restitution' such as in Germany was out of the question here. What was supposed to be restituted? Did they take away our apartment, did they ruin my career?! No, none of this happened, they themselves had been 'victims,' after all. Did people really believe this? Did they lie to themselves? Everything was so horrible, so deceitful, so inhuman! But the worst was the wall of silence. No one asked me how I had survived the years of emigration, nobody mentioned the atrocities that occurred here! The friends that suddenly disappeared, the old men whom they had seen—must have seen—wash the ground! All this did not exist, everything was as if wiped away. I lived in a paradise for fools or criminals!" Paul Neurath (1987: 535–36), a professor of sociology and statistics, describes a totally different experience: "Here I'd like to add a few general remarks about the personal aspect of my remigration—if it is possible to call it that in view of the fact that my proper residence continued to be in New York. The first refers to the extraordinarily friendly reception I enjoyed from all sides from the first day on; not only from Professor Rosenmayr and his close colleagues, who were now also mine, and from the students, but also from all colleagues beyond my immediate institute with whom I had dealings, professional or otherwise. Add to this the repeated recommendations of my Visiting Professorships to the Ministry on the part of the faculty and each time the Ministry's unhesitating approval of these requests.

"Of course I am aware that not all remigrations can go so smoothly, with such a completely cordial and friendly reception not only from the individuals and groups in question, but also from the various concerned authorities in the Ministry. What may have facilitated things, technically speaking, is the fact that it was not a question of a complete remigration in which case a whole tenured professorship would have had to be set aside."

How good the émigrés had had it [one of them remarked], sitting in safety in rich America while people in Vienna had to suffer from war and bombs. When I interjected that those who had stayed in Vienna at least did not have to experience the murder of their parents, he regretfully admitted that—unfortunately—transgressions had occurred. Another reminded me that he had always been in favor of a Greater Germany, which was the reason why he welcomed the Anschluß at any price.... A third explained to me why he had become a Nazi in the early 1930s: fascists both in Austria and in Germany, but in the latter at least no unemployment, and what happened later could not be foreseen.

Nowadays, the few of us who are not dead but merely old hear a chorus of voices denouncing the lack of welcome extended to the refugees after 1945. Let me quote merely one such appeal from a well-known political scientist (Pelinka 1990: 39):

> From today's perspective it is a great failure of the Second Republic's "founding generation" ... not to have done what was so obvious and self-evident: to direct an appeal to all those with ties to the country to return to a new Austria. Even if it is too late today for most of those who might have been reached by such an appeal—it is not too late for Austria. It is the task for the present generation to do what the founding generation failed to do, for reasons often hard to understand today, to call upon the Austrian exiles to return.

Federal Chancellor Franz Vranitzky echoed these sentiments. The postwar generation, he said, "did not ask or did not ask audibly enough what had happened to the hundreds of thousands of Austrians who had been shown the door. They neglected to ask how they had survived and continued to live and whether there was a chance to be reconciled and to build a new trust."[11] But it was more than neglect, it was the patent ill will of all parties that prevented such gestures in 1945, as Viktor Matejka experienced when he suggested that the refugees be brought back:

> As an Austrian freed [from concentration camp] and particularly in my new function as City Councillor for Culture and Education I regarded it as my obvious duty to remind my fellow countrymen that a very substantial part of the nation had been forced to leave the country and that it was our obligation and need to invite all these valuable Austrians back home. To use a typically Austrian phrase: I got the coldest feet of my life.... What I demanded from the most authoritative places and people in Austria was no less than to let all our émigrés know, at least theoretically, that they would be cordially welcomed in their liberated homeland. Such a declaration was never made by any Austrian authority. (quoted in Dusek 1990: 147)

More than half a century has elapsed since the events of 1938, and it is almost embarrassing to speak of these past wrongs in view of the atrocities

11. Prefatory comments in Stadler 1988b: 22.

that have been perpetrated in the world since then and are still being committed. Millions of displaced persons in unprecedented forced mass migrations are on the move, knocking at the doors of the fortunate who have a place to stay but are no more willing to open them than those at whose doors we were knocking fifty years ago. One writer (Keller 1990: 98) links these disparate migrations together. "Without a consensus about the extent of the pain that Jewish Austrians had to suffer," he argues, not without a semblance of plausibility, "acceptance of ethnic minorities is impossible. Without insight into the ideological sources of the extermination policies of the Nazis it is impossible to combat the hatred of foreigners." Perhaps Freud was right in believing that men are a rabble and that one must pin one's hopes on the exceptions. Fortunately for Austria, these exceptions exist. A new generation of Austrians has grown up with an understanding of human solidarity that was sadly lacking in my youth. It is for the sake of my many new friends among these younger Austrians that I don't mind visiting Austria now and then, since my old friends have been scattered all over the globe or have disappeared from it altogether.

References

Coser, L. 1988. "Die österreichische Emigration als Kulturtransfer Europa-Amerika." In *Vertriebene Vernunft II. Emigration und Exil österreichischer Wissenschaft. Internationales Symposion 19. bis 23. Oktober 1987 in Wien*, ed. F. Stadler, 93–101. Vienna.

Döblin, A. 1949. *Schicksalsreise. Bericht und Bekenntnis*. Frankfurt.

Dokumentationsarchiv des Österreichischen Widerstands (DÖW), ed. 1984. *Widerstand und Verfolgung in Wien 1934–1945. Eine Dokumentation*. Vol. 3. Vienna.

Dusek, P. 1990. "Verdrängung in C-Dur. Das Operndirektoren-Karussell 1953–1956." *Das jüdische Echo. Zeitschrift für Kultur und Politik* 39, no. 1 (October):144–47.

Eppel, P. 1988. "Österreicher in der Emigration und im Exil 1938 bis 1945." In *Vertriebene Vernunft II. Emigration und Exil österreichischer Wissenschaft. Internationales Symposion 19. bis 23. Oktober 1987 in Wien*, ed. F. Stadler, 68–81. Vienna.

Fabry, J. 1990. "Ein Emigrant wird Immigrant." *Das jüdische Echo. Zeitschrift für Kultur und Politik* 39, no. 1 (October):152–54.

Feuchtwanger, L. 1942. *Unholdes Frankreich*. Mexico City.

Goodwin-Gill, G. S. 1990. "Different Types of Forced Migration Movements as an International and National Problem." In *The Uprooted: Forced Migration as an International Problem in the Post-War Era*, ed. G. Rystad, 15–45. Lund, Sweden.

Keller, H. 1990. "Österreich 1990. Notizen zum Zustand der Republik." *Das jüdische Echo. Zeitschrift für Kultur und Politik* 39, no. 1 (October):95–99.

Kennan, G. F. 1968. "Excerpts from a Despatch of February 17, 1939, from George F. Kennan (as Secretary of Legation at Prague) to the Department of State, on the Jewish Problem in the New Czechoslovakia." In *From Prague after Munich: Diplomatic Papers, 1938–1940*, 42–57. Princeton.

Knight, R., ed. 1988. *"Ich bin dafür, die Sache in die Länge zu ziehen". Wortprotokolle der österreichischen Bundesregierung von 1945–52 über die Entschädigung der Juden*. Frankfurt.

Knoll, R. 1979. "Die Emigration aus Österreich im 20. Jahrhundert." *Austriaca*, February, special issue:253–80.

Marrus, M. A. 1990. "The Uprooted: An Historical Perspective." In *The Uprooted: Forced Migration as an International Problem in the Post-War Era*, ed. G. Rystad, 47–57. Lund, Sweden.

Mitten, R. 1992. *The Politics of Antisemitic Prejudice: The Waldheim Phenomenon in Austria*. Boulder.

Neurath, P. 1987. "Wissenschaftliche Emigration und Remigration." In *Vertriebene Vernunft I. Emigration und Exil österreichischer Wissenschaft 1930–1940*, ed. F. Stadler, 513–37. Vienna.

Pelinka, A. 1990. "Adolf Schärf. Vom Austromarxismus zum Regierungssozialismus. Aus Anlaß seines 100. Geburtstages am 20. April 1990." *Das jüdische Echo. Zeitschrift für Kultur und Politik* 39, no. 1 (October):37–40.

Remarque, E. M. 1941. *Liebe deinen Nächsten*. Stockholm.

Schmid, G. 1983. "Kinogeschichte der Zwischenkriegszeit." In *Österreich 1918–1938. Geschichte der Ersten Republik*, ed. E. Weinzierl and K. Skalnik, 705–14. Vol. 2. Graz.

Schmidl, E. A. 1987. *März 38. Der deutsche Einmarsch in Österreich*. Vienna.

Schwarz, E. 1992. *Keine Zeit für Eichendorff. Chronik unfreiwilliger Wanderjahre*. Frankfurt.

Seghers, A. [N. Radvanyi]. 1944. *Transit*. Boston.

Stadler, F. 1987. "Emigration der Wissenschaft—Wissenschaft von der Emigration. Ein ungeschriebenes Kapitel österreichischer Zeitgeschichte." In *Vertriebene Vernunft I. Emigration und Exil österreichischer Wissenschaft 1930–1940*, ed. F. Stadler, 9–41. Vienna.

_____. 1988a. "'Vertriebene Vernunft'—Rückblick und Zusammenschau." In *Vertriebene Vernunft II. Emigration und Exil österreichischer Wissenschaft. Internationales Symposion 19. bis 23. Oktober 1987 in Wien*, ed. F. Stadler, 27–47. Vienna.

_____, ed. 1988b. *Vertriebene Vernunft II. Emigration und Exil österreichischer Wissenschaft. Internationales Symposion 19. bis 23. Oktober 1987 in Wien*. Vienna.

Svoboda, W. 1990. "Politiker, Antisemit, Populist. Oskar Helmer und die Zweite Republik." *Das jüdische Echo. Zeitschrift für Kultur und Politik* 39, no. 1 (October):42–51.

Tägil, S. 1990. "From Nebuchadnezzar to Hitler: The Question of Mass Expulsion in History up to World War II." In *The Uprooted: Forced Migration as an International Problem in the Post-War Era*, ed. G. Rystad, 59–85. Lund, Sweden.

Werfel, F. 1945. *Jacobowski und der Oberst. Komödie einer Tragödie in drei Akten.* Stockholm.

Wodak, R., et al. 1990. *"Wir sind alle unschuldige Täter". Diskurshistorische Studien zum Nachkriegsantisemitismus.* Frankfurt.

Zaloscer, H. 1987. "Das dreimalige Exil." In *Vertriebene Vernunft I. Emigration und Exil österreichischer Wissenschaft 1930–1940*, ed. F. Stadler, 544–72. Vienna.

Chapter 5

THE INFLUENCE OF AUSTRIAN ÉMIGRÉS ON THE DEVELOPMENT AND EXPANSION OF PSYCHOANALYSIS IN THE UNITED STATES AFTER 1945

Bernhard Handlbauer

Introduction

The expulsion of Austria's intellectual elite in the 1930s was the most drastic rupture in Austria's cultural history of this century. By the end of 1938, the heritage of the fin de siècle, with its innovations in architecture, art, literature, medicine, music, philosophy, and psychology, had virtually disappeared from Austrian soil. The intellectual exodus (see Stadler 1987, 1988; Stadler and Weibel 1995) led to the transfer of culture and science from Central Europe to the English-speaking world, above all to the United States (see Coser 1984; Fermi 1968; Fleming and Bailyn 1969; and Heilbut 1983). This applies especially to "Psychological Vienna" of the interwar period, essentially represented by Sigmund Freud, Alfred Adler, Karl Bühler,

I would like to thank the following people for the information and for the valuable and stimulating ideas they provided: Edith Kurzweil, Peter Neubauer, Else Pappenheim, Dennis Rohrbaugh, Robert Stewart, Nellie Thompson (all in New York), Sanford Gifford (Boston), Peter Heller (Buffalo), Ernst Federn (Vienna), and Ernst Falzeder (Salzburg). Many thanks also to Caroline Schwarzacher, Uschi Sützl, Mel Greenwald and Elisabeth Wörndl (Salzburg), Else Pappenheim and Stephen Frishauf (New York), and Fay Friedman (Buffalo) for their help in translating the chapter.

and their followers. In the 1920s and 1930s, numerous important contributions to the theory and practice of clinical, educational, developmental, and social psychology, as well as psychotherapy and mental health, were made in Vienna (see Ash 1987; Benetka 1995; Fallend 1988; Gardner and Stevens 1992; Handlbauer 1984; Huber 1977, 1978; Pappenheim 1989; Reichmayr 1990; and Sterba 1982). This creative laboratory of modern psychology was almost completely exiled in 1938: approximately 100 to 150 psychoanalysts, Adlerian "individual psychologists,"[1] collaborators of the Bühler Institute,[2] and perhaps an even greater number of students in training left Austria. About two-thirds emigrated to the United States. Many achieved success as physicians, pedagogues, and social workers, exerting an enormous influence on the development of psychoanalysis, individual psychology, and other schools of psychotherapy,[3] especially in New York and California.

That psychoanalysis has had a decisive influence on modern thinking and on most of the psychotherapeutic schools remains undisputed, regardless of divergent opinions on the value of psychoanalysis as a science and a therapy or on Freud as a person. My chapter focuses on the most influential group among these émigrés and examines the impact of Viennese psychoanalysts on American psychoanalysis. I draw on the existing German and English literature[4] and on my own primary source research, especially on

1. These include Alexandra Adler, Paul Brodsky, Danica Deutsch, Rudolf Dreikurs, Alfred Farau, Carl Furtmüller, Sofie Lazarsfeld, Ernst and Helene Papanek, Lydia Sicher, and Erwin Wexberg (see Handlbauer 1988 and 1995).

2. These include Hedda Bolgar, Egon Brunswick, Charlotte Bühler, Karl Bühler, Ernest Dichter, Liselotte Fischer, Else Frenkel-Brunswick, Herta Herzog, Marie Jahoda, Paul Lazarsfeld, and Hans Zeisel. See the chapters by Ash, Eschbach and Willenberg, Fischer, Fleck, and Neurath in Stadler 1988; the chapters by Benetka and Fleck in Stadler and Weibel 1995; and Benetka 1992 and Fallend, Handlbauer, and Kienreich 1989.

3. Émigrés who came from Vienna or who were inspired by their contact with psychological circles in Vienna founded new directions in psychotherapy or even new schools: Rudolf Dreikurs, Heinz Kohut, and Jakob Moreno (psychodrama) and Fritz Perls (Gestalt therapy). Other émigrés influenced American founders of new schools: Otto Rank (Carl Rogers), Paul Federn (Eric Berne), and Wilhelm Reich (body therapists).

4. There are a number of articles and books that deal with this subject. See, for example, Bettelheim 1988; Coser 1984; Fallend, Handlbauer, and Kienreich 1989; Farau 1953; Federn 1988a; Fermi 1968; Gifford 1977; Hale 1978, 1995; Jacoby 1983; Jahoda 1969; Kurzweil 1989, 1994; May 1976; Millet 1966; Mühlleitner 1992; Mühlleitner and Reichmayr 1995; Parin 1990; Peters 1992; Reichmayr 1987, 1990; Schick 1973; Spaulding 1968; and Timms and Segal 1988. There are also many biographies and autobiographies that pertain to this subject. See, for example, Alexander, Eisenstein, and Grotjahn 1966; Buxbaum 1990; Coles 1970; Deutsch 1973; Ekstein 1987; Ekstein, Fallend, and Reichmayr 1988; Fallend and Reichmayr 1992; Flory 1976; Gerö 1994; Grotjahn 1987; Kaufhold 1993; Kestenberg 1992; Oberläuter 1985; Pappenheim 1988; Plänkers and Federn 1994; Roazen 1985; Stepansky 1988; and Wyatt 1992.

interviews, to survey the backgrounds of the Austrian emigrants,[5] to summarize their impact on American psychoanalysis and related fields, and to provide thoughts on the issue of how psychoanalysis changed due to its transplantation from Europe to the United States. I concentrate on the important period between the 1940s and the 1960s, when European[6] émigrés exerted their greatest influence on American psychoanalysis and reinforced the impact of psychoanalysis on American culture.[7]

Background of the Émigrés

Psychoanalysis was born in turn-of-the-century Vienna, which not only may have been the cradle of the modern world but also Karl Kraus's "experimental laboratory for the end of the world" and eventually Stefan Zweig's "the world of yesterday." The early history of psychoanalysis mirrors Austria's cultural history. To a large extent, its protagonists belonged to a social class of assimilated Jewish intellectuals. This class represented an important cosmopolitan element of cultural ferment during the fin-de-siècle era. The history of psychoanalysis is also connected with rising antisemitism in Vienna, and it is paradigmatic for the situation of Jewish intellectuals and scientists in society: psychoanalysis was not created within the universities but in a private circle of highly educated, nonconformist physicians and

5. Reichmayr (1987, 1990) and Mühlleitner (1992) were the first to produce basic material on the emigration of Austrian psychoanalysts and their biographies (see also Mühlleitner and Reichmayr 1995). This survey is based on and supplements their research.

6. I focus on Austrian émigrés, but there were, of course, numerous others who had an enormous influence on the expansion of psychoanalysis and the development of its theory.

7. I will touch only on aspects of the related issue of Freud and America. Similarly, I will not take part in the renewed discussion about the scientific status of psychoanalysis. See, for example, Robinson 1993 and the controversy over the contribution by Frederick Crews in the *New York Review of Books* (November 1993—February 1994). However, I would like to observe: The disappointment with the limitations of psychoanalysis and the enthusiasm for "Freud bashing" among American intellectuals can be seen as a reaction to the uncritical overvaluation and idealization of a simplified psychoanalysis in the past. The critique concerning aspects of a petrification of psychoanalysis within rigid training and dogmatic theories may well be justified (see Malcolm 1982). But the assaults can also be regarded as part of a long tradition of attacks against the emancipating potential of psychoanalysis in terms of social enlightenment. Where "liberal" has become an invective, where new prisons and the death penalty are the ultimate answers to social disintegration, and where Prozac is the general solution to depressing conditions of life, there is no longer fertile ground for psychoanalysis to thrive. According to Parin (1990: 191), "psychoanalysis does not tolerate subjecting analysts and their patients to social and political distress. Psychoanalysis is more socially sensitive than many other disciplines, comparable perhaps to historical research." But the history of the "rise and crisis of psychoanalysis" (Hale 1995), as well as its connection to the rise and crisis of American culture from 1945 to the present, is another story.

intellectuals.[8] With few exceptions, for example, Richard Sterba, the later émigrés were of Jewish or partially Jewish origin. They were, however, highly assimilated within Austrian culture, and their Jewishness meant little to most Austrian analysts, especially those of the younger generation.[9] Salomea Gutmann-Isakower was born in 1888 in Oswiecim, Galicia. She moved to Vienna in the early 1920s and was a member of the Viennese Psychoanalytic Society—Wiener Psychoanalytische Vereinigung (WPV)— from 1928 until her emigration in 1938. Neither she nor any of the other émigrés could, of course, have associated her village of birth and her Jewish origins with the terrifying place that would later be known under its German name—Auschwitz.

The early pioneers of psychoanalysis or their families had come to Vienna from all parts of the Habsburg Empire. Most of the later émigrés of the WPV were born between 1870 and World War I, half of them in Vienna and half of them in different cities of the Habsburg Empire, in particular Lemberg (now Lviv) and other towns in Galicia (Mühlleitner 1992). It is important to keep in mind that many of the later émigrés had already experienced an earlier migration from the periphery of the empire to Vienna. This earlier migration differed from the later exile: many earlier émigrés went voluntarily and were already fluent in the language they had to adopt. But the genesis and history of psychoanalysis are linked to the processes of migration characteristic of our century, both regionally (the formation of metropoles) and internationally, which were due to war, economic crisis, and underdevelopment in the areas of out-migration. An important but little-explored aspect of the history of psychoanalysis is that these people who were themselves uprooted were the ones who dedicated their lives to the restitution of the emotionally uprooted.

The émigrés were in many respects pioneers of a modern life-style. This applies especially to the women among them, who had been allowed to enroll at European universities at the beginning of this century, while women at American universities still faced admission restrictions in the 1930s. Nevertheless, around 40 percent of the Austrian émigrés were women, and they made important contributions to the history of psychoanalysis in the United States.

Freud lived in Vienna until his emigration in 1938, surrounded by his daughter Anna and an inner circle of intimate friends. His continued presence there was of psychological importance for the Viennese analysts. The activities of this circle were impressive: a flourishing psychoanalytic training institute, a very productive publishing house, which included several

8. This situation was characteristic of much intellectual creativity; see, for example, the history of the Vienna Circle (Wiener Kreis) (Stadler 1987, 1988; Feigl 1969).

9. Personal communication from Else Pappenheim.

journals, a psychoanalytic therapy center that provided inexpensive treatment for people of limited financial means, the beginnings of child analysis and psychoanalytic child guidance clinics, the first applications of psychoanalysis to social work, numerous theoretical contributions and innovations, and, above all, a climate of intellectual stimulation and exchange. Nearly all of the later émigrés were very active within this circle, many of them in important positions. This background and their experiences here were among the most important qualities they took with them when they were expelled from Austria.

During the Roaring Twenties, Berlin had become a special magnet for the German-speaking cultural and intellectual world. Many Viennese psychoanalysts went for a period of time to the German capital,[10] including some who were involved in leftist movements. The Berlin Psychoanalytic Institute, founded in 1920, was the first to enforce obligatory training standards, and it was in Berlin from 1920 to 1932 that the Viennese Hanns Sachs was the first in the history of psychoanalysis to work exclusively as a training analyst.[11] The Berlin curriculum had three basic facets: training analysis, theoretical instruction, and control analysis within the framework of a psychoanalytic polyclinic. This model later became a standard. In 1933, when the Nazis closed down the Berlin Psychoanalytic Institute and German and some Austrian psychoanalysts emigrated to the United States, it was this model that they had in their mental suitcases.[12]

Hardly any other discipline was so completely and effectively uprooted and exiled by the Nazis than soul-dissecting (*seelenzerfasernde*) psychoanalysis, the Nazi expression used at book burnings. After the annexation of Austria in 1938, the last important psychoanalytic institute on German-speaking soil was utterly destroyed by the Nazis, and within one year, about one hundred analysts and candidates in training left Vienna. Almost the entire psychoanalytical community of Vienna was destroyed; August Aichhorn,

10. For example, Annie Angel-Katan, Siegfried Bernfeld, Frances Deri, Helene Deutsch, Otto Fenichel, Marianne Kris, Eduard Kronold, Anna Mänchen, Annie Reich, Wilhelm Reich, and Theodor Reik.

11. It was not until 1925 that the International Psychoanalytic Association (IPA) decided to make training analysis obligatory. Most of the pioneers of psychoanalysis, like Hanns Sachs, Max Eitingon, Otto Rank, and Karl Abraham, had either never been analyzed or had been so only "peripatetically," for example, on brisk walks through Vienna with Freud.

12. The "export" of this model had already begun in the early 1930s, when Sándor Radó and Karen Horney went to New York, Franz Alexander to Chicago, and Hanns Sachs to Boston in order to take part in the organization of the psychoanalytic institutes in the United States. Ernst Simmel emigrated in 1934 to Los Angeles. Some German analysts like Else Heilpern and Ruth Selke went to Vienna in 1933. Heinrich Löwenfeld went to Prague and became a nominal member of the WPV. Already in 1927, the German Erik Erikson had come to Vienna, where he was analyzed by Anna Freud and trained at the WPV.

Richard Nepallek, and Alfred Winterstein were the only Viennese analysts who did not emigrate.[13]

Seventy-one members of the WPV emigrated, while two members became victims of the Nazis.[14] That the number of Nazi victims was not higher may be attributed to the successful rescue operations by the international psychoanalytic community: Anna Freud, Ernest Jones, Muriel Gardiner, Mary O'Neil Hawkins, Walter Langer, Ruth Mack Brunswick, Anne Ramer, and others, with extraordinary commitment and often at great personal risk, managed to organize dozens of affidavits (see Gardiner 1983, Langer and Gifford 1978, and Steiner 1994). The American Psychoanalytic Association (APsaA) founded the Emergency Committee on Relief and Immigration in 1938 under the chairmanship of Lawrence Kubie and Bettina Warburg in order to collect money and affidavits from Americans willing to guarantee economic support of potential émigrés so that they could get visas and enter the United States.[15]

Out of the seventy-one WPV émigrés, fifty-two went to the United States[16] (see appendix 5.1), nine to Great Britain, four to Palestine, and six to other countries. Exactly half of the fifty-two émigrés fled directly to the United States, while fourteen emigrated via Great Britain, where some of them had stayed for several years, and twelve traveled via other countries (Mühlleitner 1992).

Along with the WPV members who went to the United States, there was a large group of candidates in training who received most of their training or completed it there. This group consisted of the thirty-four people listed in appendix 5.2, but that is only an approximation of the actual number.[17]

The trauma of exile is well captured in this quotation from the émigré Heinz Kohut (quoted in Peters 1992: 263):

> I have lived two different lives, with somehow no bridges in between. One is the life of a German, an Austrian, who felt absolutely at home in this culture,… My

13. On the chronology of events, see Reichmayr 1987, 1990 and Mühlleitner and Reichmayr 1995.

14. Nikola Sugar died in the ghetto of Theresienstadt; Rosa Walk was arrested by the Gestapo in France in 1942 and died following the fall from a window of a Gestapo interrogation building (see Reichmayr 1987: 142 and Mühlleitner 1992).

15. By 1943 the committee had helped 149 people; among them were 41 medical psychoanalysts and 13 lay analysts (see Jeffrey 1989).

16. Including six Americans who left Vienna between 1936 and 1939: Dorothy Burlingham, Julia Deming, Mary O'Neil Hawkins, Edith Jackson, Estelle Levy, and Ruth Mack Brunswick.

17. It can be assumed that there were other émigrés to the United States whose names we still do not know and that there were altogether at least one hundred analysts and candidates in training from Vienna who exerted their influence on American psychoanalysis. A further large group should also be mentioned: the children of émigrés who spoke perfect English but were raised within a family of Austrian background and eventually became analysts themselves.

parents, even my grandparents spoke Viennese. In every sense I was part of what surrounded me.... Then came this incomprehensible rupture. Suddenly I was expelled from it.

Persecution, expulsion, and exile are extremely traumatizing experiences that can lead to severe emotional disruption and crisis. In some way or another, each émigré was confronted with this experience. Furthermore, almost every émigré had lost friends and close relatives in the Holocaust. They were able to save their own lives, but they had to cope with accompanying feelings of guilt for having survived.[18] Although many psychoanalysts experienced emigration themselves, psychoanalysts have scarcely examined the psychological consequences of emigration, which is quite shocking.[19] Moreover, the Holocaust is omnipresent in the biographies of the Viennese émigrés,[20] but few have dealt with it.[21] The individual traumas of the émigrés had been enormous, and perhaps it was impossible for most of them to "emotionally realize what has happened" (Funke 1989) and to reflect and write on the experiences.

The cultural change and the necessity to adapt to a new way of life undoubtedly stimulated the productivity and impressive quality and volume of work produced by these émigrés.[22] The challenge created by the new working environment in exile and the ambition to succeed in the rough competition may have played a factor. Also, success and obtaining wealth, important American values, may have provided the sense of security that was needed after having overcome the life-endangering insecurity of going into exile. The flight into work possibly kept painful memories away. Having been expelled may have fostered a desire to prove their worth to the world. Or expulsion may have created an unconscious sense of guilt, which said, in effect, "You are guilty or you would not have been expelled."

Although those who were expelled survived, they had to pay a high price: depression and emotional homelessness. The flight, the problems of adapting to a foreign language and culture, the attempts to rescue endangered relatives

18. Space does not permit the complex psychological mechanism of this paradox to be discussed here.

19. Among the few examples, see Grinberg and Grinberg 1989 and Piers and Piers 1982. Along with the few contributions of analysts, see the important book by the Austrian émigré and clinical psychologist Dorit Bader Whiteman (1993).

20. Margaret Mahler's mother was killed at Auschwitz, Judith Kestenberg's mother was killed by German invaders, and Else Pappenheim's mother removed herself from imminent deportation by committing suicide.

21. See, for example, Federn 1989, Luel and Marcus 1984, and Bergmann and Jucovy 1982. Judith Kestenberg dedicated the major part of her work to research on the effects of the Holocaust on survivors and their children; see the bibliography in Kestenberg 1992.

22. Bruno Bettelheim (1988: 216) stressed that without his emigration none of his books would have been written.

from Europe, and feelings of guilt if they did not succeed must have been an incredible emotional burden for the émigrés. The refugees remained strangers in a strange land (see Wimmer 1993). The culture that had once been a home for them had been destroyed by tyranny, war, and murder. There was no way back to a place where a major part of the population was still antisemitic and anti-intellectual. Emigration turned into permanent exile. There was no time to show how much they suffered from expulsion and the crimes that had been committed against them. Their children, born in the foreign country, had no grandparents. Some adapted by overly identifying with the America that had saved their lives. America was, in spite of all its deficiencies, a democracy, a free country. Were they to succeed in getting rid of their European ponderousness and in practicing American optimism, they would be rewarded with feelings of relief. Americanization had its advantages but also demanded its tributes.[23]

All émigrés were confronted with these difficulties. But in the case of the psychoanalysts, these realities no doubt weighed even more heavily, because psychoanalysis is, like no other discipline, transmuted in very personal and intimate ways through the lengthy training period. Whether the experience of migration left its mark on the working methods or on the self-concept of psychoanalysts remains an open, scarcely examined question, but it can be assumed that the traumas of these individuals had significant impact on the history of psychoanalysis itself.[24]

The Impact of the Émigrés on American Psychoanalysis

It is impossible here to summarize the evolution of psychoanalysis in the United States before World War II, so I will restrict myself to a few essentials.[25] The New York Psychoanalytic Society and APsaA were founded in 1911, and there was an enormous public interest in Freud, especially among the avant-garde during the 1920s. In 1922, perhaps as many as five hundred freelance psychoanalysts practiced "psychoanalysis" in New York with no theoretical knowledge (Peters 1992: 123). The main goal of the first American

23. Fifty years later, one of the émigrés said: "No one is really at home over there, don't kid yourself" (Rudolf Ekstein at the symposium, "Vertriebene Vernunft," November 1987, Vienna).

24. The question is to what extent the traumatic experiences contributed to different developments, for example, to glorification of the past and a holding on to idealizations ("orthodoxy") or to an uncritical identification with the new reality and a submission to the norms of the new culture ("dilution," "superficiality," and the loss of the psychoanalytic critique of culture). Both developments can be observed within the Americanization of psychoanalysis.

25. The details appear in Burnham 1979; Gifford 1977; Hale 1971, 1978, 1995; Lewin and Ross 1960; Lorand 1969; May 1976; Millet 1966; Oberndorf 1953; Quen and Carlson 1978; Rosenzweig 1993; and Wangh 1962.

psychoanalysts, who were mainly psychiatrists, was to stop this proliferation. This situation gave the discussion on the issue of lay analysis a totally different dimension in the United States that was hard for Europeans to understand. There was no formal psychoanalytic training in the United States before the first European analysts arrived. Until the early 1930s, the psychoanalytic training in America consisted of reading the first inadequate translations of Freud[26] and traveling to Europe, mainly to Vienna, to be analyzed by Freud or by one of his close followers. In the early 1930s, the European-trained analysts returned to the United States and started to organize training institutes using the institutes of Vienna and Berlin as models. They began inviting Europeans to serve as training analysts, which provided one reason for the emigration of prominent Viennese analysts to the United States in the early 1930s.[27] This set the pattern for the admission of the later émigrés and their strong influence on these institutes. The New York Institute was founded in 1931 and was to remain for decades the organizational center of American psychoanalysis. Within two years, the institutes in Chicago, Washington-Baltimore, and Boston were founded. Under the strong influence of the émigrés, the Council on Professional Training was created in 1935 primarily in order to establish training standards.

When émigrés arrived in the United States, public interest in psychoanalysis was very high. Between the 1940s and 1960s it flourished as a therapeutic method and as a new way of psychological thinking. Psychoanalytical concepts and terms like repression, the unconscious, oedipus complex, dream analysis, Freudian slip, infantile sexuality, defense mechanism, castration fear, penis envy, etc. passed into public discourse and infiltrated Hollywood, literature, the arts, the media, and the universities. There were various reasons for this development. A readiness to accept anything new is, of course, characteristic of American society. But there was also a great enthusiasm for achieving self-understanding and for transforming the puritan culture of America; the émigrés arrived at a time when "psychological thinking" became fashionable. After World War II, new professional fields in psychiatry and social work were developed. American medicine was not rigid and was open to principles of psychodynamic psychiatry, which created a need for reform, particularly in programs of training. Psychoanalysis became well established in postwar America due to the lasting influence of the psychoanalytically oriented army psychiatrists.

26. The first translations were made by Abraham A. Brill. But even the meticulous "standard edition" by Strachney was criticized for inadequate translations of, for example, the German *Masse* (group) and *Trieb* (instinct). See Bettelheim 1985.

27. Erik Erikson went to Boston in 1933, followed by Helene Deutsch in 1934, Felix Deutsch in 1935, and Beate Rank in 1936. Fritz Wittels went to New York in 1932, and Herman Nunberg in 1934.

Although European analysts initially faced many difficulties as new arrivals (adapting to a different culture, acquiring medical licenses, and competing with American analysts), they soon achieved a privileged status. Many other émigrés had to take jobs with much lower social status. The psychoanalysts could enter a professional field that was very much in demand and needed their know-how. Psychoanalysts became "phenomenally successful" because they "arrived at the right place at the right time" (Coser 1984: 19, 42). The three decades after 1945, during which the émigrés contributed so decisively to the expansion of psychoanalysis, have been described as "the years that were fat" (Gifford 1977: 380). Outside the clinical professions, psychoanalysis had "spread its influence over every branch of culture in the United States, with the force and speed of a forest fire" (Millet 1966: 593). The enormous influence of the émigrés can be seen in several areas. The great differences from coast to coast, from city to city, and from institute to institute must, of course, be kept in mind.

Psychoanalytic Training Institutes

In the years from 1946 to 1974, twenty-six new training institutes were sanctioned by the APsaA. The émigrés played a great role in building up these institutes, and a disproportionately large number of them worked as training analysts in them.

The largest group of émigrés worked in New York.[28] The high density of Viennese analysts there makes it possible to speak of their direct influence on a specific psychoanalytical culture in this new mecca of psychoanalysis. That New York had the largest concentration of Jews and seemed to be the most European city in the United States made it attractive. In addition, it held the promise of success and offered the possibility of coming into contact with other émigrés. In second place behind New York was Boston,[29] followed by Chicago.[30] Other émigrés influenced the development of the psychoanalytic institutes elsewhere.[31]

28. Among these were Edmund Bergler, Peter Blos, Berta Bornstein, Gustav Bychowski, Ludwig Eidelberg, Kurt and Ruth Eissler (after 1948), Ernst and Paul Federn, Salomea Gutmann-Isakower, Heinz Hartmann, Margit Herz-Hohenberg, Otto Isakower, Ludwig Jekels, Judith Kestenberg, Olga Knopf, Ernst Kris, Marianne Kris, Eduard Kronold, Margaret S. Mahler, Peter Newbauer, Herman Nunberg, Else Pappenheim, Annie Reich, Lili Peller, Theodor Reik, Max Schur, Isidor Silbermann, Melitta and Otto Sperling, René Spitz, and Fritz Wittels.

29. Edward and Grete Bibring, Felix and Helene Deutsch, Erik Erikson, Eduard Hitschmann, Beate Rank, and Hanns Sachs.

30. Bruno Bettelheim, Kurt and Ruth Eissler (before 1948), Heinz Kohut, Gerhard Piers, Maria Piers, Emmy Sylvester, and Edoardo Weiss.

31. In Washington D.C. (Jenny Wälder), Cleveland (Anny Katan), Denver (René Spitz), Detroit (Selma Freiberg, Fritz Redl, and Richard and Editha Sterba), Los Angeles (Francis Deri, Rudolf Ekstein, Otto Fenichel, and Robert Jokl), Philadelphia (Robert Wälder), San Francisco

The Austrian émigrés had special influence on the expansion of psychoanalysis in the field of psychoanalytic training. This type of work is barely noticed by those outside the field, so its influence is largely underestimated. The fact that there is solid training in the United States is to a great extent due to the work of the émigrés in this field. At one time, training analysis, theoretical instruction, and technical seminars were mainly in the hands of the émigrés, especially in Boston and in New York. Most of the Viennese émigrés there opposed the dilution of psychoanalysis and had great influence on the orthodox Freudian organization of the institutes. In a remarkable paper, Siegfried Bernfeld (1952) reflected on the negative effects of the trend toward rigid training regulations, which he argued would not promote the goals of psychoanalysis, namely, intellectual, social, and emotional autonomy.

The Viennese tradition of child analysis was carried on in the United States by many Austrian émigrés.[32] Some were committed to establishing training for child analysis within psychoanalytic institutes, including the training of nonphysicians. In doing so, they faced considerable opposition.

At this time the great teachers in the field were mainly émigrés.[33] As interesting, cosmopolitan personalities, they could mediate complex relations and impress with unexpected interpretations. In the discussions at the New York institute, they set the tone and were the éminences grises in the background. To a lesser extent, they took on official functions in the psychoanalytic societies and institutes.[34] "Surrounded by the aura of close association with the founding fathers, they imposed their vision on their American colleagues. At

(Siegfried Bernfeld and Anna Mänchen), Seattle (Edith Buxbaum), and Topeka (Rudolf Ekstein, Else Heilpern, and Robert Jokl) at the Menninger Clinic (see Friedman 1990).

32. For example, Berta Bornstein, Anny Katan, Marianne Kris, Peter Neubauer, and Jenny Wälder.

33. Coser (1984: 52ff.) conducted a poll of 692 members of the psychoanalytic institutes in New York, Boston, and San Francisco. Asked to name the leading American psychoanalyst, the results were: 1. Heinz Hartmann, 2. Ernst Kris, 3. Erik Erikson, 4. Margaret Mahler, 5. Phyllis Greenacre, 6. Edith Jacobson, 7. Rudolf Loewenstein, 8. Otto Fenichel, 9. Helene Deutsch, and 10. Bertram Lewin. Out of the ten most important analysts in America, eight were émigrés and six of them were former members of the WPV.

34. Heinz Hartmann was president of the IPA (1953–59); Grete Bibring (1962–63) and Heinz Kohut (1964–65) were presidents of the APsaA. The following émigrés were presidents of local institutes: in Boston, Helene Deutsch (1939–41), Edward Bibring (1947–49), Felix Deutsch (1951–54), and Grete Bibring (1955–58); in Chicago, Gerhard Piers (1961–62); in Denver, René Spitz (1962–63); in New York, Herman Nunberg (1950–52), Heinz Hartmann (1952–54), and Margaret Mahler (1971–73); in Philadelphia, Robert Waelder (1953–55); in New York (Downtown Institute), Ludwig Eidelberg (1958–60), Otto Sperling (1963–65), and Max Schur (1966–68); in San Francisco, Erik Erikson (1950–51) and Anna Maenchen (1955–57); in Seattle, Edith Buxbaum (1958–59); in Topeka, Rudolf Ekstein (1956–57) and Otto Kernberg (1971–73); and in Westchester, Leopold Bellak (1962–63).

the present time American analysts trained by refugees still largely dominate the psychoanalytic establishment" (Coser 1984: 20).

The Development of Psychoanalytic Theory

The Austrian émigrés had a dominating influence on the development of psychoanalytic theory, particularly in the area of ego psychology and early childhood development. The origins of these innovations went back to Vienna, but in the United States "the new wine found old bottles ready to receive it" (Gifford 1978: 339). The theoretical work on ego psychology by Heinz Hartmann, Ernst Kris, and Rudolf Loewenstein, known as the "gifted trio," dominated psychoanalytic training in the United States for several decades.[35] Hartmann was the last in a line of Freud's crown princes, which was an important factor in his rising influence. He was analyzed by Freud in the 1930s. With this aura, the work on ego psychology that he had already developed in Vienna, an impressive intellect, erudition, and great commitment, Hartmann succeeded in taking the leading position in the further development of psychoanalytic theory. His ambition was for psychoanalysis to become a science. Hartmann also promoted the application of psychoanalysis to psychology and the social sciences (see Jahoda 1969). At the same time psychoanalysis was integrated into psychiatry. Seen from today's point of view, this venture was problematic because the assessment of psychoanalysis as a science led later to disappointment and even rejection. Kurzweil (1994) sees a striking connection between the main problem of the émigrés—adapting to American society—and the leading psychoanalytic theory of that period, which was created by an émigré and focused on the problems of adaptation.[36]

Psychoanalysis as a science was no longer compatible with critical analyses of society. In the course of the Americanization of psychoanalysis, Freud's cultural critique became disregarded. His views on society and religion and his pessimistic notion of the death wish played no role within the training of American psychoanalysts.

The émigrés were unusually productive scholars; they "published four times as many books and more than one and a half times as many papers in psychoanalytic journals as did their American-born colleagues" (Coser

35. See, for example, Hartmann 1939 and 1964. An important periodical for the "gifted trio," as well as for other émigrés, was the annual *Psychoanalytic Study of the Child*, founded in 1945 by Anna Freud, Heinz Hartmann, and Ernst Kris.

36. American culture, in contrast to the picture of "rugged individualism," esteems adaptation, conformism, standardization, and popularization, especially in the sense of consciousness of community and of collaborating up to a point. These values may have coincided with the wishes of the émigrés to be part of the prestigious medical profession (personal communication by Peter Heller).

1984: 53). Many of their publications became psychoanalytic classics, such as Helene Deutsch's *The Psychology of Women* (1944–45) or Otto Fenichel's three-volume *The Psychoanalytic Theory of Neurosis* (1945).[37] Furthermore, Viennese émigrés like Siegfried Bernfeld, Kurt Eissler, Max Schur, Ernst Federn, and Herman Nunberg published outstanding contributions on the history of psychoanalysis itself.[38]

Although Anna Freud lived in London and became very influential within the politics of the IPA, British psychoanalysis was dominated by her antagonist Melanie Klein. Klein's theory on early, preoedipal conflicts was one of the most important supplements to classical, oedipal-centered psychoanalysis. Anna Freud's minority position in London stands in contrast to the support she enjoyed among American psychoanalysts (Federn 1988a). She maintained excellent contacts with the Austrian émigrés in the United States and, as one of the first ego psychologists, supported the development of ego psychology theory in America. The domination of psychoanalysis in America by ego psychology led to its isolation from the theories of Melanie Klein and from the British theorists of object relations. American psychoanalysis was also less open to dissenting therapeutic concepts, for example, those of Sándor Ferenczi. Their disputes with psychoanalytic dissidents like Otto Rank, Wilhelm Reich, Alfred Adler, Carl Gustav Jung, and their followers were also more hostile than in Europe.[39]

It was not until the 1970s that a Viennese-born émigré created major irritation within the psychoanalytic establishment. Heinz Kohut, a training

37. To mention a few other examples of important publications by the Viennese émigrés: Edmund Bergler, *The Basic Neurosis: Oral Regression and Psychic Masochism* (1949); Bruno Bettelheim, *Symbolic Wounds* (1954) and *The Empty Fortress* (1967); Peter Blos, *On Adolescence* (1962); Berta Bornstein, *Clinical Notes on Child Analysis* (1945); Gustav Bychowsky, *Psychotherapy of Psychosis* (1952); Ludwig Eidelberg, *Take Off Your Mask* (1949); Kurt Eissler, *The Psychiatrist and the Dying Patient* (1955); Rudolf Ekstein (with R. Wallerstein), *The Teaching and Learning of Psychotherapy* (1958); Erik Erikson, *Childhood and Society* (1950); Paul Federn, *Ego Psychology and the Psychoses* (1952); Eduard Hitschmann, *Great Men: Psychoanalytic Studies* (1956); Ernst Kris, *Psychoanalytic Explorations in Art* (1952); Margaret Mahler, *On Human Symbiosis and the Vicissitudes of Individuation* (1968) and (with others) *The Psychological Birth of the Human Infant* (1975); Peter Neubauer (and D. Flapan), *Assessment of Early Child Development* (1975); Herman Nunberg, *Practice and Theory of Psychoanalysis* (1948) and *Principles of Psychoanalysis* (1955); Theodor Reik, *Masochism in Modern Man* (1941); Max Schur, *The Id and the Regulatory Principles of Mental Functioning* (1966); René Spitz, *No and Yes: On the Beginning of Communication* (1957) and *The First Year of Life* (1965); and Robert Waelder, *The Basic Theory of Psychoanalysis* (1960).

38. Siegfried Bernfeld, *Bausteine der Freud-Biographik* (1981); Ernst Federn and Hermann Nunberg, eds., *Minutes of the Vienna Psychoanalytic Society* (4 vols., 1962–75); and Max Schur, *Freud: Living and Dying* (1972).

39. For biographies and the reception given to those "dissidents," see, for example, Aron and Harris 1993, Donn 1988, Grosskurth 1986, Handlbauer 1984, Haynal and Falzeder 1991, Lieberman 1985, Roazen 1984, Sharaf 1983, and Stepansky 1983.

analyst who occupied an influential position in the Chicago institute and within the APsaA, published several books (1971, 1977) on the psychology of the self and on the theory and treatment of narcissistic disorders. His critique of psychoanalytic orthodoxy and his own tendency to become orthodox "Kohutian" led to severe conflicts with the APsaA.

Another member of the younger generation of émigrés that took psychoanalytic theory in a new direction was Otto Kernberg.[40] He wrote some of the most important books on narcissistic disorders (Kernberg 1975, 1984) and skillfully integrated various and divergent theoretical trends of modern psychoanalysis (see, for example, Kernberg 1976). Of all Viennese émigrés, Kernberg exerts the most important influence on American psychoanalysis at present.

Psychiatry Depending on one's viewpoint, psychoanalysis either conquered, shaped, and dominated American psychiatry for decades, or it was swallowed up by it. Having a fixed place within a profession loaded with prestige, psychoanalysis became part of a system-preserving guild. Its triumphal march into the field of psychiatry is due to various factors. Before the beginning of World War II, William Menninger was appointed chief of psychiatry in the Office of the Surgeon General of the Army and Air Force. There he could tilt the training of army psychiatrists more favorably to psychoanalysis.[41] The image of psychoanalysis was so positive that after 1945 the American government paid for psychoanalytic training, including training analysis[42] for up to two years, for a whole generation of psychiatry students. Some psychiatric institutions like the Menninger Foundation in Topeka and the Austen Riggs Foundation in Stockbridge, Massachusetts, opened up completely to psychoanalysis and gave preference to European émigrés in admissions. Apparently their extensive psychiatric training, which was based on clinical work, was valued as much as their knowledge of psychoanalysis. In the 1940s and 1950s, more and more, chairs in psychiatry were occupied by psychoanalysts.[43] New opportunities

40. Kernberg was born in Vienna in 1928; he emigrated with his family to Chile in 1939 and received his analytic training there. In 1959 he immigrated to America and worked, among other places, at the Menninger Foundation in Topeka and, since 1973, in New York.

41. "His opposite number in the Navy was also a psychoanalyst. Increasingly, key appointments carrying large responsibilities were given to psychoanalysts, who responded enthusiastically to their new responsibilities—John ('Jock') Murray in the Air Force; M. Ralph ('Mo') Kaufman, Henry ('Hank') Brosin and Roy Grinker in the Army; Howard Rome in the Navy; and Daniel Blain in the Merchant Marine" (Millet 1966: 577).

42. Training analysis is a part of psychoanalytic education (or training). An individual studying to become a psychoanalyst goes to a training analyst several times a week to talk about his or her problems, past, dreams, symptoms, etc.

43. For example, Franz Alexander held the first chair in psychoanalysis in Chicago since the 1930s. Frederick Redlich became chief of the department at Yale; from 1955 on, Anny Katan

in the profession emerged, for example, clinics for child psychiatry and child guidance clinics, where the émigré analysts found employment.[44] In hospital departments and psychiatric clinics, analysts gained a foothold in treatment and training;[45] in the 1950s, 1960s, and early 1970s, most of these had analysts on their staffs, and many leading American psychiatrists were trained by émigrés.

Humanities Psychoanalysis definitely influenced the humanities and the social sciences in the postwar era, especially psychology,[46] ethnology, history (psychohistory, psychobiography), sociology, and literary studies.[47] But in many fields, it is hard to determine the influence of American-born analysts and European émigrés. Émigrés like Hartmann, Kris, Fenichel, and Mahler were known only to readers who were familiar with psychoanalysis, while other émigrés like Bruno Bettelheim and Erik Erikson appealed to a wide readership.

Erik Erikson had an immense influence on a wide range of intellectual issues and on several disciplines. Coser (1984: 55) argues that he "made the most consequential contemporary psychoanalytic contribution to general American culture." He was less influential in psychoanalytic debates than in public discussions outside psychoanalysis. He coined the terms "identity" and "identity crisis," which appealed directly to millions of young people in America. His life was a true American success story; he arrived as a European without credentials and became a Harvard professor. He was able to present complex psychoanalytic theories as comprehensible models that were understandable to a wide readership, and he presented psychoanalytic knowledge in a modern, journalistic way, applying it to historical, sociological, and anthropological issues.[48]

---

held a chair at the university clinic for children in Cleveland; Grete Bibring was the first female professor of psychiatry at Harvard in the years 1950–61; and since 1972 Heinz Kohut has taught at the University of Cincinnati.

44. For example, Bruno Bettelheim developed his environmental therapy in the Orthogenic School in Chicago; Rudolf Ekstein worked with psychotic adolescents in Los Angeles.

45. "By 1949 ... ninety percent of Boston analysts held academic or institutional posts of some kind" (Gifford 1978: 340).

46. On the influence of psychoanalysis on psychology, see Jahoda 1969 and Shakow and Rapaport 1964. On a local level, several émigrés worked in psychological institutes, for example, Else Frenkel-Brunswick at Berkeley and Frederick Wyatt at Ann Arbor.

47. The émigrés "encouraged the new Freudian interpretations in drama, biography, fiction, and almost every branch of literature" (Spaulding 1968: 286). The literary criticism of the 1950s was heavily influenced by psychoanalysis: Freud was read in order to understand literature and to analyze it (see, for example, the works of Lionel Trilling, Harold Blum, Susan Sontag, and Celia Brief).

48. Erik Erikson, *Childhood and Society* (1950), *Young Man Luther* (1958), *Gandhi's Truth* (1969), *Dimensions of a New Identity* (1974), and other works. On his influence, see Coles 1970, Coser 1984: 55–60, and Hughes 1975: 217–32.

Similarly, Bruno Bettelheim influenced a wide lay audience in America as a humanist critic of culture. His success derived also from "his characteristically lucid style of presentation and his flexible command of idiomatic English" (Coser 1984: 68).[49] As was true for many émigrés, some of Bettelheim's publications reflected his European heritage, for example, his book on Grimm's fairy tales, *The Uses of Enchantment* (1975).

Psychoanalysis as an Intellectual "Thrill" and the Therapy Boom

In the 1950s, it became chic in certain circles to be analyzed. Analysis was not always started because of some perceived psychological problem but with the expectation of an exotic adventure. Whoever wanted to be "in" had to have this experience, from people in Hollywood to the artists in the Village. Americans went to European analysts, so the émigrés had their hands full.[50] Psychoanalysis had never been as exciting as it was in the twenty-year period from the 1940s to the 1960s and may never be so exciting again.[51] The arrival of the Europeans stimulated an enormous interest in Freud, and, unlike today, many people who wanted to be analyzed had to be turned down.[52] As Farau and Cohn (1984: 179) note:

> In the late forties it was practically impossible to open an American paper, magazine, or a popular scientific booklet without coming across something "psychoanalytic." One ... "Freudian film" after another was made; at every party psychoanalytic terms whizzed through the air, and for dessert, dreams were interpreted just like one used to crack nuts. First-rate analysts didn't have a free minute for months but long waiting lists for their patients, and whoever could afford it some way or another had to be analyzed.

49. His major works include *Love Is Not Enough* (1950), *Symbolic Wounds* (1954), *Truants from Life* (1955), *The Empty Fortress* (1967), and *Freud and Man's Soul* (1982). On the controversy concerning Bettelheim's personality that took place after his death, see Roazen 1992.

50. From 1954 to her death, Marilyn Monroe, for instance, went to three different analysts, two of whom, Marianne Kris and Margit Herz-Hohenberg, were Austrian émigrés. See Peter Swales and Klaus Kamolz, "Marilyn auf der Couch," *Profil*, 6,13, and 20 July 1992.

51. Personal communication by Robert Stewart.

52. Assessing the influences of psychoanalysis via bestsellers, films, and other media on the everyday psychology of the American masses would be a fascinating task but difficult to do. By comparison, the influence on the political, intellectual, and artistic elite is easier to show. See Farber and Green 1993 as an example of mirroring the influence of analysts on the Hollywood elite. Although many émigrés published a lot and addressed a lay audience, many of their writings are forgotten. For example, Theodor Reik's *Listening with the Third Ear* (1948) and Hannah Green's bestseller *I Never Promised You a Rose Garden*, which portrayed the work of the German émigré Frieda Fromm-Reichmann in Chestnut Lodge, had wide influence, especially the film version after the novel reached the masses.

The boom lasted until the mid-1960s. A German or Austrian accent came to be something of an analyst's trademark and an attribute of the "shrink" in Hollywood film productions. After 1945 public interest in how to raise children "the right way" literally exploded, and Freud's views on childhood became highly popular in the United States.[53]

The émigrés were pioneers in developing a "therapy" society. According to Millet (1966: 570):

> The theoretical constructions of Freud and his followers have taken such a hold on the sophisticated public that terms and concepts once familiar only to students and practitioners of psychoanalysis are to be heard at cocktail parties, over the radio, or even from the mouths of taxi drivers. In certain circles, psychoanalysis is "the rage". Everyone has his analyst. It has almost become a status symbol. No copy of some well-known magazines is complete without a joke about the psychoanalyst; no theater season is complete without a play about a psychoanalyst, whether as villain or hero.

The origins of this can be traced in their biographies and in those of their patients. New York and a culture of psychoanalysis came to be synonymous, as the movies of Woody Allen or bestsellers like Erica Jong's *Fear of Flying* or Philip Roth's *Portnoy's Complaint* show. The concentration of Austrian émigrés and their impact on American psychoanalysis and popular culture were highest in New York. But while psychoanalysis made immense progress in classifying neuroses and narcissistic and borderline disorders in this cultural milieu, it could not answer the question of why loneliness and emotional misery spread like an epidemic in such a rich city without any taboos.[54]

The Consequences of Transplanting Psychoanalysis to the United States

The emigration of the Europeans led to a nearly complete transplantation of psychoanalysis from the German-speaking to the English-speaking culture. These traumatic events changed psychoanalysis. In the United States, a medical and therapeutic orientation of psychoanalysis experienced a meteoric rise and breathtaking expansion. This development seemed to prove Freud's earlier expressed fear that psychoanalysis could be degraded to a "handmaiden of psychiatry" in America. The discussion over lay analysis, that is, psychoanalysis practiced by nonphysicians, preoccupied Freud in the

---

53. Benjamin Spock wrote several bestsellers in this field.

54. The growing influence of psychotherapy in society has two faces: it offered help for people in need but also neglected the cause of emotional sufferings. It is noteworthy that psychoanalysts very seldom gave opinions on social questions. They could diagnose borderline disorders but were silent on the social causes of the fissures and cracks in the souls of people.

last years of his life in a highly emotional way. His vision of psychoanalysis went far beyond the treatment of neurotic people; psychoanalysis was to achieve advances in all branches of the humanities. In 1928, Freud wrote about the future practitioners of psychoanalysis: "I should like to hand it over to a profession which does not yet exist, a profession of *lay* healers of the soul who need not be doctors and should not be priests" (Freud and Pfister 1963: 126). In his polemic "The Question of Lay Analysis," Freud justified this distrust of a field dominated by medical doctors.[55] The APsaA soon went in this direction and in 1938 decided that only medical doctors should be allowed to train.

Except in England, psychoanalysis was subsequently wiped out almost completely in Europe by the Nazi regime, and as psychoanalysis in the postwar years was most powerful in the United States,[56] the American decision on training had an influence on the history of psychoanalysis that was more lasting and much stronger than it would have been had emigration not happened.[57] Views on the Americanization of psychoanalysis diverge greatly: whether this transformation brought superficiality or salvation, whether psychoanalysis was damaged or experienced an upswing, and whether it became diluted or flourished depend on whether one adopts a European or American perspective.[58] Psychoanalysis in America went in decline for those like Freud who regarded America as suspect, disagreeable, materialistic, pragmatic, and shallow (see Warner 1991). But those who admire the strength and dynamics of American society point out its impressive expansion in

55. "… in his medical school a doctor receives a training which is more or less the opposite of what he would need as a preparation for psycho-analysis. His attention has been directed to objectively ascertainable facts of anatomy, physics and chemistry…. His interest is not aroused in the mental side of vital phenomena…. Only psychiatry is supposed to deal with the disturbances of mental functions; but we know in what manner and with what aims it does so. It looks for the somatic determinants of mental disorders and treats them like other causes of illness" (Freud 1953–74: 20:230). Malcolm's portrait (1982: 162) of an orthodox psychoanalyst trained by the New York Institute seems to underscore the effect of more than forty years of a medically oriented psychoanalysis: "We psychoanalysts play with fire every day…. We steeled ourselves to this task long before we became analysts. We steeled ourselves to it in medical school and as interns and residents, when we had to do things that hurt other people." See also Federn 1990.

56. Twenty-two percent of the members of the IPA were Americans in 1931, 50 percent in 1946, and 64 percent in 1952.

57. Those Europeans who favored lay analysis, for example, Kurt Eissler, Paul Federn, Herman Nunberg, Richard Sterba, were not influential within the APsaA. Eissler's *Medical Orthodoxy and the Future of Psychoanalysis* (1965), a defense of lay analysis, was largely ignored by the psychoanalytic establishment. Sterba nearly got excluded from his psychoanalytic association because he had trained laymen. Theodor Reik, who as a layman could not get full membership in the New York society, founded in 1948 his own psychoanalytic society for nonphysicians, the National Psychological Association for Psychoanalysis.

58. See the different views of Federn (1988b) and Wyatt (1988), Bettelheim (1988), Jacoby (1983), Pappenheim (1988), and Parin (1990).

quantitative terms. It is ironic that psychoanalysis had its most sweeping success in a country Freud disliked. In America the émigrés undoubtedly had chances and possibilities they would not have had in Europe. Their propensity for innovation played a role, too, so that the concepts that had been developed in Vienna became successful in the United States. The career path of Bettelheim and Erikson would have been unheard of in Europe. Psychoanalysts who had been largely ignored in Vienna suddenly found hundreds of Americans who were eager to learn and were fascinated by their "exotic" *Weltbild*. In this encounter and exchange lies the essence of cultural transfer from Europe.

Once the émigrés arrived, psychoanalysis went through a "sea change" (Hughes 1975: 189–239). The American way of life and mentality are in many respects diametrically opposed to the European. The pessimistic perspectives of European analysis had to be changed and adapted considerably to have a chance of succeeding in the United States. Psychoanalysts on the Left faced an especially difficult situation (Jacoby 1983). None of them dared to criticize openly the social conditions in the country that had taken them in. Criticism could also be dangerous. "In the McCarthy Era, those émigrés with political conviction went into inner exile. No one wanted to risk being thrown out again. It was a justified caution. Furthermore, one would not have achieved anything politically. It would have been masochism."[59]

The early pioneers of psychoanalysis were to a great extent nonconformists who focused on pathogenic mechanisms in society from their rather marginal and sometimes "outsider" position in that very society. After the 1940s, psychoanalysis became a respected, prestigious, and profitable profession. Those seeking psychoanalytic training seem to have been increasingly influenced in their decisions by considerations of income and prestige. This orientation played a crucial role in the prevailing disinterest of psychoanalysts in questioning their own culture and society, which was reflected in their theory of ego psychology.

Techniques of psychoanalysis petrified in the United States. How to conduct psychoanalysis was taught in a narrow technical sense and not as an art, as if it could be learned from simple formulas in textbooks. For this reason, Freud's technical articles from the years between 1911 and 1915, which he himself qualified as "essentially negative" and "for beginners," were treated as sacred texts and taken literally: psychoanalysts "learned" to behave like "mirrors"[60] and "surgeons." For instance, in Vienna most analysts, like medical

---

59. Personal communication of Else Pappenheim. In this context, Erikson's steadfastness in the McCarthy era is impressive: in 1950 he refused to sign the anticommunist loyalty oath and lost his professorship of psychology at Berkeley.

60. That is, they would not show any emotion of their own; they would just mirror the patient's emotions.

doctors, received their clients in an office that was part of their apartments, whereas in the United States, more and more analysts developed an anxiety toward showing anything personal, which explains the clinical sterility of their consulting rooms. Of course, the question of how to draw a line between one's professional and one's private life is a central issue in psychotherapy. But the trend in America went toward an impenetrable barrier between the two areas. In their training, analysts learned the motto: "Never ask a question and never answer a question." This attitude encouraged the rise of a new type of analyst who came very close to the picture we know from various cartoons: the mute sitting behind the couch, inhibited and rigid, with a phobic relation toward the patient. It was considered almost scandalous to ask a patient about his or her well-being, for example, after illness or personal loss.

There were differences, too, in the goals of therapy. Recall that Freud's concept of mental health was not in line with the current trends in psychiatry and did not consider adjustment to the prevailing moral values as the predominant aim. As he noted in *The Loss of Reality in Neurosis and Psychosis* (1924), "We call behaviour 'normal' or 'healthy', if it combines certain features of both reactions—if it disavows the reality as little as does a neurosis, but if it then exerts itself, as does psychosis, to effect an alteration of that reality" (Freud 1953–74: 19:185). It seems that due to the transplantation of psychoanalysis to the United States, both the identity of the psychoanalyst and the goals of therapy shifted toward adjustment to the norms of the society of which the analyst had, by then, become a representative.

In the early history of psychoanalysis in Europe, the liberation of the "repressed" and the "unconscious" dominated therapy. After the immigration wave to the United States, the goal was to educate and improve the patient, to correct amorality and asociality.[61] In addition, Freud and the European analysts were more skeptical about psychoanalysis as a therapy, whereas in the United States the therapeutic effects of psychoanalysis were often overestimated and loudly advertised.

Conclusion

This chapter identifies eighty émigré psychoanalysts who were born or trained in Vienna and describes their specific background and their enormous influence on American psychoanalysis in various fields: on psychoanalytic training

---

61. Peter Heller sees in this development not simply an American influence but a general reaction toward the release of aggression in fascism. To promote civilized behavior and to control drives became the main goals of psychoanalysis, whereas in the Victorian period the main goal was to release the repressed eros (personal communication).

(especially in Boston and New York), on the development of psychoanalytic theory (ego psychology and early childhood development), on publications for psychoanalytic professionals (for example, by Helene Deutsch, Otto Fenichel, Heinz Hartmann, Ernst Kris, and Margaret Mahler) and a wider intellectual readership (Erik Erikson and Bruno Bettelheim), and on psychiatry and therapeutic practice within an increasing psychoanalytic boom.

The biographies and activities of the émigrés, the traumatic transplantation of psychoanalysis from the German-speaking to the English-speaking culture and its various effects on the history of psychoanalysis as well as on the émigrés themselves, the émigrés' connection to the rise and crisis of American psychoanalysis, and their impact on American culture at large are all fruitful areas for further research. The same may be said of the cultural and scientific loss that the emigration of the psychoanalysts created in postwar Austria, the ramifications of which are still felt today (see Huber 1977 and Mühlleitner and Reichmayr 1995: 110-14).

Appendix 5.1 Biographical and Geographical Information about the Émigrés to the United States: WPV Members

Name	Born	Place of Birth	WPV Membership	First Emigration	USA	City	Died
Anny (Angel-)Katan	1898	Vienna	1925–38	1936 Holland	1946	Cleveland	1992
Edmund Bergler	1899	Galicia	1928–38		1938	New York	1962
Siegfried Bernfeld	1892	Lemberg	1919–26, 1933–37	1934 France	1937	San Francisco	1953
Edward Bibring	1894	Galicia	1925–38	1938 GB	1941	Boston	1959
Berta Bornstein	1896	Kraków	1933–38	1933 Vienna*	1938	New York	1971
Edith Buxbaum	1902	Vienna	1928–38		1937 1947	New York Seattle	1982
Gustav Bychowsky	1895	Warsaw	1931–38	(from Warsaw)	1939	New York	1972
Frances Deri	1881	Vienna	1934–38	1933 Czech.*	1935	Los Angeles	1971
Felix Deutsch	1884	Vienna	1922–38		1935	Boston	1964
Helene Deutsch	1884	Galicia	1918–38		1934	Boston	1982
Ludwig Eidelberg	1898	Galicia	1928–38	1938 GB	1940	New York	1970
Ruth Eissler	1906	Odessa	1937–38	1933 Vienna*	1938 1948	Chicago New York	1989
Erik Homburger Erikson	1902	Frankfurt	1933–34		1933 1939 1951 1960	Boston San Francisco Stockbridge, MA Boston	1994
Paul Federn	1871	Vienna	1903–38		1938	New York	1950
Otto Fenichel	1897	Vienna	1920-30, 1935–37	1933 Norway* 1935 Czech.	1938	Los Angeles	1946
Salomea Gutmann-Isakower	1888	Galicia	1928–38	1938 GB	1940	New York	1974
Heinz Hartmann	1894	Vienna	1925–38	1938 France 1939 Switz.	1941	New York	1970
Else Heilpern	1896	Berlin	1935–38	1934: Vienna*	1938	Topeka	19??
Margit Herz-Hohenberg	1898	Slovakia	1925–38	1939 GB 1959 Israel	1939 1988	New York New York	1992
Eduard Hitschmann	1871	Vienna	1905–38	1938 GB	1940	Boston	1957
Otto Isakower	1899	Vienna	1925–38	1938 GB	1940	New York	1972
Ludwig Jekels	1867	Lemberg	1910-38	1935 Sweden 1937 Australia	1938	New York	1954
Robert Jokl	1890	Hungary	1921–38 remigration	1938 France 1946 Vienna	1947 1950	Topeka Los Angeles	1975
Ernst Kris	1900	Vienna	1928–38	1938 GB	1940	New York	1957
Marianne Kris	1900	Vienna	1928–38	1938 GB	1940	New York	1980
Eduard Kronold	1899	Lemberg	1928–38	1938 Czech. 1938 GB	1938	New York	1993

Appendix 5.1 *(cont.)*

Name	Born	Place of Birth	WPV Member-ship	First Emigration	USA	City	Died
Grete Lehner-Bibring	1899	Vienna	1925–38	1938 GB	1941	Boston	1977
Heinrich Löwenfeld	1900	Berlin	1937–38	1933 Prague*	1938	New York	1985
Margaret Mahler	1897	Hungary	1933–38	1938 GB	1938	New York	1985
Anna Mänchen	1902	Lithuania	1937–38	1933 Vienna*	1938	San Francisco	1991
Hermann Nunberg	1884	Galicia	1915–38		1931	Philadelphia	
					1934	New York	1970
Lili Peller	1898	Prague	1931–35	1934 Palestine	1938	Baltimore	
						New York	1966
Beate Rank	1896	Poland	1923–38	1926 France	1936	Boston	1967
Annie Reich	1902	Vienna	1928–30, 1933–38	1933 Czech.	1938	New York	1971
Theodor Reik	1888	Vienna	1911–33	1933 Holland*	1938	New York	1969
Hanns Sachs	1881	Vienna	1910-20		1932*	Boston	1947
Paul Schilder	1886	Vienna	1919–32		1928	Baltimore	
						New York	1940
Max Schur	1897	Galicia	1933–38	1938 GB	1939	New York	1969
Otto Sperling	1899	Vienna	1933–38		1938	New York	
René Spitz	1887	Vienna	1926–30	1932 France*	1938	New York	
					1957	Denver	1974
Editha Sterba	1895	Budapest	1925–38	1938 Switz.	1939	New York	
					1940	Chicago	
					1946	Detroit	1986
Richard Sterba	1898	Vienna	1928–38	1938 Switz.	1939	New York	
					1940	Chicago	
					1946	Detroit	1989
Jenny Wälder	1898	Lemberg	1928–38		1938	Boston	
					1943	Washington	
						Florida	1989
Robert Wälder	1900	Vienna	1924–38	1938 GB	1938	Boston	
					1943	Philadelphia	1967
Edoardo Weiss	1889	Trieste	1913–36	(from Rome)	1939	Topeka	
					1940	Chicago	1970
Fritz Wittels	1880	Vienna	1906–10, 1927–36		1932	New York	1950

Source: Mühlleitner (1992).

(* = emigration from Berlin)

Appendix 5.2 Biographical and Geographical Information about the Émigrés to the United States: Candidates in Training and American-Trained Émigrés

Name	Born	Place of Birth	Emigra-tion	City	Died	Lives Now In
Paul Bergman	1907	Vienna	1938	London		
			1941	Topeka		
			1950s	Washington, D.C.	1965	
Leopold Bellak	1916	Vienna	1938	Boston		
			1942	New York		Larchmont, N.Y.
Bruno Bettelheim	1903	Vienna	(1938–39	Dachau/Buchenwald)		
			1939	Chicago		
			1973	Los Angeles	1990	
Ernst Federn	1914	Vienna	(1938–45	Dachau/Buchenwald)		
			1948	New York		
			1951	Cleveland		
		(remigration)	1972			Vienna
Kurt R. Eissler	1908	Vienna	1938	Chicago		
			1948	New York		New York
Rudolf Ekstein	1912	Vienna	1938–40	New Hampshire/Boston		
			1947	Topeka		
			1957	Los Angeles		Los Angeles
Else Frenkel-Brunswick	1908	Lemberg	1938	Berkeley	1958	
John Kafka	1921	Linz	(1933 France)			
			1940	Chicago/New Haven/Washington, D.C.		Maryland/Washington, D.C.
Judith Kestenberg	1910	Kraków	1937	New York		New York
Heinz Kohut	1913	Vienna	(1939 GB)			
			1940	Chicago	1981	
Peter Neubauer	1913	Krems, Lower Austria	(1938 Switzerland)			
			1941	New York		New York
Else Pappenheim	1911	Salzburg	1938	Baltimore		
			1941	New York		
			1947–52	New Haven		New York
Gerhard Piers	1908	Vienna	1939	Chicago		
Maria Piers	1911	Vienna	1939	Chicago		Chicago
Frederick Carl Redlich	1910	Vienna	1938	Iowa/Boston/New Haven		
				Los Angeles		Los Angeles
Fritz Redl	1902	Klaus, Upper Austria	1936	Detroit		
Melitta Sperling	1899	Galicia	1938	New York	1973	
Frederick Wyatt	1911	Vienna	1938	NY/Mass./Ohio		
		(remigration)	1974	Freiburg, FRG	1993	

Source: Compiled from material collected by the author.

References

Alexander, F., S. Eisenstein, and M. Grotjahn. 1966. *Psychoanalytic Pioneers.* New York.

Aron, L., and A. Harris. 1993. *The Legacy of Sándor Ferenczi.* Hillsdale, N.J.

Ash, M. G. 1987. "Psychology and Politics in Interwar Vienna: The Vienna Psychological Institute, 1922–1942." In *Psychology in Twentieth-Century Thought and Society,* ed. M. G. Ash and W. R. Woodward, 143–64. Cambridge.

Benetka, G. 1992. "'Dienstbare Psychologie': Besetzungspolitik, Arbeitsschwerpunkte und Studienbedingungen in der 'Ostmark.'" *Psychologie und Gesellschaftskritik* 16, no. 1:43–81.

_____. 1995. *Psychologie in Wien. Sozial- und Theoriegeschichte des Wiener Psychologischen Instituts. 1922–1938.* Vienna.

Bergmann, M. S., and M. E. Jucovy, eds. 1982. *Generations of the Holocaust.* New York.

Bernfeld, S. 1952. "On Psychoanalytic Training." *Psychoanalytic Quarterly* 31: 453–82.

Bettelheim, B. 1985. *Freud and Man's Soul.* London.

_____. 1988. "Kulturtransfer von Österreich nach Amerika, illustriert am Beispiel der Psychoanalyse." In *Vertriebene Vernunft II. Emigration und Exil österreichischer Wissenschaft. Internationales Symposion 19. bis 23. Oktober 1987 in Wien,* ed. F. Stadler, 216–20. Vienna.

Burnham, J. C. 1979. "From Avant-Garde to Specialism: Psychoanalysis in America." *Journal of the History of the Behavioral Sciences* 15:128–34.

Buxbaum, E. 1990. *From Vienna to Seattle: Dr. Edith Buxbaum Remembers. An Interview with Lawrence H. Schwartz. May 14 and June 11, 1978.* Seattle.

Coles, R. C. 1970. *Erik H. Erikson: The Growth of His Work.* Boston.

Coser, L. 1984. *Refugee Scholars in America.* New Haven.

Deutsch, H. 1973. *Confrontations with Myself.* New York.

Donn, L. 1988. *Freud and Jung: Years of Friendship, Years of Loss.* New York.

Ekstein, R. 1987. "Die Vertreibung der Vernunft und ihre Rückkehr." In *Vertriebene Vernunft I. Emigration und Exil österreichischer Wissenschaft 1930–1940,* ed. F. Stadler, 472–77. Vienna.

Ekstein, R., K. Fallend, and J. Reichmayr. 1988. "'Too Late to Start Life Afresh'. Siegfried Bernfeld auf dem Weg ins Exil." In *Vertriebene Vernunft II. Emigration und Exil österreichischer Wissenschaft. Internationales Symposion 19. bis 23. Oktober 1987 in Wien,* ed. F. Stadler, 230–41. Vienna.

Fallend, K. 1988. *Wilhelm Reich in Wien. Psychoanalyse und Politik.* Vienna.

Fallend, K., B. Handlbauer, and W. Kienreich. 1989. *Der Einmarsch in die Psyche. Psychoanalyse, Psychologie und Psychiatrie im Nationalsozialismus und die Folgen.* Vienna.

Fallend, K., and J. Reichmayr. 1992. *Siegfried Bernfeld oder Die Grenzen der Psychoanalyse. Materialien zu Leben und Werk.* Basel.

Farau, A. 1953. *Der Einfluß der österreichischen Tiefenpsychologie auf die amerikanische Psychotherapie der Gegenwart.* Vienna.

Farau, A., and R. C. Cohn. 1984. *Gelebte Geschichte der Psychotherapie. Zwei Perspektiven.* Stuttgart.

Farber, S., and M. Green. 1993. *Hollywood on the Couch: A Candid Look at the Overheated Love Affair between Psychiatrists and Moviemakers.* New York.

Federn, E. 1988a. "Die Emigration von Anna und Sigmund Freud. Eine Fallstudie." In *Vertriebene Vernunft II. Emigration und Exil österreichischer Wissenschaft. Internationales Symposion 19. bis 23. Oktober 1987 in Wien*, ed. F. Stadler, 247–50. Vienna.

———. 1988b. "Psychoanalysis: The Fate of a Science in Exile." In *Freud in Exile: Psychoanalysis and Its Vicissitudes*, ed. E. Timms and N. Segal, 156–62. New Haven.

———. 1989. "Versuch einer Psychologie des Terrors." *Psychosozial* 12, no. 37:53–73.

———. 1990. "How Freudian are the Freudians? Some Remarks on an Unpublished Letter." In *Witnessing Psychoanalysis: From Vienna Back to Vienna via Buchenwald and the USA*, ed. E. Federn, 155–74. London.

Feigl, H. 1969. "The Wiener Kreis in America." In *The Intellectual Migration: Europe and America, 1930–1960*, ed. D. Fleming and B. Bailyn, 630–73. Cambridge, Mass.

Fermi, L. 1968. *Illustrious Immigrants: The Intellectual Migration from Europe, 1930–1941.* Chicago.

Fleming, D., and B. Bailyn, eds. 1969. *The Intellectual Migration: Europe and America, 1930–1960.* Cambridge, Mass.

Flory, G. 1976. "Edmund Bergler. Leben und Werk." Ph.D. diss., University of Mainz.

Freud, S. 1953–74. *The Standard Edition of the Complete Psychological Works of Sigmund Freud.* 24 vols. Ed. J. Strachey. London.

Freud, S., and O. Pfister. 1963. *Psychoanalysis and Faith: The Letters of Sigmund Freud and Oskar Pfister.* New York.

Friedman, L. J. 1990. *Menninger: The Family and the Clinic.* New York.

Funke, H. 1989. "Emigrantenansichten: 'Sich wirklich gefühlsmäßig vergegenwärtigen, was geschehen ist'. Alexander Mitscherlich aus der Sicht emigrierter Psychoanalytiker." In *Forschen und Heilen. Auf dem Weg zu einer psychoanalytischen Hochschule. Beiträge aus Anlaß des 25 jährigen Bestehens des Sigmund-Freud-Instituts*, ed. H. Bareuther et al., 305–27. Frankfurt.

Gardiner, M. 1983. *Code Name "Mary."* New Haven.

Gardner, S., and G. Stevens. 1992. *Red Vienna and the Golden Age of Psychology, 1918–1938.* New York.

Gerö, G. 1994. "The Handwriting on the Wall." In *Psychoanalyse in Selbstdarstellungen II*, ed. L. M. Hermanns, 199–230. Tübingen.

Gifford, S. 1977. "History of Psychoanalysis in the United States." In *Encyclopedia of Psychiatry, Psychology and Psychoanalysis*, ed. B. B. Wolman, 374–84. New York.

———. 1978. "Psychoanalysis in Boston: Innocence and Experience. Introduction to the Panel Discussion—April 14, 1973." In *Psychoanalysis, Psychotherapy and the New England Medical Scene, 1894–1944*, ed. G. E. Gifford, 325–45. New York.

Grinberg, L., and R. Grinberg. 1989. *Psychoanalytic Perspectives on Migration and Exile.* New Haven.

Grosskurth, P. 1986. *Melanie Klein: Her World and Her Work*. New York.

Grotjahn, M. 1987. *My Favorite Patient: The Memoirs of a Psychoanalyst*. Frankfurt.

Hale, N. G. 1971. *Freud and the Americans: The Beginnings of Psychoanalysis in the United States, 1876–1917*. New York.

————. 1978. "From Berggasse XIX to Central Park West: The Americanization of Psychoanalysis, 1914–1940." *Journal of the History of the Behavioral Sciences* 14:299–315.

————. 1995. *The Rise and Crisis of Psychoanalysis in the United States: Freud and the Americans, 1917–1985*. New York.

Handlbauer, B. 1984. *Die Entstehungsgeschichte der Individualpsychologie Alfred Adlers*. Vienna.

————. 1988. "'Lernt fleißig Englisch!' Die Emigration Alfred Adlers und der Wiener Individualpsychologen." In *Vertriebene Vernunft II. Emigration und Exil österreichischer Wissenschaft. Internationales Symposion 19. bis 23. Oktober 1987 in Wien*, ed. F. Stadler, 268–87. Vienna.

————. 1995. "The Emigration of the Viennese Individual Psychologists." In *Vertreibung der Vernunft. The Cultural Exodus from Austria*, ed. F. Stadler and P. Weibel, 122–26. Vienna.

Hartmann, H. 1939. *Ego Psychology and the Problems of Adaptation*. New York.

————. 1964. *Essays in Ego Psychology*. New York.

Haynal, A., and E. Falzeder. 1991. "'Healing through Love'? A Unique Dialogue in the History of Psychoanalysis." *Free Associations* 21:1–20.

Heilbut, A. 1983. *Exiled in Paradise: German Refugee Artists and Intellectuals in America from the 1930's to the Present*. New York.

Huber, W. 1977. *Psychoanalyse in Österreich seit 1933*. Vienna.

————. 1978. *Beiträge zur Geschichte der Psychoanalyse in Österreich*. Vienna.

Hughes, H. S. 1975. *The Sea Change: The Migration of Social Thought, 1930–1965*. New York.

Jacoby, R. 1983. *The Repression of Psychoanalysis: Otto Fenichel and the Political Freudians*. New York.

Jahoda, M. 1969. "The Migration of Psychoanalysis: Its Impact on American Psychology." In *The Intellectual Migration: Europe and America, 1930–1960*, ed. D. Fleming and B. Bailyn, 420–45. Cambridge, Mass.

Jeffrey, W. D. 1989. "After the Anschluss: The Emergency Committee on Relief and Immigration of the American Psychoanalytic Association." *American Psychoanalyst* 23, no. 2 and 3 (fall/winter):6–9.

Kaufhold, R., ed. 1993. *Pioniere der Psychoanalytischen Pädagogik: Bruno Bettelheim, Rudolf Ekstein, Ernst Federn und Siegfried Bernfeld*. Special edition. *Psychosozial* 16, no. 53.

Kernberg, O. 1975. *Borderline Conditions and Pathological Narcissism*. New York.

————. 1976. *Object Relations Theory and Clinical Psychoanalysis*. New York.

————. 1984. *Severe Personality Disorders*. New Haven.

Kestenberg, J. S. 1992. "Kindheit und Wissenschaft. Eine biographische Skizze." In *Psychoanalyse in Selbstdarstellungen I*, ed. L. M. Hermanns, 147–202. Tübingen.

Kohut. H. 1971. *The Analysis of the Self*. New York.

_____. 1977. *The Restoration of the Self.* New York.

Kurzweil, E. 1989. *The Freudians: A Comparative Perspective.* New Haven.

_____. 1994. "Vom Ödipus-Komplex zur Kultur. Der Einfluß der Emigranten auf die amerikanische Psychoanalyse." *Sigmund Freud House Bulletin* 18, no. 1B:24–50.

Langer, W. C., and S. Gifford. 1978. "An American Analyst in Vienna during the Anschluss, 1936–1938." *Journal of the History of the Behavioral Sciences* 14:37–53.

Lewin, B. D., and H. Ross. 1960. *Psychoanalytic Education in the United States.* New York.

Lieberman, E. J. 1985. *Acts of Will: The Life and Work of Otto Rank.* Amherst.

Lorand, S. 1969. "Reflections on the Development of Psychoanalysis in New York from 1925." *International Journal of Psychoanalysis* 50:589–95.

Luel, S. A., and P. Marcus. 1984. *Psychoanalytic Reflections on the Holocaust: Selected Essays.* New York.

Malcolm, J. 1982. *Psychoanalysis: The Impossible Profession.* New York.

May, U. 1976. "Psychoanalyse in den USA." In *Freud und die Folgen (1). Psychologie des 20. Jahrhunderts,* ed. D. Eicke, 482–527. Zurich.

Millet, J. A. P. 1966. "Psychoanalysis in the United States." In *Psychoanalytic Pioneers,* ed. F. Alexander, S. Eisenstein, and M. Grotjahn, 546–96. New York.

Mühlleitner, E. 1992. *Biographisches Lexikon der Psychoanalyse. Die Mitglieder der Psychologischen Mittwoch-Gesellschaft und der WPV 1902–1938.* Tübingen.

Mühlleitner, E., and J. Reichmayr. 1995. "The Exodus of Psychoanalysts from Vienna." In *Vertreibung der Vernunft. The Cultural Exodus from Austria,* ed. F. Stadler and P. Weibel, 98– 121. Vienna.

Oberläuter, D. 1985. *Rudolf Ekstein – Leben und Werk. Kontinuität und Wandel in der Lebensgeschichte eines Psychoanalytikers.* Vienna.

Oberndorf, C. P. 1953. *A History of Psychoanalysis in America.* New York.

Pappenheim, E. 1988. "Zeitzeugin." In *Vertriebene Vernunft II. Emigration und Exil österreichischer Wissenschaft. Internationales Symposion 19. bis 23. Oktober 1987 in Wien,* ed. F. Stadler, 221–29. Vienna.

_____. 1989. "Politik und Psychoanalyse in Wien vor 1938." *Psyche* 43:120–41.

Parin, P. 1990. "Die Beschädigung der Psychoanalyse in der angelsächsischen Emigration und ihre Rückkehr nach Europa." *Psyche* 44:191–201.

Peters, U. H. 1992. *Psychiatrie im Exil. Die Emigration der dynamischen Psychiatrie aus Deutschland 1933–1938.* Düsseldorf.

Piers, G., and M. W. Piers. 1982. "On Being a Newcomer." *The Annual of Psychoanalysis* 10:369–78.

Plänkers, T., and E. Federn. 1994. *Vertreibung und Rückkehr. Interviews zur Geschichte Ernst Federns und der Psychoanalyse.* Tübingen.

Quen, J. M., and E. T. Carlson. 1978. *American Psychoanalysis: Origins and Development.* New York.

Reichmayr, J. 1987. "'Anschluß' und Ausschluß. Die Vertreibung der Psychoanalytiker aus Wien." In *Vertriebene Vernunft I. Emigration und Exil österreichischer Wissenschaft 1930–1940,* ed. F. Stadler, 123–81. Vienna.

_____. 1990. *Spurensuche in der Geschichte der Psychoanalyse.* Frankfurt.

Roazen, P. 1984. *Freud and His Followers.* New York.

_____. 1985. *Helene Deutsch: A Psychoanalyst's Life.* New York.

_____. 1992. "The Rise and Fall of Bruno Bettelheim." *The Psychohistory Review* 20, no. 3 (spring):221–50.

Robinson, P. 1993. *Freud and His Critics.* Berkeley.

Rosenzweig, S. 1993. *Freud, Jung and Hall, the King-maker: The Historic Expedition to America (1909).* St. Louis.

Schick, A. 1973. "Psychotherapy in Old Vienna and New York: Cultural Comparisons." *The Psychoanalytic Review* 60:111–26.

Shakow, D., and D. Rapaport. 1964. *The Influence of Freud on American Psychology.* New York.

Sharaf, M. 1983. *Fury on Earth: A Biography of Wilhelm Reich.* New York.

Spaulding, E. W. 1968. *The Quiet Invaders: The Story of the Austrian Impact upon America.* Vienna.

Stadler, F., ed. 1987. *Vertriebene Vernunft I. Emigration und Exil österreichischer Wissenschaft 1930–1940.* Vienna.

_____. 1988. *Vertriebene Vernunft II. Emigration und Exil österreichischer Wissenschaft. Internationales Symposion 19. bis 23. Oktober 1987 in Wien.* Vienna.

Stadler, F., and P. Weibel, eds. 1995. *Vertreibung der Vernunft. The Cultural Exodus from Austria.* Vienna.

Steiner, R. 1994. "'Es ist eine neue Art von Diaspora....' Bemerkungen zur Emigrationspolitik gegenüber deutschen und österreichischen Psychoanalytikern während der Verfolgung durch die Nationalsozialisten auf der Grundlage des Briefwechsels zwischen Anna Freud und Ernest Jones sowie anderer Dokumente." *Psyche* 48:583–652.

Stepansky, P. E. 1983. *In Freud's Shadow: Adler in Context.* Hillsdale, N.J.

_____. 1988. *The Memoirs of Margaret S. Mahler.* New York.

Sterba, R. F. 1982. *Reminiscences of a Viennese Psychoanalyst.* Detroit.

Timms, E., and N. Segal, eds. 1988. *Freud in Exile: Psychoanalysis and Its Vicissitudes.* New Haven.

Wangh, M. 1962. *Fruition of an Idea: 50 Years of Psychoanalysis in New York.* New York.

Warner, S. L. 1991. "Freud's Antipathy to America." *Journal of the American Academy of Psychoanalysis* 19:141–55.

Whiteman, D. B. 1993. *The Uprooted: A Hitler Legacy.* New York.

Wimmer, A. 1993. *Die Heimat wurde ihnen fremd, die Fremde nicht zur Heimat. Erinnerungen österreichischer Juden aus dem Exil.* Vienna.

Wyatt, F. 1988. "The Severance of Psychoanalysis from Its Cultural Matrix." In *Freud in Exile: Psychoanalysis and Its Vicissitudes,* ed. E. Timms and N. Segal, 145–55. New Haven.

_____. 1992. "Warum ich Psychoanalytiker wurde – überdeterminiert!" In *Psychoanalyse in Selbstdarstellungen I,* ed. L. M. Hermanns, 345–99. Tübingen.

Chapter 6

HEIMAT HOLLYWOOD

Billy Wilder, Otto Preminger, Edgar Ulmer,
and the Criminal Cinema of the
Austrian-Jewish Diaspora

Jonathan Munby

Introduction: Austrian-Jewish Prominence in Postwar American Crime Cinema

Austrian-Jewish filmmakers who fled to Hollywood from fascism in the
1930s left their most indelible mark on a cycle of films problematically
labeled "film noir."[1] Visually dark and thematically pessimistic, these crime
films addressed the sociocultural upheavals in the United States brought on
first by the war and then by postwar redomestication. Aesthetically, the postwar crime film is generally understood as Hollywood's most experimental and
transgressive film form—a significant claim, given Hollywood's status as the
primary institution (pretelevision) for the regulation of America's self-image in
the twentieth century.

1. As film scholar Frank Krutnik (1991: 15–17) points out, the term "film noir" was first
coined by French postwar film critics who in the summer of 1946 saw five American crime
thrillers exhibited as a group: *The Maltese Falcon* (1941), *Double Indemnity* (1944), *Laura*
(1944), *Murder, My Sweet* (1944), and *Woman in the Window* (1944). Critics writing for *L'Ecran
Français, Revue du Cinema,* and *Nouvelle Critique* were able to see distinct trends that linked
these films together and distinguished them from prewar screen typology. The French critics
noted film noir's connections to American detective fiction, which they already had termed "*série*

Most critical appraisals of the postwar crime cycle note its stylistic debt to European modernism, especially Weimar German expressionism. The disproportionate presence of exiled Austrian (and German) filmmakers in the making of this crime cycle has been used to prop up an argument for the cycle's exceptionalism, something only enhanced by the use of the French word *noir*, which marks the cycle as somehow outside Hollywood norms. In attributing the cycle's anomalous status to "alien" influences, film critics and historians have overlooked that the European exiles' influence on postwar Hollywood had been profoundly shaped by their own "Americanization" in the 1930s. To know that a style has foreign origins is one thing; to define what this style communicates in the American context or why it found a *Hollywood* calling is another.

As the biographies of Billy Wilder, Otto Preminger, and Edgar Ulmer testify, these directors regarded America neither as a place of cultural banishment nor as a temporary sanctuary from the ruptures of European conflict. In fact, they tended to rationalize their journey to America in terms of pull rather than push factors, understanding themselves less as "exiles" than as "émigrés." As Jews, this positive disposition toward the host culture can only have been enhanced by the horrors of fascism in the old country. By comparison, the more pluralistic and ethnically tolerant mandate of Franklin Delano Roosevelt's New Deal administration must have held a powerful appeal. In this period, all three directors took on American citizenship. While this was in many ways a prerequisite for ensuring political asylum, none of them viewed their American citizenship cynically. Both Preminger and Wilder were notorious for their almost jingoistic defense of their adopted homeland whenever anyone (especially visiting Europeans) criticized the United States. During the Great Depression, Ulmer found affirmation for his calling in making films for ethnic and racial minorities. Advancing the interests of those on the margins of American culture and society was for Ulmer, as an "Americanizing" émigré, an appropriate task.

The Austrian-Jewish exile/émigré's influence on postwar Hollywood, then, cannot be accounted for in terms of a simple transplantation of European (modernist and/or Eurocentric) sensibilities onto the American 1940s. To understand why these particular filmmakers promoted a dark and disillusioned vision of postwar America, it is necessary to examine the complex

---

noir américaine." Although this connection is important, the American postwar crime cycle should not stand in isolation from its *cinematic* (and theatrical) predecessors, both domestic and foreign. Three of the films were indeed indebted to the work of such writers as Dashiell Hammett, Raymond Chandler, and James M. Cain, but the critics completely overlooked that three of the five—*Laura, Double Indemnity,* and *Woman in the Window*—were directed by exiles of Austrian-Jewish extraction: Otto Preminger, Billy Wilder, and Fritz Lang, respectively.

terms of their prewar "Americanization" and consequent "diasporic" self-understanding as simultaneously exile and émigré. In order to do this, it is necessary to travel back even further to uncover the unique place Jews occupied in Austrian culture before the onset of fascism. Only in this way can we more properly understand these directors' postwar aesthetic and political choices in the United States and unravel the forces that placed Austrian-Jewish film exiles at the forefront of fashioning an American cinema that dissented from sanctioning the postwar order.

Much critical space has been devoted to the analysis of so-called noir aesthetics, yet surprisingly little has been done to connect these features to the political contest for the control of Hollywood in the postwar years. The contest culminated in the ignominious inquisitions conducted by the House Un-American Activities Committee (HUAC) in 1947 and 1951–53, which directly and indirectly subjected exiled German-speaking filmmakers to a second experience of purging. Postwar political gatekeepers regarded the American film art fashioned by the exiled filmmakers as the clearest example of Hollywood's seditious "un-American" tendencies.

Modernity's Chosen Subjects: Jewry in Pre-Anschluss Viennese Culture

To speak of a purely Austrian influence on Hollywood would be to truncate the truth, for almost all Central European filmmakers who became famous in America were apprentices in Weimar Berlin's Universumfilmaktiengesellschaft (UFA) studios at Babelsberg and were influenced by a liberal artistic establishment dominated by Jews. For Austrian filmmakers, the route from Vienna to Berlin in the 1920s and early 1930s was well trodden because Babelsberg was the sole serious commercial rival to Hollywood. As the careers of Billy Wilder and Edgar Ulmer attest, Berlin served as a *Treffpunkt* (rendezvous/meeting point) for all those who would later continue their journey to Los Angeles as a *Fluchtpunkt* (point of escape/vanishing point). Wilder's first work in cinema was for UFA as a screenwriter. Ulmer served a cinematic apprenticeship in Berlin, first with Decla-Bioscope in 1918 and later with a fellow Max Reinhardt protégé, F. W. Murnau, as the latter's artistic director of such classics of the Weimar cinema as *The Last Laugh* (1924) and *Faust* (1926). Perhaps it was symptomatic of the awkward existence of the Austrian First Republic that so many Austrian film and theater artists found refuge in Berlin as a place to work out their artistic desires and as the *other* crossroads between East and West. It is precisely this double experience of exile that is most significant in explaining the specific nature of Austrian-Jewish contributions to American cinema.

I am concerned here with Otto Preminger and Edgar Ulmer, both protégés of the great Austrian theatrical innovator, Max Reinhardt. Reinhardt
was able to manufacture in both Berlin and Vienna a sense of collective
unity in his audience through his "theater of illusion and mass spectacle."
This sense of togetherness was absent beyond the confines of the theater,
lacking in a political sense from the self-understanding of both Germany
and Austria as *nation*-states, an understanding that would prove so useful in
the wrong hands. At the same time, Reinhardt's development of a small-scale,
more reflective theater (*Kammerspiel*, or ensemble theater) pointed toward
an opposite concern for individual, not collective, identity. This kind of art
clearly addressed the contradictions of the period. It was part of a quest for
unity, yet it developed a modernist sensitivity to the problem of individual
identity in an age of mass production and technology. Symptomatically,
this giant of the Austrian art scene was a Jew.

The three filmmakers I focus on here came, like Reinhardt, from Jewish
families that had moved in the early twentieth century from the far-flung
corners of the Habsburg Empire to Vienna. These filmmakers' aesthetic
treatments of the problems of postwar American society are rooted in their
formative artistic training in the complicated antisemitic context of the
post-1895, pre-Anschluss period of Austrian history. As Steven Beller (1989)
points out, this was a period when the intellectual and cultural life of
Catholic Vienna came to be dominated by Jews. Judaism itself, as Carl
Schorske (1979: 146–80, 208–78) intimates in his discussion of Theodor
Herzl and Gustav Klimt, does not seem to have influenced Austrian modernism directly, for the movement was led by predominantly secularized
and assimilated Jews. Yet antisemitism provided the context that paradoxically located the artists and intellectuals forming the core of Viennese culture on the political periphery.

Wilder, Ulmer, and Preminger were indebted, then, to a generation of
secularized Austrian Jews who had found in the rarified realm of high culture a way of maintaining a stake in Austrian modernity when all other
avenues to power were being closed to them. As protégés of this cultural
avant-garde—as writers, filmmakers, artistic directors, and theater directors—and as members of the salon and café-klatsch society, Preminger,
Wilder, and Ulmer extended the previous generation's goal of constructing
through culture an ersatz totality that could compensate for liberal Jewish
middle-class disenfranchisement in other areas of modern public life.

In a culture where antisemitism had become *hoffähig* (acceptable/pre-
sentable) following the decline of classic bourgeois liberalism, especially in
the 1890s with the victory of Karl Lueger and the Christian Right, the Austrian-Jewish middle class did not retreat into the sanctuary of ethnic and
religious traditions. Instead, they made a concerted effort to hold onto those

areas where they had made gains in secular bourgeois culture, the areas of high art and intellectual leadership. Preminger and Wilder rejected careers in law in favor of careers in film, theater, and literature, while Ulmer left the field of architecture. Their decisions showed that Austrian Jews could continue to occupy a vital space *within* an all-important domain of society, that is, the space that mediated Austrian middle-class self-representation.

Yet in making the choices they did—albeit as secularized Jews—they maintained a contradictory relationship to the gentile membership of the bourgeoisie and were constantly reminded of their estranged relationship to bourgeois identity. As fellow Austrian-Jewish film exile Fred Zinnemann described, "It was the enormous sense of not belonging, as expressed everywhere with typical Viennese charm: 'We do not have anything against the Israelites, we just want them to go somewhere else'" (quoted in Cargnelli and Omasta 1993: 9).[2] Beller (1989: 243–44) argues that the isolation of the Viennese cultural elite through antisemitism had unique consequences:

> [Jews were able] to observe and record the nature of post-liberal society and the crisis of the individual with an intensity and in a form which only emerged later in other societies. In those societies these problems had appeared only marginal, whereas for the Jews of Vienna they had become central.

When these Austrian-Jewish exiles arrived in Hollywood, they brought with them this sense of internal exile from their own class and a modernist aesthetic tradition to go with it, something that was to find its most profound transatlantic and cross-cultural application in the American context of maladjustment to embourgeoisement in the aftermath of World War II. The postwar crime cycle articulated feelings of crisis, displacement, alienation, disillusionment, and a conspiring fate that, while consistent with the legacy of the exiled Austrian-Jewish filmmaker, became a national condition in the context of the postwar era.

Exiles or Émigrés?

It is tempting to rationalize Wilder, Preminger, and Ulmer's postwar dark period as the product of Eurocentric views on the materialism of American culture. As Austrian exiles, all three directors certainly had this view at their disposal. Their critique of postwar culture, however, was launched from another perspective as well. All three had held a deep affinity for the liberating features of American culture even before they were forced to seek asylum. For these filmmakers to arrive at such a powerfully pessimistic view of their adopted

---

2. "'Mir hamm' ja nix gegen die Herrn Israeliten, wir möchten nur gern, daß sie woanders hingehn.'"

nation by the late 1940s had as much to do with a genuinely *American* concern for the postwar course of things as it did with their being transplanted Europeans. To unearth the roots of these filmmakers' investment in postwar American culture, it is necessary to turn back to the place America occupied in their formative years and evaluate the degree to which these displaced Viennese artists understood themselves as "exiles" rather than "émigrés."

In Billy Wilder's case, America had been a powerful influence in his life from day one. His mother, Eugenia, had spent a period of time in her youth with an uncle in New York. When she returned to Austria, she remained deeply attached to the United States, always dreaming of returning. This hold on her imagination extended to Eugenia's choice of names for her sons. Although originally naming Samuel and Wilhelm after deceased grandparents in accordance with Jewish tradition, she quickly Americanized her sons' names. Samuel became Billie (and Wilhelm, Willie) in accordance with Eugenia's love of Buffalo Bill, whose Wild West show she had seen at Madison Square Garden (Zolotow 1977: 21). "Buffalo" Billy Wilder, then, grew up in a household where America held a strong fascination as a positive alternative to Austria, which was, no doubt, intensified by the problems associated with being a Jew in Vienna.

In fact, in an article on jazz for *Die Stunde* in 1926, the young Billy Wilder provided an early indication of the special place America occupied not only in his but also in Europe's imagination: "For jazz? Against jazz? The most modern music? Kitsch? Art? Needed! The necessary revitalization of a decrepit Europe" (quoted in Karasek 1994: 49).[3] Jazz was symptomatic of the rejuvenating and irreverent antitraditional features of American culture. Wilder's love of jazz had enabled him to escape the provincialism of Vienna in the mid-1920s and make it to the other hub of Central European intellectual and cultural life, Weimar Berlin.

In Vienna, he had written rave reviews of the American jazz musician Paul Whiteman, who subsequently commissioned him to do the same in Berlin by paying for Wilder's ticket and meals. Yet at the same time, he became revered in Berlin as one of the few men who could dance the Charleston. Earning a living as a dance-hall gigolo and as a street-savvy screenwriter, Wilder also preserved a love of high modernist art and the waltz.[4] This split identification with old- and new-world cultures pervaded

3. "Für Jazz? Gegen Jazz? Modernste Musik? Kitsch? Kunst? Bedürfnis! Notwendige Bluterneuerung des verkalkten Europa."

4. Although Wilder's screenplays of the Weimar period display a predominant concern for street culture and crime—*Menschen am Sonntag* (1929), *Der Mann, der seinen Mörder sucht* (1931), *Emil und die Detektive* (1931), *Ein Blonder Traum* (1932), and *Scampolo, ein Kind der Straße* (1932), he was also busy collecting modernist art masterpieces. Wilder rose to the status of being Hollywood's foremost art collector, investing obsessively in everything from Klee and Picasso to Saul Steinberg and Henry Moore.

his film work throughout his career and became a trait common to all exiles/émigrés who excelled in the noir aesthetic. Thus, in spite of the difficult conditions surrounding it, Wilder's eventual entry into the United States in many ways fulfilled both his own and his mother's dream of "returning" to America.

Even more than Wilder, Preminger's journey to Hollywood cannot be described in terms of flight. Unlike Wilder, Preminger was attracted not so much to "Americana" but to the high life of New York City. Long before the onset of fascism made emigration to America a matter of necessity, the image of New York razzmatazz, its wild social scene, and Broadway held a special place in Preminger's imagination (Frischauer 1974: 59–60). In stark contrast to Wilder, he was given a red carpet welcome upon arrival in New York in 1935. Renowned as Max Reinhardt's heir and the directorial *Wunderkind* of the Josefstadt Theater, Preminger had been invited to direct both *Libel!* on Broadway, a play which was a huge success in Vienna, and films for Twentieth Century-Fox, which paid his transatlantic passage.

These pull factors were reinforced by an encounter with the antisemitic forces of Viennese society. Two years before Hollywood and Broadway executives started courting him, Viennese authorities offered Preminger the chance to become the managing director of the Burgtheater, the highest position in Austrian theater. There was only one condition: he must convert to Catholicism, as no Jew had ever held such a high position. As was typical for a member of the Jewish cultural elite in Vienna, Preminger was a highly secularized and assimilated Jew. He was, after all, the proud son of the former chief prosecutor of the Austro-Hungarian Empire. Yet he remained a man of principle and would not make this concession to antisemitic forces. His refusal to convert meant that the offer was withdrawn. The incident demonstrates the contradictory status of Jews in Viennese culture and made the option to work in America more attractive.

Edgar Ulmer had shared with Preminger the advantages of working under the tutelage of Max Reinhardt. He had received training as an architect at the Akademie der bildenden Künste in Vienna, which led him first into a career as a set designer for both the Burgtheater and Josefstadt Theater. This, in conjunction with his film work for F. W. Murnau, had enabled Ulmer to travel to the United States on a number of occasions before the onset of fascism. In 1923 he had toured with Reinhardt's *The Miracle*, for which he had designed the sets. On the strength of this, he was hired by Martin Beck to design stage sets on Broadway and by Universal Studios in Hollywood.

Several return trips to Germany in the mid- to late 1920s were motivated by his association with Murnau, which ultimately led in 1930 to a permanent decision to reside in the United States. On the strength of *The Last Laugh* (1924), for which Ulmer had been artistic director, Twentieth Century-Fox invited Murnau to make films in Hollywood. Ulmer accompanied him, again as artistic director, working on the classics *Sunrise* (1927) and *Tabu* (1931), before Murnau's tragic death in an automobile accident in 1931. Although Ulmer had returned briefly in 1929 to work on Robert Siodmak's *Menschen Am Sonntag*, his marriage to an American already signaled to those on the set, such as future Jewish exiles Siodmak, Billy Wilder, and Fred Zinnemann, that he was Hollywood bound (Karasek 1994: 74).

Collectively, then, these Austrian-Jewish filmmakers were motivated as much out of pull as push factors in their journeys to America. Their problematic status in the old country fueled an ongoing recourse to culture as an ersatz totality in which as Jews they could remain central rather than peripheral to the life of the nation. Their strong presence as Jews in Austrian arts and intellectual life gave them a concomitant ability to cross national boundaries. It is clear, too, that Wilder, Preminger, and Ulmer were attracted to and benefited from the cross-cultural possibilities and international language of cinema and theater.

America Realized: Depression America (No Auteurs Allowed)

As assimilated Jews in Catholic Vienna, Wilder, Preminger, and Ulmer were always made aware of their status as misfits. Their situation fostered suspicions toward and conflicts with authority and almost schizophrenic relationships with their Austrian and European past once they were ensconced in the United States. As Wilder was to reflect in 1945: "What I hate most about the Austrians is that I can't hate them" (quoted in Karasek 1994: 34). Wilder would go on to make many films that dealt with the culture clash between Americans and Europeans. When he eventually fled to America in 1933, he found that his first obstacle was the English language. True to his attraction for American popular culture, he set about learning English from 1930s radio soap operas and baseball broadcasts. Sports metaphors and street slang abound in his writing; they are symptomatic both of his love of American popular culture and of the increased legitimacy of all forms of popular and vernacular speech during the Great Depression.

Wilder's quest for immigrant status was far from a formality. Once his initial visitor's visa had expired, he had to leave the country—to Mexico—in order to request a more permanent immigration visa. On being asked by the immigration officer about his reasons for seeking asylum in the United States, Wilder replied that he wished to make movies. After making him sweat it out, the officer eventually granted him his request on one condition: he must make a few "good" films. Hollywood offered

Wilder a meal ticket and his chief vehicle for Americanization. Initially condemned to revamping and translating UFA scripts for Fox, Wilder was eventually given the chance to write more original "American" material. In the late 1930s, he formed an enduring screenwriting partnership with Charles Brackett at Paramount. Yet, in spite of their success, Wilder became increasingly frustrated with not having ultimate control over the films on which he worked. The final straw was the doctoring of the film *Hold Back the Dawn* (1941), in which Wilder's own experience of exile is easily discernible.

The film stars Charles Boyer as the gigolo Georges Iscovescu who is stranded in Mexico and is seeking asylum in the United States following his flight from Europe. To facilitate his goal, the protagonist seeks an arranged marriage with an American teacher (Olivia de Havilland). As the plot unfolds, Georges's exploitative intentions change as he falls in love with the reluctant American. The film asks a quintessential question for exile/émigrés: "Is it love? Or is it immigration?" (Karasek 1994: 196). Wilder was infuriated by director Mitchell Leisen's script tampering, especially in a film based on such an intensely personal experience. After this Wilder vowed never to write screenplays for others, and in 1942 he directed his first film in America, *The Major and the Minor*.

Although Wilder was grateful for the chance to earn any kind of a living in the United States, his desire for autonomy grew with the job. Like Wilder, both Preminger and Ulmer shared this quest for independence. But the conditions that governed their conflicts with authority were quite different, both having entered the United States on more favorable terms than Wilder. Preminger, for example, had been brought to America in 1935 by Joseph Schenck, who had recently merged his company, Twentieth Century, with Fox. Schenck and his chief producer, Darryl Zanuck, wished to coax Preminger into the factory system, which gave him ample time to learn the ropes. But after only two films he had a major altercation with Zanuck. Being used to having autonomy as a stage director in Vienna and naive about the power of Hollywood studio moguls, Preminger did not realize the consequences. His contract was not renewed in 1937, and owing to collusion among the moguls, no alternative offers were made. The Hollywood message was clear: "No *auteurs* allowed." He returned to Broadway, unable to make another film for six years.

Friends suggested that he return to Vienna and the Josefstadt Theater. Preminger (1977: 22), however, rejected this option:

> Though I had never in my life known as dark a time as that winter of 1937, I didn't for a second consider leaving America. I loved the country. I believed in my future. I had no desire at all to return to Vienna, not ever. Events [the Anschluss of 1938] proved I was right.

Hardly a political radical, Preminger held a strong admiration for Franklin Roosevelt and evinced a classic liberal admiration for America's freedoms, especially the chance to criticize the state (Preminger 1977: 53). This optimistic view of America was always contrasted with the repressive nature of European regimes.

Like Preminger, Edgar Ulmer had come to Hollywood in relatively benevolent conditions, basking in the wake of F. W. Murnau. Following the death of Murnau in 1931, however, Ulmer was left to fend for himself and gained a directorial contract with MGM in 1933. The experience was not rewarding, involving mainly a couple of forgettable formula Westerns under the pseudonym of John Warner. The one bright moment was *The Black Cat* (1934), now regarded as a cult classic, which first paired Bela Lugosi with Boris Karloff. Disappointed not only with Hollywood but also himself, Ulmer went into voluntary exile from Hollywood, traveling east like Preminger to New York. There, Ulmer was able to discover a more meaningful outlet for his film talents in documenting the struggles for cultural recognition of those on the sociocultural margins and in the lower classes. He teamed up with creative artists from the Jewish-, Ukrainian-, and African-American communities to address problems of cultural identity and tradition, which must have resonated deeply with his own plight as an exile.

As a secularized Jew from Austria, Ulmer came to terms with his ethnic roots only when he got to America. Throughout the late 1930s, he made a number of Yiddish films, including *Grune Felder* (1937), *Yankl der Shmid* (1937), *Di Klyatshe* (1939), and *Americaner Shadchen* (1940). Some of these drew on the talents of New York's Jewish Arts Theater. His most famous Yiddish film was *Di Klyatshe*, also known as *The Light Ahead*, which told the story of a crippled peasant's romantic attachments to a blind girl in turn-of-the-century Poland. Faced with a cholera epidemic, the superstitious villagers decide to redeem themselves in face of what they interpret as the wrath of God by exploiting the love between the two outcasts. The film dealt honestly with the strengths and weaknesses of the Jewish community, and as George Lipsitz (1990: 199) emphasizes, considering its release in 1939, it "presented its knowing audiences with a parable about the horrifying tragedy confronting European Jewry at that very moment."

Ulmer's experience in the Great Depression involved him in discovering and articulating America's promise of pluralism and in celebrating collective community action. The Harlem Players, impressed by his ability to work with low budgets and his sensitivity to "minority" causes, invited him to direct a film about street/underworld life in Harlem. *Moon over Harlem* (1939) fit well into the existing independent black cinema tradition of so-called race films, which sought both to rectify misrepresentations and compensate for the absence of black experience and identity in mainstream

American cinema. Ulmer must have drawn political optimism from his role in helping displaced and disenfranchised peoples organize. In fact, he described his attraction to the low-budget B movie and the ethnic/racial docudrama as a form of artistic vindication: "I really am looking for absolution for all the things I had to do for money's sake" (quoted in McCarthy and Flynn 1975: 409). This was as much an ironic jab at the apolitical nature of his high-art heritage in European cinema and theater as a commentary on the commercial motivations underlying his earlier work in Hollywood.

Ulmer's political coming-of-age was informed by the twin contexts of the fascist horror abroad and the struggles of ethnic and racial collectives in New York City. These mutually reinforcing contexts shaped Ulmer's positive relationship to his adopted homeland in the 1930s, which suggests compelling reasons to argue that compared to Preminger and Wilder, Ulmer was even more likely to become disillusioned with the postwar situation. Accordingly, his postwar crime films express an intense sense of blasted hopes. In sum, the 1930s were a difficult time professionally for all three filmmakers in Hollywood as they struggled to come to terms with the restrictive conditions of the studio system. But the experience also stood them all in good stead to take advantage of the opening up of the system in the 1940s.

Criminal Visions of Maladjustment in Wartime and Postwar America

In the 1940s, Wilder was offered his first chance to direct, Preminger returned to good graces in Hollywood following a hiatus spent on Broadway, and Ulmer returned to directing in Hollywood after working independently in New York. The new-found artistic autonomy of exile/émigré directors in the 1940s coincided with a shared unleashing of a darkly critical commentary on American life. Many factors explain why this was so. Most obviously, these crime films addressed the turbulent sociocultural conditions during the war and the postwar transition. That exile/émigré directors were at the forefront in fashioning this deterministic crime cinema had everything to do with both their intensifying concern for their adopted homeland and their diasporic views as both displaced Austrians and Jews in the postwar American world. Certain changes in the nature of the film industry, however, enabled them to gain the autonomy they desired at this historical moment. These changes also encouraged the postwar critique of America to take the form of the crime film.

The launching of an antitrust suit against the major studios for their alleged monopoly control in the late 1930s plus the wartime tax relief granted small-film producers led to an explosion in independent companies.

In addition, the major studios, eager to help prosecute the war and to avoid wartime objections by federal monitors to contentious and potentially seditious material, increasingly split their production into A and B production units. A units produced big-budget films that relied on the overseas market to recover initial investments and thus depended on gaining export licenses from the Office of War Information (OWI) and the State Department. As they were subject to the scrutiny of federal censors, A features tended not to advance negative images of American life. By contrast, B features were made on minimal budgets and were thus not dependent on export earnings to recover investment, which meant that B production was centered on the domestic audience. One of the chief consequences was that B and independent features became the prime venue for addressing topical and controversial issues in 1940s Hollywood. That the formula crime film would emerge as the privileged B format was partially a result of economic concerns, too. Tried, tested, and repeatable crime formulas were especially attractive to independent companies, which were not able to spread financial risk across an array of products and needed a guaranteed box-office return (Parker 1986).

As the major studios either suppressed or tried to divest themselves of socially critical filmmakers, independent companies and B units offered new and growing venues for the dissatisfied (Neve 1992: 85–144). Here was an arena where the quest for autonomy and integrity could be maintained. Not surprisingly, it was Fox's B unit that offered Preminger his second chance at making it in Hollywood, and it was the so-called Poverty Row B-movie companies that Ulmer exploited on his return to Los Angeles.

For Billy Wilder, things were somewhat different. Yet he, too, found a special calling in making the 1940s Hollywood crime cycle, despite not having left the Hollywood fold during the 1930s, where he worked for the OWI in making pro-American, anti-Nazi propaganda during the war and functioned *within* the system. Although Billy Wilder had had a long history of film work as a screenwriter, his first directing experience occurred in the mid-1940s and the early 1950s and contained his most cynical and darkest representation of American life. Collectively, *Double Indemnity* (1944), *The Lost Weekend* (1945), *A Foreign Affair* (1948), *Sunset Boulevard* (1950), and *Ace in the Hole* (1951) reflect the traumatic climate of a culture trying to adjust to the prerogatives of peacetime order. They are merciless indictments of how the once-idealized American enticements of sex, money, and status actually lead to self-destruction. This series of films is given only one moment of comic relief, *The Emperor Waltz* (1948), which was a commercial failure.

The Emperor Waltz dramatizes features of American-Austrian relations that are a twist on his 1937 screenplay for *The Champagne Waltz*. The latter reflected Wilder's optimism in the 1930s about America and his cynicism about Europe, a situation no doubt fostered by the rise of fascism. It features a staid European culture (as embodied in the Viennese waltz) being "taught a lesson" by American idealism (as embodied in the freedom of jazz music). *The Emperor Waltz* features a gate-crashing American salesman (Bing Crosby) from Newark, New Jersey, who tries to get Austrian Emperor Franz Joseph to approve his new invention, the phonograph, which symbolizes the encroachment on tradition by modernizing forces. A series of class and romantic conflicts ensue between the high-bred European Countess Johanna and the low-bred American. The conflicts are resolved in marriage. Yet this resolution is tinged with irony: the cost of the old-world Viennese countess yielding to the charms of the pioneering modern American is a future in Newark! Wilder is prepared to suggest that love may conquer all, but the reality of cultural osmosis allows him to reserve judgment on the consequences of an old-world/new-world matrimony of interests.

This theme took on a graver cast in his next film, *A Foreign Affair. A Foreign Affair* concerns the corrupting American influences of graft and the black market on bombed-out Berlin, a less humorous precursor to his treatment of the attempted Americanization of cold-war Germany in *One, Two, Three* (1961). Both films reveal how Wilder was uncertain about a future in which European traditions are forced to kowtow to American materialism. In *A Foreign Affair*, a prim Republican representative from Iowa (Jean Arthur) is sent by Congress to examine the American occupation. Discovering that GIs are suffering from "moral malaria," indulging in the black market and burlesque shows, the politician lodges a complaint about American lassitude with an American military captain (John Lund). The captain seems to be a war profiteer with a Nazi lover, who is played, decadently, by Marlene Dietrich. In spite of all the intrigue, the captain turns out in the end to be the good guy, and the way is made clear for the two to fall in love. This stock resolution, however, constitutes a small sanctuary from the general impression of a world without moral order at the mercy of black-market graft.

The cynicism of *A Foreign Affair* appears in Wilder's darker crime melodramas of the same period, *Double Indemnity, Sunset Boulevard,* and *Ace in the Hole. Double Indemnity*, which Wilder coscripted with Raymond Chandler, is ostensibly about murder committed for the victim's insurance. Barbara Stanwyck plays Phyllis Dietrichson, a classic femme fatale who tempts a bored insurance salesman, Walter Neff (played by Fred MacMurray), into murdering her husband and staging his death as though it were accidental (falling from a train), which would allow her to claim a double indemnity. Neff goes through with her plan only to find out that she does not love him and has duped him all along. He kills her in revenge but is fatally wounded in the process. The movie is told in the form of a flashback confessional, as the dying Neff narrates his story into a dictating machine. Although made before the conclusion of the war, this film set the mood for Wilder's postwar crime films. It dwelt on the nightmare consequences of a trapped organization man's attempt to make it out of Los Angeles's faceless suburbia. Part of the film's power is drawn from casting MacMurray, an actor normally associated with fatherly, nice-guy, middle-class security, against type. As such, *Double Indemnity* anticipates many concerns that prevailed in the postwar world. A story of how the twin enticements of sex and money lead to self-annihilation, *Double Indemnity* offered a foretaste of the destructive criticism of once-sacred American mores that predominated in both *Sunset Boulevard* and *Ace in the Hole.*

Ace in the Hole was, as one critic put it, one of the few films "that have come from Hollywood with an utter disregard for box-office values or potentialities" (Madsen 1969: 91). Kirk Douglas plays Charles Tatum, a ruthless reporter seeking his way back to the big time in New York. While eking out a living as a reporter for a small newspaper in Albuquerque, New Mexico, he discovers a man trapped alive in a collapsed mine. He decides to milk the story for all its worth to make it a national event. He dissuades attempts at a speedy rescue of the trapped man and encourages a gullible sensation-seeking public to come and experience the event live. Rival journalists and radio broadcasters come along with a carnival troupe, replete with Ferris wheel. Tatum, however, has secured exclusive interview rights with the trapped man. This cynical manipulation of the public and one small man's life ends in tragedy. The trapped man dies and along with him the hopes of the ruthless reporter. Tatum realizes that this story needed a "happy ending" if it were to be his ticket back to the big time. The film was perceived as a sick comment on both the tabloid news and the nature of the American public. Unredeemingly cynical, it bombed at the box office.

Perhaps the huge success of the film that preceded *Ace in the Hole* had lured Wilder into a false sense of security about how far he could go in his critique of American mores. *Sunset Boulevard* was a self-reflective, almost masochistic piece about a down-and-out screenwriter, Joe Gillis (William Holden), and his morbid dependence on an equally hapless aging silent-movie queen, Norma Desmond (Gloria Swanson). *Sunset Boulevard* extended *Double Indemnity's* vision of Los Angeles as an unredeemingly decaying space of sick relationships and in the process identified Hollywood as the prime site of American self-deception. It indicts Hollywood for selling only images of beauty, love, and financial success, images that belie the corrosive and pestilent truth that underwrites these values. The intertextual piece features forgotten stars of the silent period such as Buster Keaton, Erich von Stroheim, and, of course, Gloria Swanson herself. An indictment of the film industry's short memory, it passes judgment on the exploitative features of America's dream machine. Perhaps this constituted Wilder's indirect way of getting back at Hollywood's spineless behavior in face of HUAC's inquisition.

Although Wilder may not have set out to buck the system directly, Preminger certainly did. He was one of the few Hollywood exiles who did not receive his cinematic apprenticeship at Germany's UFA studios, coming directly from Vienna's Josefstadt Theater to Twentieth Century-Fox. Preminger's contributions to the 1940s and 1950s crime cycle—*Laura* (1944), *Fallen Angel* (1945), *Where the Sidewalk Ends* (1950), *The Thirteenth Letter* (1951), and *Angel Face* (1952)—perhaps best demonstrate how far film noir was indeed an extension of preexisting Hollywood film traditions and not an anomaly. Yet it would be wrong to say that Preminger's crime films do not betray his European aesthetic training. Moreover, this group of films articulates concerns about the host culture that could only have been catalyzed by the experience of exile.

Preminger was finally accepted back into the Hollywood fold only after he had been left to fend for himself on Broadway. Ironically, in *Margin for Error*, which he also directed, this Jewish refugee from Hitler gained a reputation for his powerful stage performance as a vicious Nazi consul, a stereotype so successful that it paved the way for his return to Hollywood. Having accepted Preminger back to direct a film version of *Margin for Error* (1943), Fox producer Darryl Zanuck then relegated him unceremoniously to B-movie production to keep him out of harm's way. What ensued was Preminger's first box-office smash and his best known crime melodrama, *Laura*.

In many ways Preminger's success in working with a B-movie format, with a low budget and low cut-and-take ratios, was rooted in his experience as a theater director. His skills lay less in editing than in the effective use of mise-en-scène (lighting, set design, costume, blocking of actor movement, and camera angles) with minimal resources, a craft learned as a stage entrepreneur in both Vienna and New York. On the basis of *Laura*'s box-office success, Zanuck promoted Preminger to A features, where on larger budgets he was able to extend his theatrical skills to the screen.

Preminger's predisposition to a socially critical yet politically uncommitted cinema turned on problems common to many exiles: identity confusion, disillusionment with the host culture, hatred of the society that had forced exile, and difficulties with societal integration. While such problems of maladjustment relate to the particulars of the exiled director's personal history, they say even more about the general condition of postwar American society.

Laura's world is one of sexual obsession, where "everyone is implicated, in which everyone not only has a motive for, but is seemingly capable of, committing a heinous crime" (Silver and Ward 1992: 169). A clever use of mise-en-scène forges primary identification between audience and male protagonist, Detective McPherson (Dana Andrews), as he becomes infatuated with the portrait of Laura (Gene Tierney). The camera is perversely privy, much like a peeping Tom, to his detective work as he searches her apartment.

An erotic attachment is forged in the climate of murder. When it turns out that not Laura but her friend has been murdered, the lower-class detective's infatuation with the image of a girl of class leads him to compromise his objectivity before the lure of a real relationship. This situation not only blurs his reasoning powers but obfuscates the distinction between himself and the actual murderer.

An unbalancing obsession for sex and money again proves to be the prime destructive enticement in both *Fallen Angel* and *Angel Face*. In the former, promoted as the follow-up to *Laura*, Eric Stanton (Dana Andrews) rides penniless into town. Posing as a medium, he attempts to divest one of the town's most respected citizens, June Mills (Alice Faye), of her personal fortune. At the same time, he falls for Stella (Linda Darnell), a seductive and gold-digging waitress, whom he plans to marry. Stella is murdered, and Eric, as the leading suspect, is forced to flee town with June. In the process he finds out that he really does love June. They return to town and clear Eric's name, which leaves the path open for their marriage. The complete moral uncertainty of the relationship between the film's main protagonists undermines easy resolution in the old conventions of romantic love. This is underscored repeatedly by Preminger's expert use of mise-en-scène, including one dance sequence filmed as a long take where the two contrasting women (Stella versus June) are comparatively represented as moral opposites split by the male protagonist who, as the title suggests, is the "fallen angel" on his way to hell.

Angel Face constitutes a variation on the same theme, featuring a lower-class ambulance driver who falls for the deceptive charms of a wealthy beauty. A heady mix of sex and money again traps the male protagonist into an obsessive and fatal relationship. By contrast, *Where the Sidewalk Ends* signals a move away from depictions of the corrupt and decadent upper class toward a film that comments on the generally corrupting force of the everyday urban milieu. It features a violent cop who inadvertently kills a robbery suspect and tries to pin the blame first on a taxicab driver and then on a notorious underworld figure. The latter tactic succeeds, but in a strange twist the detective owes up to the killing and is sent to prison. This scene of moral redemption constitutes a forlorn and hardly rewarding attempt by one man to rise above a society corrupt to the core. Our male hero is psychologically unstable, morally ambiguous, with a propensity to violence. And these qualities in a cop!

Where the Sidewalk Ends was a film made in 1950 at the height of both the postwar crime cycle and the "red scare," and it was symptomatic of a general mistrust of traditional authority figures and conventions. The film was bound to be read as evidence of a Hollywood at odds with the goals of postwar power interests. More than Wilder and Preminger, Ulmer had a declaredly political investment in releasing the American cinema's democratic possibilities from the stranglehold of top-down studio control. Wilder and Preminger, too, had had their fights with Hollywood authorities in order to establish creative autonomy. Over time, however, they became establishment figures in an institutional sense. Although this probably only fueled the consternation over the attempt by external policing forces to dictate Hollywood's postwar responsibilities, Ulmer was more suspicious about Hollywood's co-optive power. He later professed that he "did not want to be ground up in the Hollywood hash-machine" (quoted in Bogdanovich 1974: 222), so in the 1940s he made a conscious decision to make films beyond the confines of the major studios. Even though B-feature directors were stuck with limited budgets, the payoff was that producers exerted minimal interference on the end product. Ulmer believed that this afforded him maximum creative freedom to make honest statements about American life.

In a series of crime films now regarded as classic film noir—*Detour* (1945), *Strange Illusion* (1945), *Ruthless* (1948), *Strange Woman* (1946), and *Murder Is My Beat* (1955)—Ulmer made perhaps the most sustained critique of postwar society that was possible within the Hollywood system. In these films he displayed an aesthetic prowess that was rooted in his European heritage yet motivated by his experiences making low-budget docudramas for ethnic and racial minorities during the Great Depression in New York.

The problems of returning to peace were also the problems of reestablishing a sense of roots, place, and community, the prerequisites for establishing a secure sense of self. Ulmer's films were laments about the costs of fighting the war, the loss of local identity in the name of identifying with the nation-state, and the consequent difficulties of returning to a culture that had lost the pluralist momentum of the prewar years. Instead, individuals came out of the war to the anonymity and sameness of a Levittown future. The alienating effects of discontinuous mise-en-scène that proliferate in Ulmer's postwar crime films are not simply aesthetic experimentation or transplanted European style. Rather, these aesthetic devices in conjunction with a predilection for fatalistic/deterministic plots are a product of a genuine engagement with the problems of the day—the product of someone's disappointment with the present given the promise of the past.

Ulmer's postwar crime melodramas turn on problems of mistaken identity and identity confusion, as in *Murder Is My Beat*, in which an innocent person might take the rap for a murder, or *Detour*, in which the protagonist projects fears of being falsely accused of murder, which leads the person through a self-injection of paranoia to kill someone inadvertently. Deterministic devices abound in *Ruthless*, scripted secretly by blacklisted socialist and Hollywood Ten member Alvah Bessie, which portrays the dehumanizing and alienating effects of capitalist desire on an individual.[5] *Strange Illusion* is a reworking of Hamlet in which the protagonist is almost hoisted by his own petard. It is the oedipal story of a youth's suspicion that his father's death and his mother's planned remarriage have something to do with each other. He feigns insanity to try to catch his father's murderer and mother's new lover. However, he is committed to a mental asylum by his mother, and the experience almost sends him into real madness. Such stories speak to a crisis in modern subjectivity in an unanchored culture ruled by the corrupting mores of sexual obsession and the unfettered desires for wealth and status.

Detour best demonstrates Ulmer's historical sensibility about America's postwar problems. As a road metaphor, the title conveys from the outset a concern about a society derailed from some "truer" path. The narrative has strong autobiographical references, telling the story of a frustrated pianist, Al (Tom Neal), who hitchhikes his way across America to try to hook up with his sweetheart in Hollywood.[6] Along the way, things go terribly wrong as the driver dies suddenly. Fearing that the cops might accuse him of murder, he decides to adopt the identity of the dead driver and commandeers the car. His bad luck gets worse as he picks up a female hitchhiker, Vera (Ann Savage), who turns out to have had a lift with the former owner of the stolen car. Vera blackmails Al into following her scheme to sell off the car once they get to Los Angeles. Once there, her plans change when she discovers that the dead man is heir to a huge fortune. Al refuses to go along with Vera's idea that he impersonate the dead man in front of his family, who haven't seen him for years, in order to claim his fortune. Vera threatens to call the police if he doesn't follow her orders. Al grabs the telephone line unaware that it is coiled around Vera's neck, as she is calling from behind a locked door, and inadvertently strangles her to death.

This story of an outrageously conspiring fate was shot in six days at a ratio of one-and-a-half feet to one foot used, which is remarkable at a time when the average cutting ratio was thirty to one. A triumph in how to exploit minimal resources, *Detour* abounds in riotous extended dialogue to fill out the long takes and compensate for limited film stock. The pessimistic mise-en-scène is provided by the clever use of minimalist set design, lighting, and oblique camera angles. Individual scenes are linked together through off-cuts from the spent materials of other directors. These skills were the culmination of training in European theater and film, with its preference for

5. The "Hollywood Ten" were the ten accused of being communists and indicted for contempt when they refused to answer questions after being called to testify before HUAC in 1947. All ten claimed that the committee infringed on their First Amendment rights.

6. In his youth, Ulmer had entertained ambitions of becoming a professional classical concert pianist.

mise-en-scène over action, and his experiences of working with the bare minimum of resources for his ethnic and racial docudramas in the 1930s.

Such aesthetic tricks were dialectically related to the film's commentary on the contemporary disorder of things. The film replayed Ulmer's own anxieties concerning the illusory appeal of Hollywood as a "hash-machine." The journey from New York to Tinsel Town by the frustrated pianist, who really wants to play Brahms waltzes but is condemned to playing chestnuts in sleazy night bars, plays out Ulmer's worst fears about artistic capitulation. New York, Ulmer's site of optimism during the Great Depression, is abandoned as the protagonist succumbs to the "detour" of Hollywood's enticements. Told in flashback, *Detour* laments dashed possibilities and resonates with Ulmer's own sense of postwar frustration.

The Postwar Political Stakes: "No More *Grapes of Wrath*"

In 1946, Eric Johnston, the former head of the U.S. Chamber of Commerce and champion of liberal corporate consensus, was appointed as the new leader of the Motion Picture Association of America (MPAA). The MPAA was the supervising organization of Hollywood's producers and distributors, as well as the overseer of Hollywood's internal censorship agency, the Production Code Administration (PCA). Johnston saw himself as a prophet of "democratic capitalism," arguing that the postwar era should be built on the principles of full production, without the divisive ideologies that characterized the New Deal era, especially those employing the rhetoric of class conflict. He warned against a Hollywood that would return to conveying negative impressions of America:

> We'll have no more *Grapes of Wrath*, we'll have no more *Tobacco Roads*. We'll have no more pictures that show the seamy side of American life. We'll have no more pictures that deal with labor strikes. We'll have no more pictures that deal with the banker as villain. (quoted in Schumach 1964: 169)

Instead, Johnston advocated a consensus philosophy in the belief that capitalism would be the rising tide that would lift all boats. The legitimation of this new order was to be found in the threat of communism abroad and of "un-American" domestic alternatives, largely residues of New Deal thinking. Johnston used his office to persuade Hollywood to join in this divesting of the past as a way of legitimizing America's rise to globalism:

> It is no exaggeration to say that the modern motion picture industry sets the styles for half the world. There is not one of us who isn't aware that the motion picture industry is the most powerful medium for the influencing of people that man has ever built.... we can set new styles of living and the doctrine of production must be made completely popular. (quoted in May 1989: 126)

Such statements coalesced with the policing interests of McCarthyites such as J. Parnell Thomas, the leader of HUAC's investigation of Hollywood in the late 1940s. As a scaremonger of the "red threat," Thomas possessed, like many of his fellow McCarthyites, an almost xenophobic hatred of Hollywood as a proponent of the pluralist popular culture that had redefined American-ism during the 1930s. Otto Preminger (1977: 116) noted that, for Thomas, Hollywood "was an old-hunting ground.... He believed the entertainment industry to be a breeding ground for sedition. He had once attacked the Federal Theater as a hotbed of 'Communism and the New Deal.'"

In many ways, then, HUAC's intervention in Hollywood had less to do with the communist threat abroad than in rooting out and delegitimizing Hollywood's affiliations with the New Deal legacy. To this extent, HUAC ser-viced, even if inadvertently, the needs of men like Johnston who represented corporate capitalism, which had emerged as a powerful force after the war. It is more than coincidence that Johnston, after initially resisting HUAC's inqui-sition in Hollywood, bowed to its pressure and helped instigate behind closed doors, at the Waldorf-Astoria in late 1947, the infamous Hollywood blacklist.[7]

Learning from the experience of Hollywood's propaganda role in World War II, many postwar interest groups, including the State Department, saw the necessity of making the film industry its ally rather than its enemy in their quest for power. In 1947, Franklin Fearing (1947: 59), the pioneering social psychologist in film studies, stated that he admired the military's "frank recognition that film and radio do shape attitudes" and were "the proper media for expressing ideas and values." He advised changing the attitude of prewar film research, which had concentrated on "how *harmful* the movies were, rather than exploring their possibilities in a democratic society."

This described the crucial difference between McCarthyism and corpo-rate liberalism in their attitudes toward Hollywood. At the same time, even for those power groups trying to make friends with Hollywood, the problem remained of trying to dissuade producers from revitalizing film genres that might contradict its potential as an agent of positive reinforcement for America's postwar global responsibilities. In June 1945, in response to the release of the gangster film *Dillinger*, the PCA received correspondence not only from moral interest groups, as might be expected, but even from a con-cerned director, Frank Borzage (1945):

> I have viewed with growing alarm the trend toward another cycle of gangster and racketeer films. Nothing can do this country and the motion picture industry

7. The studio heads met secretly at the Waldorf-Astoria in New York in an attempt to stave off HUAC's momentum, especially for a federally instituted form of Hollywood censorship. They drew up a list of film personnel whom they supposed might have communist affiliations. The bosses agreed that everyone on that list was to be fired and blacklisted until they had cleared their names.

more harm at this particular time than films designed to glamorize gangsters and their way of life.

At present our entire nation is working desperately on a plan which will bring peace and prosperity and good will to all the world. Foreign nations are looking to the United States for guidance. Much of the guidance and influence we will wield on the outside world will be transmitted through the medium of the motion picture.

This is certainly an inopportune time for us to convey the impression that America is made up of largely of gangsters, black market operators, petty racketeers and murderers.... Only too well do we in Hollywood remember that once before we gave this impression to the world.

Borzage's fear of the crime cycle was driven by two related issues. Most obviously he was concerned about the damaging image of the United States such films communicated and the kinds of attitudes this might feed. Second, and more interestingly, he understood that this way of representing the American way of life was connected to a 1930s Hollywood tradition. The crime films of the 1930s, especially the gangster genre, were the subject of that decade's biggest struggle between the film industry and external policing agencies. It was a fight that ended in Will Hays, then head of the PCA, declaring a moratorium on gangster film production in 1935, the first enforcement of the Production Code. Whatever Borzage's motivations for writing this letter, he was at least sensitive to how the crime cycle engaged a troublesome collective memory of one of Hollywood's most controversial moments.

Yet Hollywood could ill afford to turn away from audience demand for films that tried to represent the uncertain conditions of postwar America. The postwar 1940s became marked as the most strike-ravaged period in American history. Such struggles were interpreted as New Deal residue, the return of unresolved disputes between labor and management, hangovers from the Great Depression that had been put on hold by the need to prosecute the war collectively. The link of this reality with a particular political order from the past clearly undermined the efforts of emerging postwar power groups that were seeking to capitalize on the consensus brought about by the war. Consequently, bringing about a collective amnesia with respect to the Great Depression became a primary task for right-wing interest groups and corporate liberals alike. In this context, Hollywood's crime film could only be perceived as an obstacle to this task. In many ways, then, the emergence of a new crime cycle after the war constituted a return of the repressed.

The topical nature of these social and psychological crime features helped account for their box-office appeal, and they rose to constitute about a quarter of Hollywood production in the late 1940s (Jones 1956). Significantly, it was the exiles who were the driving force behind this resuscitation of a taboo "criminal" film form. That this was to prove problematic to those seeking authority in postwar America did not matter to them. If anything, it probably fed the exiles' well-grounded disdain for totalizing doxologies and moral and political interference in their work.

Moreover, we have to contextualize the exile/émigré's contribution to the modernist critique of bourgeois weltanschauung in Hollywood in the light of the Holocaust abroad and the "red scare" at home. The searing indictments of postwar American life as dehumanizing and hopeless, which characterize the collective noir oeuvre of the Austrian-Jewish directors I have dealt with here, were no doubt affected by the horror of the gas chambers. Billy Wilder, for example, found out at war's end that his mother, grandmother, and stepfather had all perished at Auschwitz. The climate of the "red scare" and its attendant nationalist chauvinism must have heightened the anxiety of the whole host of film émigrés that postwar America, in contrast to the New Deal America of their Americanization, could no longer provide sanctuary from the xenophobic and oppressive forces that had defined life in the "old country."

Not accidentally, Preminger gained a reputation during the 1950s for his campaigns against all forms of censorship. *The Moon Is Blue* (1953) was identified with the court case that effectively ended the Production Code's censoring powers; *Exodus* (1960) broke the blacklist, as Preminger gave screen credit to the formerly banned Dalton Trumbo, who had written the screenplay. Despite his outspoken objections to HUAC, Wilder was not subjected to the blacklist. He explained later that he was probably protected by his screenwriting association with Charles Brackett, who was a right-wing Republican (Karasek 1994: 363–67). Ulmer never had a high enough profile in the Hollywood establishment to warrant censorship, even though his films were perhaps the most openly critical of capitalism and bourgeois mores. By his own admission, this was the advantage of working in B-movie production; people tended to leave you alone. Yet HUAC's effect on Hollywood was profound in its suffocation of the socially critical potential of the Hollywood cinema that exile filmmakers had done so much to nurture.[8] In this regard, I leave the last word to Otto Preminger (1977: 115):

> Freedom of expression is the most powerful defense of democracy. No totalitarian government, right or left, can exist without censorship. It must firmly control the speech and writing of its citizens. When Senator Joseph McCarthy was playing on the uncertainty of Cold War fears by charging that America was riddled with Communist spies, the consequence was a repression of dissent and a black period in the history of American liberty. The studio heads in Hollywood were among the first to panic.

8. As Silver and Ward's study (1992: 335) reveals, the production of so-called noir crime melodramas almost halved after 1951. While structural changes certainly contributed to the demise of the B crime feature, the downfall of this socially critical film tradition cannot be disengaged from the contemporaneous political climate.

Filmography

Title	Date Released	Director	Produced By
Ace in the Hole	1951	Billy Wilder	Paramount
Americaner Shadchen	1940	Edgar G. Ulmer	Fame Films
Angel Face	1952	Otto Preminger	RKO
The Black Cat	1934	Edgar G. Ulmer	Universal
Ein Blonder Traum	1932	Paul Martin	UFA
The Champagne Waltz	1937	A. Edward Sutherland	Paramount
Detour	1945	Edgar G. Ulmer	PRC
Dillinger	1945	Max Nosseck	Monogram Pictures Corp.
Double Indemnity	1944	Billy Wilder	Paramount
Emil und die Detektive	1931	Gerhard Lamprecht	UFA
The Emperor Waltz	1948	Billy Wilder	Paramount
Exodus	1960	Otto Preminger	United Artists
Fallen Angel	1945	Otto Preminger	Twentieth Century-Fox
Faust	1926	F. W. Murnau	UFA
A Foreign Affair	1948	Billy Wilder	Paramount
Grune Felder	1937	Jacob Ben-Ami Edgar G. Ulmer	Collective/New Star
Hold Back the Dawn	1941	Mitchell Leisen	Paramount
The Last Laugh	1924	F. W. Murnau	UFA
Laura	1944	Otto Preminger	Twentieth Century-Fox
The Light Ahead	1939	Edgar G. Ulmer	Ultra Film/Collective
The Lost Weekend	1945	Billy Wilder	Paramount
The Major and the Minor	1942	Billy Wilder	Paramount
The Maltese Falcon	1941	John Huston	First National Pictures/ Warner Bros.
Der Mann, der seinen Mörder sucht	1931	Robert Siodmak	UFA
Margin for Error	1943	Otto Preminger	Twentieth Century-Fox
Menschen am Sonntag	1929	Curt Siodmak Robert Siodmak Edgar G. Ulmer Fred Zinnemann	Filmstudio Berlin
The Moon Is Blue	1953	Otto Preminger	Otto Preminger
Moon over Harlem	1939	Edgar G. Ulmer	Meteor Productions
Murder Is My Beat	1955	Edgar G. Ulmer	Allied Artists Pictures
Murder, My Sweet	1944	Edward Dmytryk	RKO

Filmography *(cont.)*

Title	Date Released	Director	Produced By
One, Two, Three	1961	Billy Wilder	United Artists/Mirsch Co./ Pyramid Productions
Ruthless	1948	Edgar G. Ulmer	Eagle Lion
Scampolo, ein Kind der Straße	1932	Hans Steinhoff	Bayerische Filmgellschaft
Strange Illusion	1945	Edgar G. Ulmer	PRC
Strange Woman	1946	Edgar G. Ulmer	United Artists
Sunrise	1927	F.W. Murnau	Fox
Sunset Boulevard	1950	Billy Wilder	Paramount
Tabu	1931	Robert J. Flaherty	Paramount
The Thirteenth Letter	1951	Otto Preminger	Twentieth Century-Fox
Where the Sidewalk Ends	1950	Otto Preminger	Twentieth Century-Fox
Woman in the Window	1944	Fritz Lang	International Pictures
Yankl der Shmid	1937	Edgar G. Ulmer	Collective

Compiled from The Internet Movie Database (IMDb) (http://www.imdb.com/) and Walker 1995.

References

Beller, S. 1989. *Vienna and the Jews, 1867–1938: A Cultural History.* Cambridge.

Bogdanovich, P. 1974. "Edgar G. Ulmer, An Interview." *Film Culture,* no. 58–59–60:189–234.

Borzage, F. 1945. Letter. MPAA/PCA file, *Dillinger.* Academy for Motion Picture Arts and Sciences, Los Angeles.

Cargnelli, C., and M. Omasta, eds. 1993. *Aufbruch ins Ungewisse. Österreichische Filmschaffende in der Emigration vor 1945.* Vienna.

Fearing, F. 1947. "Summary." *Journal of Social Issues* 3, no. 3:58–60.

Frischauer, W. 1974. *Behind the Scenes of Otto Preminger.* New York.

Jones, D. 1956. "Communism and the Movies: A Study of Film Content." In *Report on Blacklisting: I, — The Movies,* ed. J. Cogley, 196–304. New York.

Karasek, H. 1994. *Billy Wilder. Eine Nahaufnahme.* Munich.

Krutnik, F. 1991. *In a Lonely Street: Film Noir, Genre, Masculinity.* London.

Lipsitz, G. 1990. *Time Passages: Collective Memory and American Popular Culture.* Minneapolis.

Madsen, A. 1969. *Billy Wilder.* London.

May, L. 1989. "Movie Star Politics: The Screen Actor's Guild, Cultural Conversion, and the Hollywood Red Scare." In *Recasting America: Culture and Politics in the Age of Cold War,* ed. L. May, 125–53. Chicago.

McCarthy, T., and C. Flynn. 1975. *Kings of the Bs.* New York.

Neve, B. 1992. *Film and Politics in America: A Social Tradition.* London.

Parker, J. J. 1986. "The Organizational Environment of the Motion Picture Sector." In *Media, Audience, and Social Structure,* ed. S. J. Ball-Rokeach and M. G. Cantor, 143–60. Beverly Hills.

Preminger, O. 1977. *Preminger: An Autobiography.* New York.

Schorske, C. 1979. *Fin-de-Siècle Vienna: Politics and Culture.* New York.

Schumach, M. 1964. *The Face on the Cutting Room Floor: The Story of Movie and Television Censorship.* New York.

Silver, A., and E. Ward, eds. 1992. *Film Noir: An Encyclopedic Reference to the American Style.* 3d ed. Woodstock.

Walker, J., ed. 1995. *Halliwell's Film Guide.* New York.

Zolotow, M. 1977. *Billy Wilder in Hollywood.* New York.

Part Three

AMERICA AND AUSTRIAN POLITICAL CULTURE

Chapter 7

ROBERT WISE'S *THE SOUND OF MUSIC* AND THE "DENAZIFICATION" OF AUSTRIA IN AMERICAN CINEMA

Jacqueline Vansant

Introduction

When Maria von Trapp watched the final scene of *The Sound of Music* as "her" family escaped into Switzerland, she allegedly exclaimed, "Don't they know geography in Hollywood? Salzburg does not border on Switzerland!" (quoted in Hirsch 1993: 75). Questioned later on set design in general, director Robert Wise blithely replied, "In Hollywood you make your own geography" (quoted in Hirsch 1993: 75). One could just as easily say, "In Hollywood you make your own history." But as Hollywood is not known for its historical accuracy, to state that Hollywood representations of Austria may stray from historical fact is not a startling revelation. Significant is rather how, why, and with what result Hollywood has chosen to construct Austria, Austrian history, and Austrian identity.

Post-1945 Hollywood has presented Austria, Austrians, and Austrian history in a way Germany, Germans, and German history could never have been portrayed. While Germany is most often associated with its Nazi past, Austria has been exploited for its beautiful scenery, stately historical buildings, and rich musical history. Although many Austrians welcomed the Anschluss, the years 1938–45 are strangely missing from most postwar American films featuring Austria. This period of Austrian history is rarely the subject or even the backdrop for American movies. If Austria is associated at all with the period of National Socialism, Austrians are usually seen as victims of it rather than complicitous in its crimes. Perhaps one of the crassest examples of Austria's "denazification" in American cinema is Robert Wise's film *The Sound of Music* (1965).

In this film, Austria has been radically dehistoricized, and the Anschluss is portrayed in such a political and social vacuum that Austria almost appears to be an overrun fairy kingdom. Ironically, more than any other postwar film, *The Sound of Music* has profoundly influenced the way Americans view Austria. After having seen the film, many Americans believe they have had an "Austrian" experience. However, the only thing Austrian about the film is the scenery and even that is not entirely Austrian (Hirsch 1993: 86).

To date, no one has looked at *The Sound of Music* in the context of Austria's position in American cinema or investigated the construction of Austria and Austrian history in the film. Except for reviews, the literature on *The Sound of Music* is limited to one analytical article and two informative books. In his article "The Sound of Music," Richard Dyer (1992) argues that the aim of the film is to resolve the tension created by the struggle between freedom and order and between music and the world. Christian Strasser (1993) and Julia Antopol Hirsch (1993) offer a wealth of information about the film but do not provide in-depth interpretations. My chapter discusses *The Sound of Music* in a broader context and, at the same time, systematically examines the representation of Austria in the film version of this American musical.

To introduce my analysis of *The Sound of Music*, I briefly discuss Austria's position in American films prior to it in comparison to Germany. This contextualizes my discussion of the film and facilitates speculation on why and how Austria has attained a position in American cinema unthinkable for Germany. In my analysis, I examine how Austrian history is dismantled and how an Austrian identity is constructed in a historical void. Further, I suggest that Wise created an American *Heimatfilm* that has had a lasting impact on Americans' image of Austria. As in the traditional German and Austrian *Heimatfilm*, a form that reached its height in the 1950s, in *The Sound of Music* an opposition is established between the decadent city and the wholesome countryside, where the stock fairy-tale-like love story is set (Steiner 1996; Westermann 1990: 157–58).

The Representation of Germany and Austria in Hollywood

The most striking contrast between Hollywood's Germany and Austria is the position of each country's history in film representations. The difference is especially apparent in American movies made after World War II. While

Germany's history in the twentieth century, particularly Nazi Germany or the legacy of Nazi Germany, has been the focus of the majority of Hollywood films featuring Germany and Germans, Austria and Austrians have been disassociated from that country's recent history. Primary examples are Billy Wilder's *A Foreign Affair* and *The Emperor Waltz*. Both released in 1948, they illustrate very different treatments of the two countries by one and the same director. *A Foreign Affair* is set in a postwar Germany still full of National Socialists, while *The Emperor Waltz* is set during the first decade of the twentieth century in an Austria inhabited by counts and countesses. Austrian-born Billy Wilder clearly associated Germans with National Socialism but depicted Austrians as a people outside of history. The dichotomy seen in these two Wilder films typifies postwar films featuring Germany and Austria.

In post-1945 representations of Germany, three primary subject areas can be pinpointed: Germany's connection with the Nazi period, the confrontation of American troops with occupied postwar Germany, and Germany as the site of the East-West conflict (see Avisar 1988, Bredella 1990, Schmundt-Thomas 1992, and Tatar 1995). How historically accurate these films are is another matter (Avisar 1988: 96; Tatar 1995: 190), but, in any case, Germany's recent history, particularly its National Socialist past, figures prominently in American films (Bredella 1990: 51).

In contrast, post-1945 representations of Austria largely disassociate the country from its recent past. American films with Austrian settings that were made after 1945 fall roughly into three categories: (1) those that were shot in Austria but take place elsewhere, (2) those where Austria is only one of many locales and as such is not integral to the plot, and (3) those where a major role is played either by an Austrian locale or by Austrian historical figures.[1]

1. My sources for post-1945 films were Strasser 1993 and Walker 1995. I have tried to be as complete as possible, but I cannot claim completeness. The categories I set up are not always clear cut and occasionally overlap. For the purposes of this discussion, however, they are useful and not too imprecise. The first group—films that feature Austria as a backdrop but whose action is located elsewhere—includes Henry Hathaway's *Diplomatic Courier* (1952), Andrew Marton's *The Devil Makes Three* (1952), Harold Prince's *Something for Everyone* (1970), and, most recently, Stephen Herek's *The Three Musketeers* (1993). The second group—films where part of the action takes place in Austria—includes Michael Ritche's *Downhill Racer* (1969), Ronald Neame's *Hopscotch* (1980), John Glen's James Bond film *The Living Daylights* (1987), and Steven Spielberg's *Indiana Jones and the Last Crusade* (1989). With the exception of the Indiana Jones film, all are set in contemporary Austria, and Austria functions largely as an attractive background. In the Indiana Jones film, Austria was chosen because of its physical proximity to Nazi Germany. The third group—films where Austrian historical figures, Austrian history, or an Austrian locale plays a major role—includes Billy Wilder's *The Emperor Waltz* (1948), George Sidney's *The Red Danube* (1949), Georg Tressler's *The Magnificent Rebel* (1961), Steven Previn's *Almost Angels* (1962) and *The Waltz King* (1963), Arthur Hiller's *The Miracle of the White Stallions* (1963), Robert Wise's *The Sound of Music* (1965), Andrew L. Stone's *The Great Waltz* (1972), Lee H. Katzin's *The Salzburg Connection* (1972), Herbert

Even Hollywood movies in which an Austrian locale or Austrian history plays an important role rarely portray political and social upheaval. Several post-1945 films set in imperial Austria are removed from any political or social conflict. In *The Emperor Waltz*, an Austrian countess falls in love with an American phonograph salesman in an Austria that Wilder portrays as outside of history. Max Ophuls's *Letter from an Unknown Woman* (1948) is a story of unrequited love in turn-of-the-century Austria, Georg Tressler's *The Magnificent Rebel* is a Beethoven story, and both Steven Previn's *The Waltz King* (1963) and Andrew L. Stone's *The Great Waltz* (1972) are Johann Strauss films. Herbert Ross's *The Seven-Per-Cent Solution* (1976) has Sherlock Holmes and Sigmund Freud working together to solve a mystery, and Milos Forman's *Amadeus* (1984) is a film based on the play about Mozart and his mediocre rival Salieri.

Films set in post-1919 Austria also reveal little about Austrian history. Lee H. Katzin's *The Salzburg Connection* (1972) only obliquely deals with politics and is basically a spy story set in the midst of the cold war. There are some former Nazis, but their existence in Austria appears only incidental. Steven Previn's *Almost Angels* (1962) tells the story of a young boy who joins the Vienna Boys Choir, and Richard Linklater's *Before Sunrise* (1995) portrays how a French and an American college student who have just met on a train spend twenty-four hours in 1990s Vienna and fall in love.

Even when films make historical events central to the plot, Austria and Austrians are viewed largely as victims of historical crises rather than active participants in history. As I describe below, Robert Wise's *The Sound of Music* has music-loving Austrians overrun by somber, disagreeable Germans. In Arthur Hiller's *The Miracle of the White Stallions* (1963), which is set at the end of World War II, the Lipizzaner horses are victims of both the Nazis and the Soviets. Set in divided postwar Vienna, George Sidney's *The Red Danube* (1949) is a love story with a decidedly anticommunist slant. Fred Zinnemann's *Julia* (1977) offers a somewhat more differentiated picture of Austria than the majority of films with an Austrian theme. A small but significant part of *Julia* is situated in Vienna during the civil war of 1934. But Austrofascism, National Socialism, and the rise of fascism elsewhere in Europe are conflated, and what actually happened in Austria is not very clear to the average viewer.

Austria's unique position in Hollywood, that is, outside of history or radically disengaged from its post-1919 status and political institutions, was

---

Ross's *The Seven-Per-Cent Solution* (1976), Fred Zinnemann's *Julia* (1977), Milos Forman's *Amadeus* (1984), and most recently Richard Linklater's *Before Sunrise* (1995). Movies such as *Where Eagles Dare* and *The Third Man* were left out of the first and third groups, respectively, because they are British films. Even though the latter was a British-American coproduction, the Americans had little influence on the film itself (Vansant 1995). In the two latter groups, I include films, such as *Amadeus*, that were not necessarily shot in Austria but "take place" there.

not new to post-1945 films. The majority of films made in the interwar period portray Austria as the home of dashing, sophisticated barons and Austrians as the personification of gaiety, often bordering on decadence. In contrast, the few films set in Germany focus either on World War I or postwar conditions in Germany. The literary sources for some of the films also reflect the different weight Hollywood has given each country's history and its contemporary daily life. For example, American directors drew on the work of Erich Maria Remarque (Frank Borzage's *Three Comrades*, 1938, Lewis Milestone's *All Quiet on the Western Front*, 1930, and James Whale's *The Road Back*, 1937) and Hans Fallada (Frank Borzage's *Little Man, What Now?* 1934) to portray contemporary German life, but they chose Arthur Schnitzler's turn-of-the-century plays (Cecil B. de Mille's *The Affairs of Anatol*, 1921, and Jacques Feyder's *Daybreak*, 1931) as models for films set in Austria.

According to Ilan Avisar (1988: 92), Hollywood directors were reluctant to portray Germany critically in the 1920s and 1930s because they did not want to threaten the German market. This, he maintains, explains the dearth of films on Germany or set in Germany in the interwar period. Nonetheless, when directors did choose to set a film in Germany, contemporary post-World War I life and social issues were the main topics. By contrast, numerous films set in Austria, with its dashing barons, offered an escape, if not the opportunity to critique prewar European decadence. Such topics were neither offensive to Americans nor a serious threat to the foreign market. Thus, directors like the German Ernst Lubitsch (*The Smiling Lieutenant*, 1931) and Austrians Josef von Sternberg (*The King Steps Out*, 1936) and Erich von Stroheim (*Merry-Go-Round*, 1923, and *The Wedding March*, 1928) found in Austria a vehicle for exploring topics that skirted overtly touchy political issues. This practice continued during and after World War II.

If Austria's presence in Hollywood films was stronger than Germany's before 1940, Germany's prominence in Hollywood films soon eclipsed that of Austria in the 1940s. Moreover, the position of the two vis-à-vis National Socialism was portrayed quite differently. Films relating to Germany and National Socialism skyrocketed, whereas those featuring Austria were fewer than ever before. "In the years 1940–1945, Hollywood produced five hundred narrative films on the war and war-related themes, out of a total of seventeen hundred feature films" (Avisar 1988: 96). Undoubtedly, not all the war films are about Germany, but a quick perusal of *Halliwell's Film Guide* yields easily over thirty film titles from 1939–45 that associate Germany with National Socialism. Although Jewish persecution plays a minimal role in these films, Germans are implicated as National Socialists (Avisar 1988: 90–133), which is not the case with Austrians in films made during the same period.

Of the five titles I located in *Halliwell's Film Guide*, three deal with Austrians and National Socialism, but it is the Germans, not the Austrians, who are National Socialists. Bernhard Vorhaus's *Three Faces West* (1940), James Whale's *They Dare Not Love* (1941), and Clarence Brown's *Come Live with Me* (1941) portray Austrians (one prince, a doctor and his daughter, and a girl refugee) running from (German) Nazis. The other two films share imperial Austria as the backdrop. Reinhold Schunzel's *New Wine* (1941) revolves around Schubert, and Edwin L. Marin's *Florian* (1940) deals with two young lovers and a Lipizzaner in early-twentieth-century Austria.

In summary, since they first appeared in Hollywood films, Germany and Austria have had a very different status. Germany and Germans have been associated with the upheavals of post-1919 history, while Austria and Austrians have been radically disassociated from this period's political and social conflict. Hollywood's "denazification" of post-1945 Austria echoes Austria's status laid down by the Allies in the Moscow Declaration of 1943, which declared Austria "the first victim of Hitlerite aggression" (quoted in Commager 1971: 479). The few postwar Hollywood films that deal with this period of Austrian history chose to inflate Austrian resistance to National Socialism or ignore the reminder to Austria, which is also delineated in the Moscow Declaration, "that she has a responsibility, which she cannot evade, for participation in the war at the side of Hitlerite Germany" (quoted in Commager 1971: 479).

One is tempted to seek the explanation for the depoliticization of Austria in the strong Austrian presence in Hollywood.[2] Approximately 240 Austrians have worked as directors, actors, screenplay writers, composers, and choreographers in more than five thousand Hollywood films (Steiner 1996). Many former Austrians in Hollywood were no doubt sentimentally attached to Austria and contributed to the creation of an Austria outside of time. But considering the high number of Jewish Austrians and other Austrian exiles active in Hollywood, this would seem unlikely. Nonetheless, it is surprising that Fred Zinnemann is the only former Austrian director who explicitly indicts Austria, in his film *Julia,* for its fascist and antisemitic tendencies. The attachment of Hollywood's "Austrians," even its Jewish Austrians, to pre-1938 Austria and its cultural heritage may have paralleled that of other Austrian émigrés who despite escape under sometimes harrowing conditions were committed to reestablishing an independent Austria after 1945.[3]

In the case of Hollywood's Austria, nostalgia for Austria cannot be the sole or even the main reason that Austria receives radically different treatment from Germany with respect to National Socialism. A memo from David O. Selznick to Carol Reed and Graham Greene dated 25 October

---

2. See the chapter in Spaulding 1968 entitled "Austrians of Screen and Stage," pp. 293–307.

3. For example, writers Ernst Lothar and Elisabeth Freundlich sought to point out the differences between Austria and Germany during their exile in the United States, and both relinquished their newly gained American citizenship after returning to Austria.

1948 concerning the portrayal of the Viennese in the film *The Third Man* (1949) suggests that by the late 1940s the image of waltzing aristocrats had already gained a strong foothold in Hollywood portrayals of Austria and firmly established itself in the American imagination. In his memo, Selznick complained that the Viennese in the film were all "weird-melodramatic characters." He continues his argument by stating:

> [T]here is nothing of the sadness about Vienna and the Viennese which is so peculiarly touching because of Vienna having been for so long the world capital of glamor and of gaiety. It was this sort of material which, after the First World War, gave greatness to several films, such as the von Stroheim FAIR, MERRY-GO-ROUND, and THE BLIND HUSBAND. (Selznick 1948: 12–13)

Richard Koszarski's descriptions (1983) of von Stroheim's Austrian films suggest that Selznick may have missed the point of them and was blind to a decadence that he probably would have found distasteful. However, more significant than Selznick's failure to understand the complexities of Stroheim's portrait of Austria is Selznick's image of Austria and Vienna as the "world capital of glamor and gaiety." In addition, Selznick also suggested to Reed and Greene that they read an article on Vienna that appeared in *Life* on 18 October 1948 in order to get a realistic picture of the city. Entitled "Vienna: It Is a Strategic City of Want, Waltzes and Quiescent Struggle," the article in the popular American magazine offers an image of Austria that harkens back to the pre-1918 era. The title and the opening paragraph set up Vienna (and by extension Austria) as a place trying to reestablish its unique identity after having been overrun by history:

> To the millions of Americans who have never visited Europe the city of Vienna has always been more of an idea than an actuality. The idea has been compounded of Strauss waltzes, wiener schnitzel and dashing Habsburg princes in surroundings of baroque elegance. It is no use saying that such a Vienna never existed. It did. The surprising thing is that in 1948, after three decades of depression, revolution, dictatorship and war, to some degree it still does. ("Vienna" 1948)

According to this article, Vienna, then, despite the vicissitudes of history, struggled successfully in overcoming its recent past and "reestablished" itself as the capital of charm, gaiety, and superficiality.[4]

In most Hollywood versions of Austria, the audience is presented with an Austria that conforms to this popular vision of the country. The Austria of dashing waltzing aristocrats introduced by von Stroheim and subsequently popularized in later films was left intact despite Austrian involvement in National Socialism. As in the *Life* article, Hollywood removed any tarnish of

---

4. Billy Wilder parodies this popular image of Vienna and Austria in his *The Emperor Waltz* (1948), but many of the contemporary critics failed to see the film as a parody.

National Socialism from Austria. While Germany in postwar films has functioned as a means to formulate "America's new global role in the wake of World War II" (Schmundt-Thomas 1992: 3), Austria has remained largely a locus of escape. After the disintegration of the Austro-Hungarian monarchy in 1918, Austria would never be the kind of military or economic threat posed by Germany and could be bestowed in Hollywood a unique position outside of history. This is particularly true of *The Sound of Music*, which has come to symbolize a nostalgic retreat into a world of conservative values.

The Sound of Music

A Brief History

The story behind the American movie went through several incarnations before the film's release in 1965. The movie *The Sound of Music* is based on the Rodgers and Hammerstein musical *The Sound of Music* (premier 16 November 1959), written by Howard Lindsay and Russel Crouse, which in turn is based on the German movie *Die Trapp-Familie* (1956), directed by Wolfgang Liebeneiner and written by Georg Hurdalek, which is itself based on Maria von Trapp's autobiographical text *The Story of the Trapp Family Singers* (1949).

While Lindsay and Crouse scaled down the German film, Ernest Lehman, the screenplay writer, expanded the musical and drew on elements in both the film and the musical, in addition to adding plot twists of his own.[5] Among other things, he rearranged some songs, cut two others ("How Can Love Survive?" and "An Ordinary Couple"), and had two written ("Confidence" and "Something Good"). Moreover, he omitted some significant references to political conflict present in the stage musical.[6] For example, the Baroness and Captain no longer break up because of political differences but rather because of incompatibility and the Captain's recognition that they do not share the same values (Hirsch 1993: 29).

The film, which could be produced and released only after the musical was no longer on Broadway, premiered on the East Coast on 2 March 1965 at the Rivoli Theater in New York and on the West Coast in Los Angeles on 10 March 1965. It was later distributed as a road show, that is, as "a 70mm movie with six-track stereophonic sound, released in a limited number of theaters" (Hirsch 1993: 175). Part of the rationale behind the road show was to create an "event," thereby increasing audience interest.

East Coast reviewers criticized the movie for being "icky sticky" and "sugar coated," whereas those from the local California newspapers and trade

---

5. See Hirsch 1993: 28–34 for a full description of the differences.
6. Note particularly pp. 25, 59, 73, 78, and 101–7 (*The Sound of Music* 1960).

papers praised it as "three hours of visual and vocal brilliance" and "a warmly pulsating, captivating drama" (quoted in Hirsch 1993: 174–75). As we know, despite the skeptics, the film was and continues to be a tremendous success:

> The original release, both as a road show and in general release, lasted an unprecedented 4 1/2 years in the United States. By December 1965, just nine months after the film opened, *The Sound of Music* had been number one 30 out of 43 weeks and amassed $50 million in worldwide box-office receipts—after taxes. (Hirsch 1993: 176)

The movie brought in more money than had been hoped for or even dreamed of and revived an ailing Twentieth Century-Fox.

The release of *The Sound of Music* also affected the Austrian tourist industry. In 1965 the number of American tourists shot up 20 percent from the previous year (Strasser 1993: 291). Americans continue to travel to Austria in search of traces of the Trapp family, as is evidenced by the continued popularity of *The Sound of Music* tour, which caters especially to American tourists.

Dehistoricization and Historical Falsification

Screenplay writer Ernest Lehman and director Robert Wise combine ahistorical and antihistorical elements to disassociate Austria from its past and then construct an Austria divorced from time. Indeed, it was this lack of interest in the political reality that led William Wyler, the original director, to drop the project.[7]

Not at all interested in portraying the historical reality or the "true story" of the Trapp family, Lehman sets out to choreograph a scene that "goes beyond realism" (Lehman 1963: 4) in order to create a fictitious Austria for the purpose of motivating the love story:

> I will not describe the specific locations. I will tell you the mood, the feeling, the effect that I would like to see. We are floating in UTTER SILENCE over a scene of spectacular and earthly beauty.... Isolated locales are selected by the camera and photographed with such stylized beauty that the world below, however real, will be seen as a lovely never-never land where stories such as ours can happen, and where people sometimes express their deepest emotions in song. (Lehman 1963: 1)

The spectacular nature shots in the opening of the film and the accompanying sound set the stage for the dehistoricization of Austria. The first shot captures clouds with no sound other than the wind. The camera moves from clouds to the mountains, to a view of a valley, then to a beautiful mountain

---

7. Wyler's biographer writes of his attitude toward *The Sound of Music.* "Lehman kept telling Wyler that Nazism was not what *The Sound of Music* was about. Wyler agreed. 'I knew it wasn't really a political thing. I had a tendency to want to make it, if not an anti-Nazi movie, at least say a few things'" (Madsen 1973: 367).

lake. The next shots show scenes of Austria, including a river valley, a small village, and small castles. Austria appears as a timeless fairy kingdom.

The camera then pauses on a hilltop with mountains in the background as Julie Andrews appears on the horizon. As the camera moves from the initial picture of the clouds over the breathtaking scenery to Julie Andrews, the soundtrack is used to construct Austria as a place outside of time that exudes music. The sound of the wind changes to that of a bird, which gradually evolves into *The Sound of Music* theme, culminating in Andrews singing "The Sound of Music." The lyrics of the song, "The hills are alive/With the sound of music,/With songs they have sung/For a thousand years" suggest that music and nature are inextricably bound in this mythical Austria (compare Dyer 1992: 48).[8]

Upon hearing the bells of the convent calling the nuns to vespers, Andrews interrupts her song and heads back to the convent. The credits are then displayed over stills of more beautiful scenery in and around Salzburg. As the overture is played, the audience is treated to sights such as the glockenspiel, the fortress, and the cathedral in Salzburg. Wise and Lehman's Austria is devoid of people, which suggests an enchanted place whose identity is not constituted by its citizens but whose essence is determined by nature and the music inspired by it.

After dehistoricizing Austria in the introduction, the director then totally falsifies history by introducing an antihistorical pseudodocumentary element. The introductory "travelogue," first song, and credits close with a picture of the city of Salzburg labeled: "Salzburg, Austria in the last Golden Days of the Thirties," which situates the action in a particular location at a vaguely specified historical moment. The caption suggests an intact paradise in imminent danger, which will no doubt leave those familiar with the Austria of the interwar period bemused.

Totally missing from this "paradise" are references to the social problems or political upheaval of the time, let alone a discussion of the "Austrian question." As historian Karl Stadler (1971: 125) writes, Austria was "in a state of civil dissension" during the 1930s, when it suffered severe political and economic strife. Parliament was suspended in 1933 and civil war broke out in February 1934. By 1934 all but the Austrofascist parties had been outlawed, and in 1937, 20.3 percent of the total workforce was unemployed (Stadler 1971: 124). In his memoirs, Bruno Kreisky (1986: 179), the former chancellor of Austria, aptly described this period of Austrian history: "Massive unemployment, chronic misery, and starvation wages shaped life in Austria and influenced political events." However, in this Hollywood version of Austria, there is no mention of political dissension, no civil strife,

---

8. Although Dyer views music and nature as inextricably bound, he does not connect them at all to the construction of an Austrian identity.

and no Austrofascist government. Austria is constructed as the epitome of beauty, grace, and music, a "never-never land" vulnerable to an invasion by a type of Captain Hook.

The pattern of historical falsification continues with references to the old monarchy. Referring to the emperor and Georg von Trapp's naval service at the same time and using the "von" in his name, a practice outlawed in the First Republic, lead the audience to believe that Austria is still a monarchy. In light of Austria's position in Hollywood films up to this point and in the context of the breathtaking scenery, lavish castles, and aristocrats, the existence of a monarchy seems quite plausible. Moreover, in this setting American audiences are more likely to view Austria nostalgically and to interpret the country as a type of fairy-tale kingdom rather than to associate the reference to royalty with a nondemocratic form of government.

Wise sets up Austria as a country removed from political and social conflict, only to reintroduce a historical event, the Anschluss, into the vacuum he has created. He does this convincingly by establishing an inner logic in the film that results in the portrayal of Austrians unambiguously as victims, which leads the viewer to identify with the loss of the paradise represented by Austria.

Despite the inner logic, the portrayal of the Anschluss and the events leading up to it nonetheless concerned Darryl Zanuck, one of the producers. He worried that the Nazi menace was not made clear enough and wrote a letter to Richard Zanuck that if the threat of an invasion was not obvious, the logical end of the picture would be the wedding scene.[9] In a handwritten note on the letter, Ernest Lehman comments on this years later. "I must say I agreed with Darryl. His instincts were always unfailing. And yet, at the time, we all decided to ignore his suggestions, and the movie triumphed despite flaws" (Zanuck 1964). Lehman conceded a flaw in the screenplay. Yet, within the context of the film story and as the audience reaction bears out, this appears not to have been problematic.

Richard Dyer (1992) suggests that the break is not as illogical as it first appears. The musical does end with the wedding scene because there are no new numbers after it. But Dyer argues that the seemingly unmotivated continuation of the story is believable because it is tied to an ongoing opposition between freedom and order set up from the very beginning of the film and only temporarily resolved with the wedding. In this context, the National Socialist threat is transformed into yet another "mountain" to be climbed and a reminder that life's challenges are never ending.

Through the falsification of historical events leading up to and including the Anschluss, as well as the composition of the scene depicting the Anschluss,

9. This was actually where the Germans cut the film off when it was first released in Germany, which caused quite a scandal (Hirsch 1993: 181–82).

Wise lends credence to Austria's victim status, affirming the Moscow Declaration.[10] In the film there is no mention of the scheduled plebiscite for a free Austria nor of the negotiations between Austria's Chancellor Schuschnigg and Hitler. Neither Schuschnigg's famous radio broadcast nor Hitler's arrival in Austria is referred to. Signaled initially only by the change in wedding bells, the Anschluss appears to have transpired without warning, at an unspecified date in summer, rather than in March, when it actually occurred. "And a transition takes place in the sound of the bells. During a dissolve, the bell-music becomes harsh, discordant, mournful, something has happened, it is not joyful" (Lehman 1963: 114).

The reactions of Austrians in the film also set Austria up as a victim of National Socialism. Contrary to historical fact, the film portrays no public display of enthusiasm after the Anschluss. The square remains ominously devoid of civilians, suggesting that most people are at home scared.

Although it is possible that the director wanted to show Austrians greeting the Nazis, this would ultimately have seemed out of place since there never appears to be any reason why the Austrians, other than a few renegades, would welcome the Germans. The identifiable Austrian Nazis are the butler, Rolf (the young admirer of the Captain's daughter), Herr Zeller, and an unnamed person at the party. Thus, the Austrians who wish to be German are outsiders—either someone from the lower class (the butler), an impressionable teenager (Rolf), or nonaristocratic Austrians who appear able to advance only through the help of the Nazis.

Other than a few Austrian Nazis, there is no overt Austrian support of Germans, and the Anschluss appears to be strictly a German import. Moreover, other plot elements strengthen the logic of the Austrians as victims. Although the only family not flying the Nazi flag in the Salzburg area is the von Trapp family, the open display of patriotism at the music festival when the Austrian audience joins the Captain in his rendition of the pseudo-Austrian folk song "Edelweiss" implies two things: the majority of Austrians did not support National Socialism, and they were powerless to resist because of the military power of the German National Socialists. The Captain vehemently opposes the Anschluss, but the very fact that he leaves Austria for his honeymoon suggests that the danger of a take-over must not have seemed so imminent; otherwise, he would not have left.

10. The depiction of the Anschluss in the German film also offers a surprising twist. In *Die Trapp-Familie*, Ruth Leuwerik, the film's Maria, is from Cologne and her German accent lends a more "neutral" tone to the Austrian accents in the film. The other actors are Austrian but speak in High German. The Anschluss is announced on the radio with Austrians wildly greeting the Germans. This in itself is not surprising. But when a National Socialist shows up to demand that the Baron hang the Nazi flag, the actor plays a rather uncultured oaf who speaks with a decidedly Austrian accent bordering on dialect. Through the use of the radio coverage and language, it almost appears as if the Austrians, rather than the Germans, are the villains.

The use of sound and color and a carefully composed mise-en-scène in the Anschluss scene clearly mark Austria as a defenseless target of German aggression:

> We are CLOSE on the final bell-tower sequence. The bell is still tolling mournfully. Now it comes to a stop. At first there is a complete void of sound. And then we HEAR an ominous SOUND in the distance, the SOUND OF MARCHING FEET. The CAMERA PANS DOWN from the tower to the square below, and we know then what has happened to Austria. A detachment of Storm Troopers is marching across the square. *Anschluß* has come. (Lehman 1963: 114)

The sound of the joyful bells obliterated by the mournful bells signals the Anschluss and symbolizes its deeper meaning for Austria. The silence that follows immediately contrasts somber Germanness with Austrian musicality. The "sound of music" has been replaced by marching feet. The transformation is also underscored in the Anschluss scene through the use of color. The storm troopers march across the sterile square whose only decoration is the Nazi flag. In addition, the composition of the scene conveys the threat that the new order poses to Austria. The bird's-eye shot is framed by the buildings on the square, creating a feeling of being trapped.

Although the Austrians are shown as victims, the Anschluss scene was evidently troublesome to some Austrians:

> The City of Salzburg was quite cooperative with the film crew and even went as far as issuing a *Sound of Music* postmark commemorating the picture. But there was one scene in the movie that the town elders did not support—the depiction of the Anschluss, where Nazis march across the Residenzplatz and take over Austria. (Hirsch 1993: 146)

The town fathers did not want the Americans hanging up swastikas on the square, exclaiming: "Oh no, you can't do that, because the people of Salzburg were not sympathizers" (quoted in Hirsch 1993: 146). Only when the Americans suggested that they could use newsreel showing Austrians welcoming Hitler did the Austrians budge. But the Austrians insisted that the banners be removed immediately after shooting, and the Americans were not allowed to use a cheering crowd (Hirsch 1993: 146). Nonetheless, Maurice Zuberano, the sketch artist and second unit supervisor stated: "The only thing we still weren't allowed to do was use a crowd cheering, but I think we made our point without it" (quoted in Hirsch 1993: 146).

The question remains: What *was* the point they were trying to make? From statements made by director William Wyler, the logic of the screenplay, and the physical appearance of the screenplay itself, this exchange can only be interpreted as a power play and a cynical ploy in which the Americans let the Austrians know that they were aware that the Austrians were not so innocent. An overwhelmingly overt show of Austrian approval would have destroyed the logic of the screenplay. Moreover, William Wyler gave up on the project in part because he had wanted to make a political statement, which Lehman reminded him was not the purpose of the movie. There is also no evidence in or written on the screenplay indicating that the Americans ever intended to show Austrian approval. This and the response to Zanuck's concerns make it clear that the Americans were very well aware they were creating a "fairy tale."

Because it has been constructed as a place outside of time, devoid of social and political strife, Austria is logically seen as a victim of National Socialism within the context of the film. Consequently, the Anschluss appears to have been instigated by a few Austrian aberrants and Germans—an event that surprised the citizens despite some warning signs. The lack of dynamic development also signals that in the film the Anschluss is not the center of the conflict and dramatic activity; it is merely a secondary conflict in which true "Austrian" values provide the strength for opposing National Socialism.

"Austrian" Identities

Although the main characters are "all Austrians," as the Captain's eldest daughter Liesl tells her young Nazi admirer Rolf, some are more Austrian than others. But because the Anschluss has been removed from its historical context and the circumstances that gave rise to the debate surrounding Austrian identity have been eliminated, "Austrian" identity is not defined in political terms. Nonetheless, the audience leaves the movie with a sense that the Trapp family are exemplars of "Austrianness." Rather than being expressed in political terms, an Austrian national identity is defined through personal traits and values coded in the film as "Austrian."

In the spectacular opening sequence, Wise codes music and nature as the cornerstones of Austrianness. Wise reiterates and amplifies this by associating a series of "positive" traits related to the love of nature and music with the Captain, Maria, and the children, while opposing "negative," supposedly non-Austrian traits to these. Musicality is opposed to lack of interest in music, the rural to the urban, naturalness to worldliness, and unquestioned love of things Austrian (rooted in nature and music) to either a resigned attitude toward the Anschluss or a pro-Anschluss attitude. On a superficial level, the Trapp family is connected to Austria through overt statements of allegiance by the Captain, but more than this it is their embodiment of "Austrian" qualities that sets them up in the viewers' mind as Austrian.

Throughout the film, Wise uses music and pseudofolk elements to form the nexus of the traits constituting a personal and "national" identity. Expressions of love for country, family, and mate are conveyed in song, or song serves as the catalyst for these emotions. Maria's appearance and song in the opening sequence binds her to Austria through her closeness to nature and the music of "nature." "Austrian" folk music brings the Captain back to his family. Immediately after he has told Maria she must leave the house and return to the convent, he hears his children singing "The Sound of Music." It draws him into the house, and he is visibly moved. The song "breaks the spell" the Captain appears to have been under since the death of his wife. He joins his children in song, and the number culminates in a very emotional "homecoming." In addition, the first time the Captain sings "Edelweiss," a song which has been mistaken for Austria's national anthem by some Americans, he is brought even closer to his children. During this scene, the audience also witnesses the first indication of his budding feelings for Maria. We see the power of music to draw the Captain away from the Baroness and decadent Vienna to a suitable mate. When the Captain sings the song again, the second time at the festival, he is joined by his Austrian compatriots. The "homeland" he sings about is associated with nature, devoid of any class distinctions or ideological conflict (Dyer 1992: 56).

Wise employs the Austrian folk dance, the ländler, to underscore and valuate the opposition between rural and urban Austria reflected in the Captain's relationships to Maria and the Baroness. As the predecessor to the waltz, the ländler is a "purer" form of that dance. The Captain does not seem particularly fond of Viennese society and his waltzing days there. However, in the scene with the ländler, the Captain's feelings for Maria and hers for him become obvious. The Captain cuts in on his son to dance with Maria. During the dance, Maria is overwhelmed by the realization of her feelings for von Trapp. By having the Captain prefer to dance the ländler with Maria than to waltz with the Baroness, Wise conflates love of homeland with love of a suitable mate.

The figure of the Baroness also acts to further highlight "true Austrian" traits by being in opposition to them. In one of first the scenes in which the audience sees the Baroness, she remarks that she understands von Trapp more after having seen him in this environment:

Elsa: You're much less of a riddle when I see you here, Georg....

Georg: ... more at home here than in Vienna, in all your glittering salons, gossiping gaily with bores I detest, soaking myself in champagne, stumbling about the waltzes by Strausses I can't even remember.

The opposition between rural and urban Austria set up here is echoed in practically every scene with the Baroness through her reaction to the family's music, to Maria, and through her own manner of dress.

Through careful editing during the scene in which Captain von Trapp sings the pseudo-Austrian folk song "Edelweiss," the director clearly shows that the Baroness perceives the "folk music" as a threat. Through a series of rapid cuts, the audience sees that the Baroness is aware of the chemistry between the Captain and Maria, something the two of them are not yet conscious of. She realizes that the music, particularly "folk music," threatens her chances with the Captain since it is something he and Maria love deeply. She tries to regain control of the situation by suggesting that von Trapp throw a party for her. A society party would clearly put her in a superior position to Maria. The editing of these scenes underscores her attempt to regain control of the situation. As the Baroness suggests the party, she stands up and walks over to the Captain, separating him physically from Maria in the frame.

The Baroness's manner and dress also mark her as a sophisticate with values clearly in opposition to Maria. Not only does she smoke—something no one else does in the movie—she wears dresses that clearly label her as a sophisticated urbanite. The red sequined dress in her final scene with von Trapp, which contrasts with the light, airy natural-looking dress of Maria, further stamps her as a woman of worldly experience, someone estranged from her "Austrian" roots.

Not only her outward appearance but also the Baroness's personal qualities tie her to decadent Austria. The Captain describes her as "lovely, charming, witty, graceful, the perfect hostess." Because of her lack of a genuine connection to music, nature, and children, however, she does not share the characteristics of a "true Austrian" and for this reason is clearly not the suitable mate for von Trapp.

By virtue of the fact that *The Sound of Music* is a musical, an American idiom, the material from which Wise was drawing had already been removed from its cultural context. But Robert Wise continues to represent Austria as a type of paradise lost. In such a world there is no place for a national identity based on social, political, or historical reality. Nonetheless, the audience leaves with a feeling of having gotten to know an Austrian family. Wise builds on the Captain's overt patriotic statements and Maria's connection to nature and music to construct his version of an "Austrian" identity based on the love of nature, "Austrian" music, children, and a country best preserved in a loving patriarchal family.

The Sound of Music: *An American* Heimatfilm?

In the introduction to Julia Antopol Hirsch's *The Sound of Music: The Making of America's Favorite Musical,* Robert Wise speculates as to the reasons for his film's success. He attributes it in part to the timing of the release:

> Nineteen sixty-five was a volatile year in the United States and throughout the world. Newspapers carried headlines of the war in Vietnam, a cultural revolution was beginning to spread throughout the country, and people needed old-fashioned ideals to hold on to. (Hirsch 1993: x)

Not discounting the charm of Julie Andrews, the adorable children, the music, and the spectacular scenery, the escape the film offered at the time of its release no doubt played a major role in its success. At a time when large segments of the population were questioning American foreign policy and patriarchal values, *The Sound of Music* was a respite from a highly politicized world. Through it, Wise presented unquestioned patriotism and a loving patriarchal family as a bulwark against uncertainty.

The movie's continued success reflects this but so, too, does Wise's careful construction of Austria as a fairy tale outside of time, which increases the long-term possibilities of audience identification (compare Dyer 1992: 45; Strasser 1993: 300–2).[11] The film evokes a nostalgia for a destroyed idealized world that never existed. By taking the musical that had emptied the German film of its cultural specificity and adding elements common to the German/Austrian *Heimatfilm*, Wise creates an American *Heimatfilm*. Removed from its cultural context, this "homeland" is grounded in a family that can take its "country," that is, its value system, along wherever it goes.

Both Liebeneiner, who directed two German Trapp family films, and Wise emptied the story of historical content and showed the "Austrian" family as embodying a set of values that can best respond to a particular historical situation. Like *The Sound of Music*, Liebeneiner's two Trapp films are a response to a particular moment in German history. In her study, Bärbel Westermann (1990) argues that in the first German film, *Die Trapp-Familie* (1956), Liebeneiner used the Austrian family to embody certain values prevalent during the Adenauer era. As opposed to the American film, the family in the German film loses its money and is resourceful in its struggle to keep above water, a topic that millions of refugees and other *Heimatvertriebene*, German-speaking Eastern Europeans forced to leave their homes after 1945, could relate to. In his study, Johannes von Moltke (1996) argues most convincingly that the second German film on the Trapp family, *Die Trapp-Familie in Amerika* (1958), is not one of exile but rather a parable of Germans' confrontation with American culture. In both cases, the German films imply the importance of adaptability and suggest the need for a strong but not necessarily patriarchal family to survive in Germany during the 1950s. In contrast, the American film offers escape and retreats into conservative values that were being questioned in American society in the 1960s.

11. Dyer specifically links the success of the film to its embodiment of problems central to the lives of the predominantly female audience. Strasser enumerates a variety of reasons for the film's success. In addition to their fascination with the Alps, Americans were deeply impressed with the religious devotion of the family. He also argues that the family is the embodiment of Europeans who were forced to leave their homelands because of their opposition to Hitler and adopted America as their new home.

The type of music used reflects how the original story of an Austrian family was adapted to a particular cultural context. In *Die Trapp-Familie*, the music is limited to folk and classical music. Westermann (1990: 143) suggests that the music in *Die Trapp-Familie* plays an important role in the construction of a national identity that is bound to the security of the family.

> The fostering of cultural treasures—in this case folk songs—is held up at the end of the film as an important quality that ensures the coherence of the family. Here, culture not only assumes the role of an element for constituting the identity for the family, but it also ensures its longevity and continuity within the family.

"Culture"—German folk songs in the German film and pseudo-Austrian folk songs in the American film—is the glue that holds the family together. The family that sings together, stays together.

The music that endowed the Trapp family films with cultural specificity also partly determined whether it was a success. The German film, a hit in Germany and Austria, did not do particularly well in the United States. By the same token, the American film was a total failure in Germany and Austria and a great success in the United States and throughout the rest of the world. No doubt, the Rodgers and Hammerstein music masquerading as Austrian folk music alienated both German and Austrian audiences.

Perhaps, however, the combination of the American music with the Austrian scenery seemed particularly incongruous and jarring to Austrian and German audiences. Ironically, Wise's use of nature as a dramaturgical component and the oppositions of tradition versus progress and country versus city were reminiscent of the German/Austrian *Heimatfilm*. Wise transformed a German film that was not originally a *Heimatfilm* in the strict sense of the word into an American *Heimatfilm* (Westermann 1990: 158).

In writing all new American music, the creators of the musical took the first step in removing the story from its "German/Austrian" context and making it more suited for American audiences. In the film *The Sound of Music*, the screenplay writer Ernest Lehman and director Robert Wise combine ahistorical and antihistorical elements to dismantle Austrian history and construct Austria anew. For this Austria, as for the Austria of the German film, an "Austrian" national identity arises out of characteristics and values that are needed to face the challenges to the Austria portrayed on the screen. To bring these out, oppositions typical of the German/Austrian *Heimatfilm*, such as tradition versus progress and the rural versus urban, are set up. The sum total is the creation of an American *Heimatfilm*.

Conclusion

Vienna's image as the home of "dashing Habsburg princes in surroundings of baroque elegance" that was popularized in the interwar period prevailed in the United States after World War II despite Austria's involvement in the National Socialist regime. *The Sound of Music* follows in a long Hollywood tradition of dehistoricizing Austria. However, Wise creates a new vision of Austria and Austrian identity in opposition to the earlier dominant Hollywood portrayal of Austria as the home of dashing, decadent aristocrats. Instead of portraying the Trapp family in an Austria grounded in political reality, he constructs an Austrian national identity based on love of nature, country, and family. In creating an American *Heimatfilm* set in Austria, Wise offered audiences temporary escape from the politically charged atmosphere of the 1960s and at the same time effectively shaped American perceptions of Austria for generations to come. Austria is seen not only as a victim of National Socialism but as a victim of history itself.

Filmography

Title	Date Released	Director	Produced By
The Affairs of Anatol	1921	Cecil B. DeMille	Famous Players-Lasky Corporation
All Quiet on the Western Front	1930	Lewis Milestone	Universal
Almost Angels	1962	Steve Previn	Disney
Amadeus	1984	Milos Forman	Saul Zaentz
Before Sunrise	1995	Richard Linklater	Castle Rock Entertainment/Columbia/Detour Film Production/Filmhaus Wien Universa Filmpro/Sunrise Production
Come Live with Me	1941	Clarence Brown	MGM
Daybreak	1931	Jacques Feyder	MGM
The Devil Makes Three	1952	Andrew Marton	MGM
Diplomatic Courier	1952	Henry Hathaway	Twentieth Century-Fox
Downhill Racer	1969	Michael Ritchie	Wildwood
The Emperor Waltz	1948	Billy Wilder	Paramount
Florian	1940	Edwin L. Marin	MGM
A Foreign Affair	1948	Billy Wilder	Paramount
The Great Waltz	1972	Andrew L. Stone	MGM
Hopscotch	1980	Ronald Neame	Avco Embassy Pictures
Indiana Jones and the Last Crusade	1989	Steven Spielberg	Lucasfilm Ltd./Paramount
Julia	1977	Fred Zinnemann	Twentieth Century-Fox
The King Steps Out	1936	Josef von Sternberg	Columbia
Letter from an Unknown Woman	1948	Max Ophüls	Universal International/Rampart
Little Man, What Now?	1934	Frank Borzage	Universal
The Living Daylights	1987	John Glen	United Artists/Danjaq Productions/Eon
The Magnificent Rebel	1961	Georg Tressler	Disney
Merry-Go-Round	1923	Rupert Julian Erich von Stroheim	Universal
The Miracle of the White Stallions	1963	Arthur Hiller	Disney
New Wine	1941	Reinhold Schünzel	United Artists
The Red Danube	1949	George Sidney	MGM

Filmography *(cont.)*

Title	Date Released	Director	Produced By
The Road Back	1937	James Whale	Universal
The Salzburg Connection	1972	Lee H. Katzin	Twentieth Century-Fox
The Seven-Per-Cent Solution	1976	Herbert Ross	Universal
The Smiling Lieutenant	1931	Ernst Lubitsch	Paramount-Publix Corp.
Something for Everyone	1970	Harold Prince	Media Productions Inc.
The Sound of Music	1965	Robert Wise	Twentieth Century-Fox/ Argyle Enterprises
They Dare Not Love	1941	James Whale	Columbia
The Third Man	1949	Carol Reed	British Lion Film Corp./ Selznick Releasing Org./ London Film Productions
Three Comrades	1938	Frank Borzage	MGM
Three Faces West	1940	Bernard Vorhaus	Republic Pictures Corp.
The Three Musketeers	1993	Stephen Herek	Disney/Caravan Pictures
Die Trapp-Familie	1956	Wolfgang Liebeneiner	Divina-Film
Die Trapp-Familie in Amerika	1958	Wolfgang Liebeneiner	Divina-Film
The Waltz King	1963	Steve Previn	Disney
The Wedding March	1928	Erich von Stroheim	Paramount Famous Lask Corp.

Compiled from The Internet Movie Database (IMDb) (http://www.imdb.com/) and Walker 1995.

References

Avisar, I. 1988. *Screening the Holocaust: Cinema's Images of the Unimaginable.* Bloomington.

Bredella, L. 1990. "How to Cope with Evil? References to the Holocaust in American Films of the 1970s and 1980s." In *Germany and German Thought in American Literature and Cultural Criticism,* ed. Peter Freese, 51–92. Essen.

Commager, H. S. 1971. *Documents of American History.* Vol. 2. New York.

Dyer, R. 1992. "The Sound of Music." In *Only Entertainment,* 45–59. London.

Hirsch, J. A. 1993. *The Sound of Music: The Making of America's Favorite Movie.* Chicago.

Koszarski, R. 1983. *The Man You Loved to Hate.* Oxford.

Kreisky, B. 1986. *Zwischen den Zeiten.* Berlin.

Lehman, E. 1963. *The Sound of Music.* Cameraman's script. Box 39a #8. Harry Ransom Humanities Research Center, University of Texas-Austin.

Madsen, A. 1973. *William Wyler.* New York.

Moltke, J. von. 1996. "Trapped in America: The Americanization of the *Trapp-Familie,* or 'Papas Kino' Revisited." *German Studies Review* 19, no. 3 (October):455–78.

Schmundt-Thomas, G. 1992. "America's Germany: National Self and Cultural Other after World War II." Ph.D. diss., Northwestern University.

Selznick, D. O. 1948. Memo, 25 October. Box 2733.7. Harry Ransom Humanities Research Center, University of Texas-Austin.

The Sound of Music. 1960. Music by Richard Rodgers, lyrics by Oscar Hammerstein II, book by Howard Lindsay and Russel Crouse. New York.

The Sound of Music. 1965. Directed by R. Wise. Twentieth Century-Fox. Film.

Spaulding, E. W. 1968. *The Quiet Invaders: The Story of the Austrian Impact upon America.* Vienna.

Stadler, K. R. 1971. *Austria.* New York.

Steiner, G. 1996. "Exile and Eldorado: Austrian Filmmakers in Hollywood." Keynote address presented at symposium, "Beyond the Sound of Music," 16–18 February, at the Center for Austrian Studies, University of Minnesota.

Strasser, C. 1993. *The Sound of Klein-Hollywood. Filmproduktion in Salzburg. Salzburg im Film.* Vienna.

Tatar, M. 1995. "'We Meet Again, Fräulein': Hollywood's Fascination with Fascism." *German Politics and Society* 13, no. 3:190–98.

Trapp, M. A. 1949. *The Story of the Trapp Family Singers.* Philadelphia.

Die Trapp-Familie. 1956. Directed by W. Liebeneiner. Divina-Film. Film.

Vansant, J. 1995. "Harry Lime und Maria von Trapp treffen sich am Stammtisch: Die 'Entnazifizierung' Österreich in amerikanischen Filmen." In *The Sound of Austria,* ed. J. Bunzl, 169–84. Vienna.

"Vienna: It Is a Strategic City of Want, Waltzes and Quiescent Struggle." 1948. *Life,* 18 October.

Walker, J., ed. 1995. *Halliwell's Film Guide.* New York.

Westermann, B. 1990. *Nationale Identität im Spielfilm der fünfziger Jahre.* Frankfurt.

Zanuck, D. 1964. Letter to Mr. Richard Zanuck from Darryl Zanuck on 30 January 1964, handwritten note from Lehman dated 31 March 1986. Box 114e #9. Harry Ransom Humanities Research Center, University of Texas-Austin.

Chapter 8

....

POLITICAL CULTURE AND THE ABORTION CONFLICT

A Comparison of Austria and the United States

Maria Mesner

Introduction

L aws concerning abortion have been at the center of public discussion during the last third of the twentieth century in many Western democracies. Unlike other issues with important legal implications that tend to be left to experts, the abortion debate has transcended expert circles and passed into the public realm. In addition, the discussion on abortion has opened up societal cleavages and fanned emotions to the point of mass demonstrations, civil disobedience, and even murder.

The considerable public attention given to the abortion debate has led to many studies of the issue. These works provide a good understanding of the situation in individual countries but leave the task of making comparisons and generalizations to the reader.[1] Therefore, a cross-national perspective seems worthwhile in two respects. First, it avoids the errors of concentrating too much on national developments and the danger of turning national

1. For Austria, see Lehner 1989 and Mesner 1994; for the United States, see Luker 1984, Ginsburg 1990, and Petchesky 1984. For other countries, see Eser and Koch 1988–89; the articles under the heading "Abortion: The International Agenda" in *Feminist Review*, no. 29 (spring 1988), pp. 23–132; Sachdev 1988; and the chapters on abortion in Nelson and Chowdhury 1994.

peculiarities into absolutes. Second, it sharpens the profile and the weight of national institutional or cultural characteristics and provides insight into their interdependence. Exemplary in this regard are two international comparisons that deal, at least in part, with the abortion debate: Soper's study (1994) on Evangelical Christians in the United States and in Great Britain and the work of Hadley (1994).

The political conflict over abortion lies at the center of my analysis. I examine the conflict between two antagonistic worldviews in Austria and in the United States, two countries with very different political traditions and cultures. I analyze these worldviews, generally labeled "pro-choice" and "pro-life,"[2] as social movements that mobilize for similar goals under very different social, institutional, and political conditions. I look at how these differences shaped the social movements and the outcome of the conflict in each country. I show how national political traditions, political culture, and the specific "grammar" of national political discourse in each country influenced the institutional developments and the outcomes of these two abortion movements despite similar ideologies and goals.

Some recent literature attributes the particular course and results of the abortion debate in Austria in the late 1960s and early 1970s to the impact of the American women's movement there (see, for example, Grillenberger 1989). My study modifies this view and suggests why the abortion debate developed so differently in each country after the mid-1970s. While abortion has nearly ceased to be a political issue in Austria, the struggle over abortion in America has gone beyond debate to an emotional confrontation with sometimes deadly consequences.

The Story before the 1970s: Traditions and Protagonists

On 23 January 1974, the Austrian Nationalrat, the legislative body comparable to the U.S. Congress, passed a law allowing abortion on demand during the first term of pregnancy. One year before this, on 22 January 1973, the U.S. Supreme Court handed down its decision in *Roe v. Wade*, which forbade the state from interfering in a woman's decision to have an abortion before the fetus is viable, thereby ruling unconstitutional the abortion laws of all states. In both countries these events were seen as a victory of the "second" or "new" women's movement.

2. I also use the term "anti-abortion." In America, especially, the usage of the terms "anti-abortion" and "pro-life" is highly polemical, but subtle distinctions between these terms are worth noting. "Anti-abortion" focuses on abortions and how to ban them, though further topics could be touched upon; "pro-life" points to a broader range of issues: adoption, financial aid for single mothers, etc. At least in Austria, there are "pro-life" groups for which the term "anti-abortion" would not be appropriate.

The formation of both national movements had occurred during the previous decade on the basis of a very similar ideology. At the core was the notion that gender is an important category determining societal divisions and defining hierarchies in society. Thus, gender became a force for mobilizing identification for those women who started to organize during the late 1960s, first in the United States and then in many Western European countries. These movements had in common their rejection of traditional family patterns and the one-dimensional role of women as mothers and homemakers. The activists demanded self-determination and sexual liberation for women. In this context, abortion and birth control became focal points in mobilizing the women's movement in both America and Austria, despite differences in their resources and organizational frameworks. To understand these differences, it is important to gain some historical perspective.

The Early Abortion Debate in the Women's Movement and in Party Politics

Before World War I, the organizational foundations of the "first" women's movement in Austria and in the United States differed, but both held similar positions on abortion for much the same ideological reasons. Both adhered to a theory that specified a male public sphere and a female domestic sphere and did not question the "natural duty" of women to bear children and fulfill their societal role as mothers and nurturers. As a result, neither movement advocated liberalizing the strict abortion laws that were in effect in both countries (Anderson 1992; Luker 1984).

Abortion became a political topic in Austria during the 1920s. Due to the weakness and ineffectiveness of the communist women's movement, socialist women formed the only important organization of female workers as a branch of the Social Democratic Party (SDAP), the most powerful opposition party after it left the governing coalition in 1920. While in the United States the women's movement started lobbying and mobilizing for the Equal Rights Amendment (ERA), that is, for the legal equality of women in the working place, in Austria the socialist women's movement made abortion law reform an important issue. The language and implementation of this campaign were, however, marked—at least partly—by a discourse on eugenics led by medical experts. One of these experts was the Social Democrat Julius Tandler, a physician who was very active in creating communal health programs as a town councillor in Vienna during the 1920s and early 1930s and who was influential in his party concerning all health-related matters. He and his colleagues discussed abortion law reform within the framework of eugenics. By controlling female reproductivity, they wanted to improve "human resources." Thus, the needs of individuals, especially the wishes of pregnant women, did not stand at the core of the socialist argument. Nevertheless, the proposals for legal reform introduced by the Social Democrats would have extended the right of women to decide about their pregnancies.

The Social Democrats did not succeed in passing a new law because Catholic-conservative forces strictly opposed any liberalization. Yet the socialist women's movement did establish abortion as a subject of public political discourse. Meanwhile, the "century of silence" (Luker 1984: 40) on abortions that were performed secretly in backrooms for the poor or in the private consultation rooms of physicians for the privileged remained unchallenged in the United States.

In 1934, Austrofascism brought an end to the socialist women's movement and the public debate on abortion. The authoritarian government continued and even reinforced the pronatalist policy of its predecessor. After Austria became part of the Third Reich in 1938, the Nazis introduced a split policy on abortion consistent with their racial policy.[3]

After World War II, once the democratic political system had been reconstructed, the socialist women's movement was rebuilt and resumed its prewar efforts for abortion law reform. At least in the beginning, the content of its resolutions was nearly identical to its prewar demands, but it faced a quite different political climate and discourse. Nazi racist population policy and the crimes and atrocities it justified totally discredited eugenics. As a result, eugenics lost much of its influence on public discourse after World War II and disappeared from socialist positions.[4]

Structural conditions had changed as well. The Social Democratic Party (now called the SPÖ) had joined in a three-party government with the People's Party (ÖVP), successor to the interwar Christian Social Party, and the Communist Party (KPÖ). After the KPÖ left the government in 1947, the SPÖ and the ÖVP formed a coalition government. Under these circumstances, the mainstream of the SPÖ had little interest in reforming the abortion laws. Given the continuing opposition of the Roman Catholic Church, which was very influential in the ÖVP, strong pressure for liberalizing the laws would have caused enormous conflict within the governing coalition. The paramount goal of the two governing parties was to maintain cooperation. Consistent with this post-1945 political culture in Austria, socialist

---

3. Abortion was absolutely banned for "fit" women, that is, "healthy Aryans," who were threatened with the death penalty in specifically serious cases; "unfit" women, that is, the "racially impure," the ill, or the disabled, were coerced into having abortions or sterilized (Bock 1986; Czarnowski 1991).

4. Eugenics residues remained only in far-right, mostly national-Catholic appeals aiming at protecting the Western Christian "superiority" against the Eastern "enemy" by having a lot of children.

women neither tried to find allies outside their own party to support their demands, which would have been breaking a long-held Social Democratic taboo, nor did they continue to lobby within the partisan realm after their long-maintained claim had been turned down. But the abortion law debate did not stop entirely. It survived in small inner-party circles under the leadership of some female politicians and a few medical and legal experts.

In the United States, the first women's movement, which had its roots in "moral movements" aimed at temperance and the abolition of slavery, was dominated almost exclusively by the views of white, Protestant, middle-class, native-born women who did not question the gender roles grounded in prevailing assumptions about human nature. The protagonists of the first women's movement adhered to a theory of two separate spheres based on the different nature of each sex: the home as the female realm of caretaking, childbearing, and child rearing and the public sphere as the male realm of business, moneymaking, and politics. In this view, being a mother was an indispensable, absolutely essential part of being a woman. Abortions were seen as the outcome of uncontrolled, irresponsible, raw, and untamed male sexuality (Hymowitz and Weissman 1978: 67), which in the words of Elizabeth Cady Stanton brought the "degradation of woman" (quoted in Ginsburg 1990: 29). The existence of female sexuality was simply denied. Perhaps the lack of organized female resistance to the legal restrictions on abortions was an "outgrowth of sexual and class conservatism," as Faye Ginsburg (1990: 33–34) suggests, especially if it went together with the view that associated birth control and abortion with "race suicide." But advocating abortions would have meant challenging the very same "motherhood" that in the Victorian age was "a woman's source of dignity in a world that all too often denied it to her" (Gordon 1977: 236).

In summary, although the women's movement in America was very active in trying to influence political decision making, due to its perception of womanhood, women's rights, and women's interests, it not only raised no voices against the legal restrictions on abortions but agreed with the ban. In Austria, continuity within the party structures, especially the persistence of socialist organizations and politicians, resulted in a continuous debate on the reform of abortion laws, although the SPÖ leaders attached varying importance to the issue.

Reconstruction, the Cold War, and the Baby Boom

Changes in reproductive and marriage behavior that occurred outside politics were very important in shaping the abortion debate in the United States and in Austria. The high-water mark of the family was during the late 1940s in the United States and in the mid-1950s in Austria and lasted to the mid-1960s.

Several trends were significant in both countries.[5] Young people married more often and at a lower age had more children than their parents, thereby reversing the long-term demographic trend of falling birth rates. The parents of the "baby boomers," who came of age during World War II in the United States and during the late 1940s and early 1950s in Austria, became the "most marrying generation on record" (May 1988: 20).

Even more interesting and decisive for the purposes of this study than a change in marriage and birth rates was the renaissance of traditional family patterns with clearly distinct and separate gender roles; the mother became totally wrapped up in her role as the homemaker and the father served as breadwinner outside the home. Correspondingly, the young women of the postwar era seemingly cared less about careers outside their homes or saw less opportunities for themselves than had their mothers. As birth rates rose, the number of women in college dropped (Hymowitz and Weissman 1978: 326). What took place in the middle of the twentieth century was unique in the history of modern societies: "the first wholehearted effort to create a home that would fulfill virtually all its members' personal needs through an energized and expressive personal life" (May 1988: 11). An Austrian author called the years after 1955 the "golden age of marriage and having children" (Münz 1985: 12).

The acceptance of traditional gender roles precluded a public debate on abortion. Demanding facilities for performing abortions meant questioning the assumption that bearing children was a woman's only purpose in life. Favoring legal abortions meant accepting that a woman might have good reasons for not wanting to have a child at a particular point in her life. The claim that women might have other priorities than procreation challenged the notion that gender roles are embedded in human nature and not socially defined or constructed. It is important to note that young women did not object to their new "old" roles for the time being, at least judging from the lack of publicly articulated opposition and from the weakness of women's movements. As Hymowitz and Weissman (1978: 326) note, the "postwar years saw an almost total rejection of feminist programs and awareness; building a home and bringing up a family seemed to be enough for most women." In this context, the American women's movement, already split and weakened, nearly vanished (Hoff 1991: 206–8). In Austria, attempts by female SPÖ politicians to push for women's rights failed for lack of public response and support. This deliberate wrapping up of women in their domestic roles did not happen without contradictions and frictions. All available evidence suggests that the number of abortions, mostly illegal, remained high during the entire postwar era in both the

5. For detailed figures and statistical data, see May 1988 for the United States and Münz 1985 for Austria.

United States and in Austria (Luker 1984: 53; Mesner 1994: 74–75).[6] Yet the postwar family model and its related gender roles were not challenged publicly before the 1960s.

Most authors believe that the lack of challenge was rooted in the "postwar desire to return to 'normalcy'" (Hymowitz and Weissman 1978: 326) and that after the chaos of the war and reconstruction era the family became the focus of individual and collective needs for happiness, stability, and harmony (Sieder 1987: 241). Although the explanations sound quite similar for both Austria and the United States, it is useful to distinguish between the two countries. May (1988: 6) points out that in America birth and marriage rates did not rise after World War I as they did after World War II. She attributes the post-World War II pattern of family formation and reproduction to the dynamics of the cold war. She believes that the flight into homes as "fortresses" reflected fears of the external enemy, the Soviet Union, and the internal enemy, communism, that were whipped up by McCarthyism.

I agree with her suggestion that the cult of the family was not only a private, individual postwar reaction to the Great Depression and World War II but also had an important political component. The export of American family ideology was part of American cultural policy in Europe against the backdrop of the cold war and the competition against the Soviet Union and the ideologies it represented. In Austria as elsewhere, the European Recovery Program (ERP) provided support for reconstruction and helped families acquire at least some typical modern household appliances. At the same time, the high number of American movies shown in Austrian theaters throughout the 1950s delivered the pictures and images of a successful "American way of life" that helped shape Austrian ideals about the family.[7] From an Austrian perspective, the United States became the symbol of modernity, progress, affluence, freedom, and democracy. Thus, American mass media, above all the film industry, provided the models for reconstructing Austria, a process that went beyond rebuilding something that had previously existed and established a new type of economic, social, and cultural system. The American cultural impact on Austria, together with the consequences of fascism and war, formed the socially conservative postwar climate that made it impossible to challenge traditional gender roles and discouraged public debate on abortion.

6. Especially if laws prohibiting abortion are in effect, the number of unreported cases is presumably high and all estimates concerning the amount of abortions actually performed tend to be unreliable and usually coincide with the political aims of their authors. Yet it seems reasonable to assume a relationship of one abortion for every three to ten births.

7. In 1955, for example, out of 468 movies shown in Austrian theaters, 440 of them were foreign ones, and 229 of these were American made (Wagnleitner 1991: 299).

The Path to Abortion Rights

Abortion law reform became a symbolic issue at the end of the 1960s in both the United States and Austria. Why in the end the conflict got so violent in the United States is due in part to the characteristics of the American political system, especially its openness to pressure from well-organized interest and single-issue groups. In addition, the impact of religious groups on American politics should not be underestimated.

By contrast, political life in Austria has historically revolved around political parties, which have provided nearly the only channel into the political decision-making process. Compared to the United States, parties in Austria are strong, centralized institutions that nominate candidates without much influence from outside political groups. During the long period of the Second Austrian Republic, they functioned as representatives of historically grounded, socially and culturally distinct constituencies. Up to the 1970s, parties had almost a monopoly as "transmission belts" (Ebbinghaus 1976: 26) between the needs of certain constituencies and the executive or legislative branches of the state, and they still largely determine the shape of politics.

Abortion as a Symbolic Issue

Joseph Gusfield (1963) has described the temperance movement in America as a "symbolic crusade" by Protestants, who believed that their social status was endangered by the rivalry of immigrant groups. The attitude toward drinking alcohol became the pivotal point, the symbolic issue, that Protestants used to demonstrate their superior status in society. They turned to the government for ratification of their point of view because "governments affect the distribution of values through symbolic acts" (Gusfield 1963: 167) and succeeded in achieving a victory when state legislatures ruled out the practices of immigrant cultures that did not oppose drinking alcohol. The actual goal of the crusade was not to stop the consumption of alcohol but to institute legal prohibition as a symbolic act. In the conflict between native-born white Protestants and immigrants in the late nineteenth century, attitudes toward drinking alcohol symbolized a set of values, a life-style, and a worldview of society.

Justified criticism arose because Gusfield concentrated too much on economic status in analyzing social movements (Soper 1994: 11). In my interpretation of the abortion conflict, I modify Gusfield's notion of status; I measure the status of a group not only in economic terms but also in terms of how easily it can impose its norms within society. Symbolic crusades are not only designed to maintain economic status during eras of social change but are undertaken if a group believes that its worldview and norms are endangered. Their aim is to ensure that a group's values and norms concerning desirable social behavior in a changing society prevail. In the abortion debate, I argue that conflicting worldviews and their related values, not the economic status of a group, have been at stake. I argue further that feminist groups also used abortion as a symbol to foster change in society, that is, to promote their ideas about how the world should be. Laws concerning abortion are suitable for such a purpose because they regulate the social relations of reproduction and gender, and negotiating them potentially challenges the traditional gender hierarchy.

Abortion became a symbolic issue for social movements during the 1960s, as social changes in that decade challenged the traditional gender hierarchy. In both the United States and Austria, the participation of women in the labor force rose. More importantly, women were better educated than in the past. At the same time, divorce rates were rising and marriage rates were falling, which called into question middle-class notions of the "perfect family." Birth control became more available as the pharmaceutical industry provided safe oral contraceptives that were increasingly used by women in both the United States and Austria. In America, the Supreme Court, referring to the right of privacy, ruled against measures that restricted efforts by married couples to exercise birth control (*Griswold v. Connecticut*).

Apparently more and more women believed that having children was no longer the only goal in their lives; getting control of their reproductive behavior became a crucial goal. As Kristin Luker (1984: 118) puts it:

> When women accepted the definition that a woman's role was as wife and mother, control of one's own body meant little. When the biological working of one's body and one's social status (or intended social status) are congruent, who needs control? In everyday terms, if one's role in life is to be a mother, it is not such a problem that one's biology often seems single-mindedly bent on producing children.... Once [women] had choices about life roles, they came to feel that they had *a right to use abortion in order to control their own lives.* (emphasis in original)

At the end of the 1960s, new women's groups entered the political stage, first in the United States, then in Western Europe, including Austria. In many countries, these groups changed the character of the abortion debate. Where the debate had existed, it had been restricted to small circles of physicians and lawyers. This second women's movement fundamentally challenged all concepts grounded in naturally determined gender roles. Women found abortion and birth control to be valuable symbols in their fight for self-determination.

In the words of one of the first pro-choice activists in California 1967:

> When we talk about women's rights, we can get all the rights in the world—the right to vote, the right to go to school—and none of them means a doggone

thing if we don't own the flesh we stand in, if we can't control what happens to us, if the whole course of our lives can be changed by somebody else that can get us pregnant by accident, or by deceit, or by force. So I consider the right to elective abortion, whether you dream of doing it or not, is the cornerstone of the women's movement.... if you can't control your own body you can't control your future, to the degree that any of us can control futures. (quoted in Luker 1984: 97)

Another contemporary activist said:

To advocate the right of abortion … meant destroying the ultimate punishment of sex and allowing the pleasure of sex for its own sake without the concomitant obligation of childbirth. Abortion stood at the apex of all our nightmares and inhibitions about sex. (quoted in Luker 1984: 97)

A history of the American women's movement summarized the situation in the United States: "Without the right to abortion many women felt there could be no true sexual freedom for women" (Hymowitz and Weissman 1978: 360).

The European evidence is quite similar. According to a document written at the beginning of the second women's movement in Western Europe, which was also published by Austrian women's rights activists:

The availability of abortions on demand and free of charge is *not* the end of the women's struggle. It is only one of the most fundamental demands. Without this demand being met the political struggle cannot start. For this fight, it is necessary that women achieve the right to their bodies, that they are free to do what they want with them.... We do not demand a better law, we demand the repeal of law. We do not demand charity, we demand justice.... We demand our due: the freedom of our bodies.[8]

A leaflet spread in Vienna by the first postwar feminist group in the early 1970s also attached great importance to the abortion issue: "The fight against the law prohibiting abortions is part of the fight for the women's right of self-determination, for their equal rights, in the law, in public, in the work place, and within the family!" (quoted in Mesner 1994: 207).

Thus, for pro-choice women in both the United States and Austria the right to have an abortion served as a symbol of women's liberation and self-determination. But what represented the vehicle for change for activists in the women's movement stood as a symbol of moral decay for their opponents. In both countries, the demand for a woman's right to decide about her pregnancy soon evoked countergroups that favored upholding the laws prohibiting abortions. While the pro-choice activists developed different notions of gender, family, reproductivity, and womanhood, the pro-life

8. "Manifeste des 343," a manifesto of the French women's movement published in *Nouvel Observateur* (April 1971) that was central to the young German and Austrian women's movements (quoted in Mesner 1994: 178).

activists tried to defend a society based on "naturally" grounded sex roles and gender relations. The defense of laws prohibiting abortion can be interpreted as a defense of the "old" order in a time of accelerated social change. The ban on abortion, in this sense, acts like a dike, a bulwark against the evil results of modernity, materialism, and decadence.

To support my argument I give only a few examples, the first a quotation from the newsletter of the LIFE coalition, a pro-life group in North Dakota:

> Could it be that we have allowed idols of materialism, drugs, alcohol, money, sex, power or success to bind us … and now our children and our families are being destroyed and taken away captive by satan? We must return to the God of the Bible [who] speaks clearly what we must do to reclaim our land and our beloved State of North Dakota from the enemy. (quoted in Ginsburg 1990: 109–10)

In Austria, a conservative judge who criticized the reform efforts said:

> The natural order of things is for a child to be raised in the family, where the father and the mother fulfill their duty to the child in a morally good, responsible, sacrificing way. The precondition is a respectable marriage. The lack of concern about the consequences of an immoral and disorderly life and about the value of life is one of the main causes of all further offenses against the sacredness of life covered by the Penal Code—from abortion to murder. The descendants of morally good marriages do not become murderers. Parents who love each other wish to have children and do not have to abort any unwanted results of disorderly relationships. (quoted in Mesner 1994: 147)

One of the founders of the most important Austrian pro-life group called the protection of the "unborn" the "limit of tolerance" that must not be crossed in order to prevent the foundations of a well-ordered community from being endangered (quoted in Mesner 1994: 185–86). In 1993, the former Catholic cardinal of Vienna said:

> I ask you to keep in mind … that nobody has the right to dispose of the life of another human being—no matter how this life may look; at that point there will be nothing to protect us against total availability, against the total manipulation of human beings. Then the individual will only be a substance that is measured by utility. (König 1993)

Although this last quotation is quite moderate, it shows how abortion is linked to the idea that modernity threatens and endangers humanity.

Feminism: A Challenge to the Old Order

After scrutinizing the institutional and organizational conditions of the pro-choice campaign and the way it reached its goals, it becomes obvious that the underlying political system and ideological traditions of each country shaped both movements in specific and typical ways. Four patterns are observable. First, the new American women's movement had the first women's movement and the civil-rights movement as its models, while Austrian feminism began within traditional party structures.[9] Second, the American women's movement hesitated to adopt the abortion plank in its basic policy statement but eventually broke new ground by doing so, while Austrian advocates of unrestricted abortion could refer to already existing traditions. Third, in the United States pressure groups, initially at the state and later at the national level, lobbied legislators to pass liberal abortion laws or repeal existing ones. In contrast, the Austrian women's movement gained its first great success, a law legalizing abortion on demand within the first three months of pregnancy, by using traditional party networks. Finally, the American activists addressed the courts when it became difficult to reach their goals through state legislatures, which led to the landmark Supreme Court decision *Roe v. Wade*. In Austria, the Parliament, although deeply divided along party lines, passed the new abortion law.

The American Pro-choice Campaign until Roe v. Wade

The new American women's movement, the most important agency for abortion rights, had it origins in the mid-1960s. Like its predecessor in the 1920s, it mobilized mainly white middle-class and upper-class women who wanted to take "action to bring women into full participation in the mainstream of American society *now*, exercising all privileges and responsibilities thereof in truly equal partnership with men" (Hymowitz and Weissman 1978: 344). As in the 1920s, the chief goal and main mobilizing issue was lobbying for the ERA in order to achieve equity in the work place. In the beginning, the National Organization for Women (NOW), the first and largest mainstream women's organization of the second women's movement, avoided talking too much about reproductive rights because the activists correctly feared that advocating unrestricted access to abortion would split the movement and put off the white middle-class women they addressed.

NOW came to be seen as reformist, so some former civil-rights and anti-war activists formed groups of "radical" feminists. These women were disappointed with the traditional attitudes toward gender relations they had experienced within the New Left and the students' movement and decided to form their own organizations. While NOW relied on steady organizational work and traditional reform tactics, the radical feminists carried out

9. Although I cannot elaborate on this point here, the focus on individual rights that marked the pro-choice stance in the United States is related to the American tradition of liberalism and (liberal) individual civil rights. In Austria, the pro-choice position was connected to a larger extent with a concern for societal—that is, state—responsibility for the social circumstances of reproduction and child rearing.

acts of provocation, so-called zap actions, which they took over from the students' movement. The first occurred in 1968 on the occasion of the Miss America beauty pageant, when protestors crowned a sheep Miss America and threw high-heeled shoes, cosmetics, and bras into a "freedom trash can."

The radical feminists' demand for repeal of abortion laws was eventually taken over by the mainstream women's movement. At its second annual convention in 1967, NOW added a plank to its Bill of Rights that called for "the right of women to control their own reproductive lives" and demanded the repeal of all laws restricting birth control and all penal laws governing abortion. This marked the first time in American history that any major women's organization focused on the issue of abortion; the resolution was very controversial and, as expected, caused a split within the mainstream women's movement.[10]

These women's groups publicly rejected a reform proposal introduced by the highly renowned American Law Institute, which permitted abortions under certain conditions.[11] Through their nationwide campaigns against state laws, the women's movement brought discussions on abortion law reform out of small expert circles into the public domain. The public response was overwhelming; a mass movement evolved and even groups like Church Women United and the YWCA supported the National Association for the Repeal of Abortion Laws (NARAL), the first national pro-choice group. The public debate was not only a discussion about the redefinition of who should decide about abortion, on what grounds, and with what kind of legitimation but also a discussion about women's rights, the position of women in American society, and the societal values connected to childbearing, reproduction, and the traditional family structure. The pro-choice activists adopted the language of democratic and human rights. They viewed abortion on demand as the *right* of a woman, not just something she had to request from her husband, her doctor, or the state.

Pro-choice activists began to engage in civil disobedience by establishing illegal abortion referral services and using them for political mobilization. In California, for example, the Society for Humane Abortions did not inform women about how to get an abortion until they had written a letter to their legislators urging the repeal of abortion laws (Luker 1984: 98).

At first, pro-choice activists were successful, getting laws passed by the state legislatures of Hawaii, Alaska, New York, and Washington. But soon the campaign for repeal came to a standstill at the state level due to rising resistance

10. Betty Friedan, NOW's first president, spoke of "a very painful confrontation with our own conflicts on abortion" (quoted in Ginsburg 1990: 39).

11. An abortion would be justifiable if a doctor decided that the pregnancy threatened the life or health of a woman, if the child would be born seriously disabled, or if the pregnancy resulted from rape or incest or began when the woman was under the age of sixteen.

by quickly emerging pro-life groups. So the pro-choice activists changed their tactics and pressured the courts to declare laws restricting abortions unconstitutional. They finally succeeded when the Supreme Court ruled in its decision in *Roe v. Wade* on 22 January 1973 that the state must not interfere in a woman's decision to have an abortion before the fetus is viable.

Austrian Feminists: Between Provocation and Accommodation

The American women's movement and its views on abortion had an enormous influence in Western Europe, especially in West Germany and eventually in Austria. Although socialist women in Austria had never stopped discussing abortion law reform, the public demand for repeal of these laws was new, and it polarized and accelerated a reform debate that had been only simmering for the previous twenty years. In the early 1970s, mostly young women pushed for liberalizing abortion laws, typically within the traditional party structures.

The origins of the new feminism lay in a study group called the Emancipation Working Group within the Active Left (Arbeitskreis Emanzipation im Offensiv Links), formed by members of the KPÖ youth organization in 1969 and a group of young women who had gathered within the Young Generation (Junge Generation), the youth branch of the SPÖ. In 1971, the head of the Department of Justice, a member of the SPÖ, introduced reform plans for abortion. His proposals specified the conditions for legal abortions; they were permitted if the life or health of the pregnant woman was endangered, if the woman could not afford having a child, or if there was the possibility that the child would be born mentally or physically disabled. At this time, the success of American pro-choice activists, for example, in pushing for passage of New York's liberal law, was reported in Austrian newspapers. This provoked intense discussions and inspired the socialist women's group to found the Action Committee for the Repeal of Article 144 (Aktionskomitee für die Abschaffung des §144), that is, the penal code article that prohibited abortions. This committee used new ways of campaigning within the traditional political framework to advance their proposal to repeal abortion laws or, at a minimum, to permit abortions within the first three months of pregnancy.

At the same time, they transcended the boundaries of traditional political culture and addressed a broader nonpartisan public. They gathered signatures from prominent people who supported their demands and spoke publicly in the streets and marketplaces. Like their American counterparts, the Austrian activists succeeded in making abortion a subject of public discussion in a way that changed the content of the debate. Discussions on medical or juridical regulations within small expert circles were replaced by calls for abortion on demand, which was to result, as the contemporary activists put it, in "women's liberation from the coercion to bear children" (quoted in Mesner 1994: 189).

In April 1972 the committee eventually succeeded in having the SPÖ convention pass a resolution demanding new abortion laws permitting abortion on demand within a certain term after conception. This was perhaps the most important single step on the way to a new liberal law. The legislative majority of SPÖ representatives eventually voted for a law reflecting the party resolution and passed it against fierce resistance from other legislators on 23 January 1974.

According to the prevailing role of parties in political culture, members of one of the two major parties had to be approached and persuaded from within, that is, by those who were official party members and had campaigned within the organizational structure of the party. Had political parties not been used as a channel or a transmission belt during the 1970s, it would have been impossible to liberalize abortion laws. In addition, due to its ideological traditions, the SPÖ was the only potential policy channel for the pro-choice activists of the 1970s. Even the second women's movement, one of the first social movements outside traditional party structures in Austria after World War II, had its earliest roots within exactly these structures. As shown above, it was in the SPÖ and the KPÖ that the first groups of mostly younger people dealt with issues relating to women's emancipation and liberation.

At the climax of the abortion conflict, the efforts of socialist women were backed up by the "autonomous" or "new" women's movement. Its activists had withdrawn from traditional parties, which they perceived as institutions defined and dominated by males, during the abortion campaign. Their goal was to form their own autonomous organizations, groups, and committees. Like their American counterparts, they organized on the basis of *gender*, not *class*, as had been the case in the earlier socialist or communist movements. The feminist activists came together on grounds of "womanhood" and the related oppression they had to share. They did not refer to their Austrian predecessors from the turn of the century, whose traditions had been disrupted by fascism. Instead, they found their ideological and organizational model in the women's movement in the United States, especially in its radical branch. The conditions of its emergence, however, were shaped by Austrian political culture and traditions.

War and Containment

The most obvious difference between the abortion debate in Austria and in the United States lies in its character after strict abortion laws were repealed in both countries. To understand why the abortion conflict settled down in

Austria while it escalated in the United States, it is necessary to look at attempts to reduce access to abortion after it was legalized.

As shown above, abortion had not been a major issue in the United States until *Roe v. Wade*. The subsequent conflict, however, has resulted in bombings and arson attacks at clinics, death threats to clinic staffers, acts of vandalism, and several killings. The escalation in part was rooted in the nature of the political system. Compared to Austria, America's federal system and its weak political parties provide more opportunity for access by interest groups (Soper 1994: 128; McSweeney and Zvesper 1991). Because legislation on abortion is the responsibility of the individual states, the opportunities for lobbying and mobilizing multiplied. Considering the symbolic potential of abortion, these provided manifold chances for provoking fierce emotions.

In addition, the United States has strong religious groups with corresponding organizational resources and ideological traditions. Both Evangelical Christian groups and the Roman Catholic Church were determined to take advantage of their resources and institutional mechanisms to push their moral agendas. They took advantage of the decentralized political system to put pressure on every candidate running for public office and on unelected officials, and they eventually succeeded in making the stand on abortion a kind of "litmus test" (Hadley 1994: 107–8). In 1994, for example, Dr. Henry Forster came under the fire of pro-life advocates because he had performed (legal) abortions; consequently, he was not appointed surgeon general.

To elaborate on these points, it is necessary to review the abortion debate in each country since the mid-1970s. In Austria, the passing of a new abortion law in 1974 was the climax of a public debate that had intensified after 1971, when the socialist government introduced a law permitting abortions only under certain conditions. This proposal evoked the resistance of socialist women's and feminist groups and of religious groups. When the pro-choice activists succeeded in getting a law passed that permitted abortion on demand within the first three months of pregnancy, a pro-life group, supported by the Roman Catholic Church, started a petition for a referendum. During the following campaign, which garnered the largest number of signatures to date, the conflict spread to every parish, including rural towns and villages. At the same time, the legislature of the province of Salzburg tried to defeat the law by requesting that the Verfassungsgerichtshof, equivalent to the U.S. Supreme Court, examine its constitutionality.[12] Pro-life activists picketed a reproductive health center in Vienna and the homes of doctors who performed abortions in smaller towns and harassed arriving patients.

After the Verfassungsgerichtshof had ruled the abortion law constitutional and the Austrian Parliament had turned down the pro-life petition, all

---

12. In 1974, the court ruled the Austrian abortion law constitutional, stating that the Austrian constitution does not contain an absolute right to life.

legal possibilities for reversing the law were exhausted. From this point, pro-life activity in Austria weakened and by the early 1990s had nearly vanished. The ÖVP, though possessing strong ties to Catholic lay organizations, with-drew its political support for anti-abortion legislation. It had avoided dis-cussing abortion during electoral campaigns since the end of the 1970s because polls showed that the majority of voters favored parties with liberal views on the issue. The Roman Catholic Church, whose membership com-prises over 80 percent of the Austrian population, returned to its position of keeping distance from politics, which it had gradually taken after World War II as a consequence of the civil war in 1934 and Austrofascism.

Once the ÖVP and the Roman Catholic Church stopped advocating anti-abortion legislation, a kind of compromise developed between groups opposing abortion and those advocating unrestricted access to abortions. Although federal law permits abortions on demand within the first term of pregnancy, in some regions of the country, especially in the rural and Catholic areas, abortions are not available because some clinics and doctors refuse to perform them. Women seeking abortions have to travel to one of the larger cities. The national health insurance system does not cover abor-tions (except for medical reasons), although the pro-choice movement had demanded public funding during the 1970s. In 1979, 1984, 1993, and, most recently, 1997, small groups have formed in support of stricter abor-tion legislation. For example, using the well-known American label, the group going public in 1993 called itself Prolife-Spot. Though some of these groups were supported by individual conservative Catholic bishops, none could mobilize mainstream Catholicism or a political party. As a result, these groups exerted little influence on public debate.

In summary, pro-lifers in Austria generally refrained from demanding new laws, while groups advocating unrestricted access to abortion usually made little effort to make it everywhere available. In the meantime, feminist movements have split and turned to other issues.

In the United States, the abortion debate began on a national level only after *Roe v. Wade*. Duly elected legislative bodies did not decide the political conflict over abortion—further evidence of the decentralized nature of American politics—but the courts, which are more open to pressure from individuals and small but well-organized groups like the pro-choice move-ment. The decision in *Roe v. Wade* was not expected by most people (Blake 1977). It came as "a bolt from the blue" (Luker 1984: 141). Under these conditions, it was easy for Christian groups using their dense networks of churches, parochial schools, and other religious institutions to mobilize against abortion on demand. The National Conference of Catholic Bishops was the first to work for limiting access to abortion and for a human-life amendment that would criminalize it. This initiative was soon followed by

Evangelical and Fundamentalist Protestant groups, which eventually became the most dynamic branch of pro-life agitation.

The Evangelical groups presented themselves as a reform movement within mainstream churches, which, according to them, had strayed from the path set out in the Bible and had become too permissive toward the vices of modernity. Several of these had gained a large membership since the 1960s, thereby filling a void left by more liberal churches and providing the kind of clear moral rules seemingly desired by many people. They did not want to accommodate a liberal pluralist society and advocated traditional family values and norms concerning sexuality. Furthermore, according to their interpretation of the Bible, Evangelical Christians saw it as a duty to use political action as a way of realizing the social goals and norms they believed were consistent with God's will (Soper 1994). Their appeals attracted people who felt threatened and frightened by the social changes and the changes in sexual mores that had occurred during the 1960s and 1970s. "America is now facing a grave crisis. Unless we, God's faithful, stand up and are counted, we could see our entire nation destroyed from moral decay," wrote the *Christian Voice*, a publication founded in 1978 (quoted in Soper 1994: 56). As shown above, abortion, as in the case of school prayer, became an important symbolic issue in the defense of the Evangelical worldview.

During the late 1970s and the 1980s, the pro-life movement actively used the American political system and the media to influence the decision-making process; it made contributions to political candidates and launched television advertising campaigns, grassroots mobilizations, and legislative initiatives designed to impose waiting periods, requirements for "informed consent," and cuts in public funding. At the end of the 1970s, the New Right, a coalition of traditional right-wing politicians, religious leaders, and "pro-family" groups, succeeded in gaining influence in the Republican Party, thereby pushing the abortion conflict into the arena of partisan politics in a way that demonstrates the openness of the American party system to pressure groups. Until then, neither the Democratic Party nor the Republican Party had been very sympathetic to cultural issues such as abortion, school prayer, or pornography because these issues cut across the social bases of both parties. Ronald Reagan was the first president to use an anti-abortion stance as a political appeal aimed at Evangelical and Fundamentalist Christians and single-issue groups advocating traditional roles of family, church, and school (Ginsburg 1990: 47).

Unlike in Austria, the Roman Catholic Church in the United States did not shy away from the political fight against access to abortion. The reason no doubt lies in the competitive struggle among churches in the United States for members. In contrast, the Catholic Church in Austria has no fear of losing members to alternative and Fundamentalist religious groups. The activism of the Catholic Church in America is typified by the decision in 1975 by the Family Life Division of the National Catholic Conference to outline and implement a "Pastoral Plan for Pro-life Activity," which led to the foundation of eighteen thousand pro-life committees across the country to monitor and influence national and local elections (Ginsburg 1990: 44). The Catholic bishops continue to support pro-life activities with millions of dollars.

It may seem paradoxical that religion continues to be more influential in politics in America than in Austria. The First Amendment of the U.S. Constitution prohibits the establishment of a state church, which has made it difficult for individual churches and denominations to build formal ties to the state. Yet religion does influence American politics due to the nature of the American political system, that is, its openness to pressure groups and its highly competitive character. By contrast, there were strong institutional ties between the Roman Catholic hierarchy and the Austrian state in the past, and these still exist today. But as a consequence of the turmoil in the inter-war period, the Roman Catholic Church has generally refrained from exerting direct political influence on Austrian politics, politicians, and parties, although there still exist personal ties between members of the ÖVP and Catholic lay organizations.

Beginning in the mid-1970s, the pro-life movement in America took advantage of American political culture the way the pro-choice activists had done before and was very successful on the national and state levels. The Hyde amendments (1976), for example, have prevented public funding of abortions unless they are performed for medical reasons. Many states reduced access to abortion by establishing waiting periods and cutting funding, neither of which were hindered by the courts. At the same time, the pro-life demonstrations and acts of civil disobedience associated with the picketing of clinics reduced the number of clinics and doctors performing abortions so that by 1988, 83 percent of all counties in the United States lacked any facilities for abortion (Hadley 1994: 102).

As time passed, it seemed that pro-life activists would be successful in their attempt to reverse *Roe v. Wade*. Both Presidents Reagan and Bush used their appointments to the Supreme Court to establish a pro-life majority. The Republican Party platform in all presidential elections from 1980 to 1992 contained an anti-abortion plank. But the threat of the renewed criminalization of abortion eventually mobilized the women's movement, which started to defend abortion rights more actively. Once again, the women's movement made abortion rights a symbolic issue. Between 300,000 and 600,000 people participated in the march "Women's Equality, Women's Lives" on 9 April 1989, one of the largest ever held in Washington. The membership drives and the fund-raising efforts of NOW and NARAL rose to new heights (Ryan 1992: 144–46).

The revived pro-choice efforts were at least partially successful. Although the executive branch under President Bush repeatedly demanded the reversal of *Roe*, the Supreme Court upheld its 1973 decision, at least in principle (Goldstein 1994). In the presidential election campaign of 1992, abortion was once again a central issue; the battle between pro-life George Bush and pro-choice Bill Clinton ended with Clinton's victory. As a result of this defeat, the Republican Party gradually distanced itself from aggressive pro-lifers: "I will not allow abortion to be a litmus test for membership," a senior Republican said in 1993 (quoted in Hadley 1994: 197). As the congressional elections of November 1994 approached, the Republican "Contract for America" contained no anti-abortion plank (*International Herald Tribune*, 29 September 1994). Under Clinton's presidency, federal legislation forbade protesters from obstructing clinics and from threatening to use force near them. The "gag rule," which prevented public employees from informing their patients about abortion, was also lifted.

As the influence of pro-lifers weakened, the legal possibilities for prohibiting access to abortion dwindled. In my view, it was the frustration of pro-life activists that radicalized them and led in March 1993 to the first murder of a doctor who performed abortions. This and subsequent murders were not simply the acts of mentally ill fanatics; they were an unintended but not surprising outcome of Fundamentalist anti-abortion campaigns, which were supported, or at least not rejected, by mainstream institutions like the Catholic Church and the Republican Party. Religious anti-abortionists introduced the language of war and killing into the discourse: "Abortion is the greatest war of all time," says a pamphlet of Human Life International (*New York Times*, 15 January 1995). The cardinal of Boston withdrew his support for clinic picketing only after the shooting of two clinic staff members in December 1994 (*New York Times*, 4 January 1995). A Nonviolent Action Project exhorted that "the mandate in Scripture is clear.… Enough looking. Enough talking. Enough ignorant evasion of responsibility. When you know that an innocent and helpless child is about to be killed, you must intervene" (quoted in Soper 1994: 113). Those who killed in their anti-abortion struggle may have taken these exhortations too seriously.

In summary, the reasons why the abortion conflict escalated in the United States and not in Austria lie in the countries' different ideological and institutional traditions. In Austria, Evangelical traditions were missing, and the Roman Catholic Church, despite the attitudes of some conservative dignitaries, had no incentive to push seriously within the political process for renewed anti-abortion legislation. Furthermore, the centralized political system in Austria gave few if any points of access to radical anti-abortionists. The American polity is more open to small but highly organized pressure groups that represent only a small number of people. Paul Weyrich, director of a right-wing interest group, said at a meeting of fifty leaders of anti-abortion groups in 1980: "It doesn't matter what the majority of American people think on a poll. What matters is the perception members of Congress have about your issue and their future" (quoted in Nelson and Carver 1994: 747). In this way, Fundamentalist religious groups seized numerous opportunities for mobilizing emotions that were difficult to channel and contain.

Conclusion

The abortion debate in Austria and the abortion debate in the United States show differences in evolution and outcome. These differences are rooted in the institutional and ideological peculiarities that determine political culture and the grammar of political discourse in each country.

One of the most important elements of political culture is the political system and how it works. In Austria, political parties and their organizational structure had almost a monopoly in channeling political demands and interests up to the 1970s and still form the most important "transmission belt" between key interest groups and the executive and legislative branches of the government. In contrast, the federal character and relatively weak party structure of the American polity offer many points of access for single-issue pressure groups and lobbies. Given this weakness and the parties' inability to deal with internal conflicts, the courts in America, especially the Supreme Court, became influential in cultural conflicts like the struggle over access to abortion.

The national protagonists in the conflict also showed some crucial differences that determined the nature of the debate. The American women's movement had its roots in moral movements such as those promoting temperance and the abolition of slavery. By defining motherhood as the core of womanhood, the American women's movement prior to the late 1960s not only did not call for the liberalization of abortion laws but supported the ban on abortion. America lacked a political movement of women that could advocate an alternative position. Although the Austrian bourgeois women's movement did not make abortion its political concern either, Austria has had a tradition of discussing abortion as a political issue since the 1920s due to the reform efforts of the socialist women's movement. In the early 1970s, advocates of repealing the abortion law could draw on these ideological and organizational traditions. The socialist networks were used to introduce and push through proposals for a liberal abortion law, and it was out of these efforts that an autonomous women's movement emerged.

In America, Evangelical traditions, which were all but absent in Austria, also fueled the conflict after the repeal of the strict abortion laws. Abortion became and remained a symbolic issue within which worldviews and social norms were negotiated. A dynamic arose that could no longer be contained; it led to physical violence and ultimately to the killings of clinic staff members.

In Austria, political culture and ideological and religious traditions did not fuel an escalating, polarized conflict. None of the institutionalized societal forces, including the Roman Catholic Church, had an interest in making abortion its crucial rallying point after the 1970s. The Austrian feminist movement turned its attention to other issues, for example, equal pay and violence in families. Once the movement had achieved its main demand concerning abortion laws, the issue lost its mobilizing effect. Most likely it would not have been possible to continue campaigns on abortion-related issues, for example, the public funding of them or the expansion of facilities throughout the country. In addition, the feminist movement split into a number of small groups and failed to create an effective political structure of its own. The centralized political system in Austria, which offers very few channels of decision making, prevented the small anti-abortion groups from having much political clout. Under these conditions, abortion laws lost their symbolic importance.

References

Anderson, H. 1992. *Utopian Feminism: Women's Movements in Fin-de-Siècle Vienna.* New Haven.

Blake, J. 1977. "The Abortion Decisions: Judicial Review and Public Opinion." In *Abortion: New Directions in Policy Studies,* ed. E. Manier, W. Liu, and D. Solomon, 51–82. Notre Dame.

Bock, G. 1986. *Zwangssterilisation im Nationalsozialismus. Studien zur Rassenpolitik und Frauenpolitik.* Opladen, Germany.

Czarnowski, G. 1991. *Das kontrollierte Paar. Ehe und Sexualpolitik im Nationalsozialismus.* Weinheim, Germany.

Ebbinghaus, R. 1976. "Legitimationsproblematik, jüngere staatstheoretische Diskussion und der Stand historisch-empirischer Forschung." In *Bürgerlicher Staat und politische Legitimation,* 9–39. Frankfurt.

Eser, A., and H.-G. Koch, eds. 1988–89. *Schwangerschaftsabbruch im internationalen Vergleich. Rechtliche Regelungen – Soziale Rahmenbedingungen – Empirische Grunddaten.* 2 vols. Baden-Baden.

Ginsburg, F. D. 1990. *Contested Lives: The Abortion Debate in an American Community.* Berkeley.

Goldstein, L. F. 1994. *Contemporary Cases in Women's Rights.* Madison.

Gordon, L. 1977. *Woman's Body, Woman's Right: Birth Control in America.* New York.

Grillenberger, S. 1989. *Eine Chronologie der Frauenbewegungen in der Bundesrepublik Deutschland und in Österreich in den siebziger Jahren unter besonderer Berücksichtigung der Abtreibungsdiskussion.* Diplomarbeit, University of Vienna.

Gusfield, J. 1963. *Symbolic Crusade.* Urbana.

Hadley, J. 1994. "God's Bullies: Attacks on Abortion." *Feminist Review,* no. 48 (autumn):94–113.

Hoff, J. 1991. *Law, Gender, and Injustice: A Legal History of U.S. Women.* New York.

Hymowitz, C., and M. Weissman. 1978. *A History of Women in America.* Toronto.

König, F. 1993. "Jenseits von Kosten und Nutzen." *Der Standard,* 3 June.

Lehner, K. 1989. *Verpönte Eingriffe. Sozialdemokratische Reformbestrebungen zu den Abtreibungsbestimmungen in der Zwischenkriegszeit.* Vienna.

Luker, K. 1984. *Abortion and the Politics of Motherhood.* Berkeley.

May, E. T. 1988. *Homeward Bound: American Families in the Cold War Era.* New York.

McSweeney, D., and J. Zvesper. 1991. *American Political Parties: The Formation, Decline and Reform of the American Party System.* London.

Mesner, M. 1994. *Frauensache? Zur Auseinandersetzung um den Schwangerschaftsabbruch in Österreich.* Vienna.

Münz, R. 1985. *Soziologische Aspekte der Familienentwicklung und die Instrumente ihrer Beeinflussung.* Habilitationsschrift, University of Vienna.

Nelson, B. J., and K. A. Carver. 1994. "Many Voices but Few Vehicles: The Consequences for Women of Weak Political Infrastructure in the United States." In *Women and Politics Worldwide,* ed. B. J. Nelson and N. Chowdhury, 738–57. New Haven.

Nelson, B. J., and N. Chowdhury, eds. 1994. *Women and Politics Worldwide.* New Haven.

Petchesky, R. 1984. *Abortion and Woman's Choice.* New York.

Ryan, B. 1992. *Feminism and the Women's Movement. Dynamics of Change in Social Movement, Ideology and Activism.* New York.

Sachdev, P., ed. 1988. *International Handbook on Abortion.* New York.

Sieder, R. 1987. *Sozialgeschichte der Familie.* Frankfurt.

Soper, J. C. 1994. *Evangelical Christianity in the United States and Great Britain: Religious Beliefs, Political Choices.* New York.

Wagnleitner, R. 1991. *Coca-Colonisation und Kalter Krieg. Die Kulturmission der USA in Österreich nach dem Zweiten Weltkrieg.* Vienna.

Chapter 9

AMERICANIZATION, CULTURAL CHANGE, AND AUSTRIAN IDENTITY

Edward Larkey

Introduction: Americanization and U.S. Hegemony

A mericanization is an ideological strategy that has attempted to propagate a consumerist social utopia in post-1945 Europe. My chapter analyzes its impact on popular-music traditions as it diffused through the mass media and elicited responses from different types of audiences and consumers. I focus on the particular case of Austria. Using a "productionist" approach that emphasizes consumption as active construction of identities, I analyze how global relations of power under the hegemony of the United States shaped the diffusion of popular music; the re-construction, reinterpretation, and representation of popular-music traditions in Austria; and the representations of Austrian identities within their institutional structures.

My central hypothesis is that Americanization entails a discourse strategy of a consumerist social utopia with far-reaching and long-term impacts that still function today. Americanization is an economically motivated, comprehensive ideology that diffused into Austria after 1945 through advertising, economic policies, and changes in the mass media. It has had ambiguous results: it has helped construct a modern "non-German" Austrian identity yet has brought the homogenizing tendencies of global cultural industries into Austria.

The Approach

As a cultural boundary-setting device, Americanization sought to accomplish three historical tasks in post-1945 Austria: (1) to establish historical and cultural distance between postwar Austria and its immediate German/Nazi past, (2) to stake out space for an anticommunist social utopia based on consumer capitalism, and (3) to integrate Austria culturally, politically, and economically into the Western market economies. As Wagnleitner (1994: 7) argues, "Americanization" is a "process of cultural transformation, a process in which the parts of the social memory that refused to identify themselves with the logic of the consumer society—the equation 'survival = consumption'—had to be worked over by propaganda and advertisement." As a cultural strategy, Americanization projects a utopian image of the "good life" that connects leisure, relaxation, and entertainment to the consumption of material goods (Maase 1992: 240; Bogart 1995: 66). Its foundations lie in the expansion of a materially based commercial culture driven by advertising (Wagnleitner 1991: 8; Bogart 1995: 68), which reaffirms "mainstream middle class values," portrays human conflict only as a playful exercise, and depicts people as "uniformly happy, healthy and vigorous" who lead lives "devoid of unpleasantness, grief, stress or pain" (Bogart 1995: 82–83).

In the postwar period, the United States was a relatively attractive hegemon. It possessed

> a mighty domestic economy, a progressive ruling class (in comparison with most others actually existing), and at least some desirable cultural ideological features particularly attractive to modernizing elites, that opened the global door to them and ensured their creation, persistence and often aggrandisement of social classes in countries all over the world willing and eager to adopt their transnational practices. (Sklair 1991: 7)

Although the United States established and maintained hegemonic core-periphery relations on a global scale (Wallerstein 1990: 41; Said 1993: 324), its policies of Americanization in Austria functioned through its regional hegemon, West Germany, which served as the economic force behind the ideological penetration of the "American way of life" in Austria. West Germany could "realistically claim to share hegemony" as a propagator of a consumerist social utopia that could serve as a model of consumer democracy for postwar Austria to emulate (Sklair 1991: 7).

As in Germany, Americanization diffused through Austrian society from the "bottom-up" (Maase 1992: 238) by influencing a cultural avant-garde of youths (Luger 1991: 112), who used it to repudiate conservative, nationalist values (Schou 1991: 156) rooted in the past and to sustain an "illusory hedonism" (Campbell 1994: 60) in the present. Its "presentist" thrust negates the authority and legitimacy of the past as a valid realm of social experience (Schou 1991: 155).

Americanization is a contested ideology that transcends class and reinforces, but also modernizes, traditional patriarchal gender roles (Thurner 1995: 61). It shifted discourse on the nation from a production-oriented, industrially based economic model of self-sufficiency to a culturally oriented model of consumer democracy (Ewen 1988: 59) under the economic tutelage of transnational corporations (TNCs) (Sklair 1991: 42) within a broad network of dependencies. It limited the sovereign activities of the Austrian government with regard to choices in *economic* policy making (compare Morawetz 1990: 98), while it *increased* the available repertoire of symbols, signs, styles, and images for recreating, reinterpreting, and reconstructing Austrian identities.

American culture had a broad impact in Austrian society, especially by promoting the spread of the English language as an international means of communication. It also undermined and competed with traditional European elitist cultural traditions (Wagnleitner 1991: 223; Schou 1991: 156) by legitimating popular cultures, discourses and practices, and everyday experiences in narratives about collective national belonging. It emphasized commercial culture, advertising, and the market as legitimizers of authority (Bogart 1995: 66) and ultimately assisted in undermining the state monopoly in the electronic media, while providing more access for the commercial interests of the TNCs. The class-transcendent vision of Austria as a consumerist democracy was shared by both major political camps, the People's Party (ÖVP) and the Social Democratic Party (SPÖ), and thus reinforced consensual structures such as the Social Partnership (*Sozialpartnerschaft*) and the neocorporatist organization of social life (Botz and Müller 1995: 27), which typified Austrian political culture in the postwar period.

Americanization has had a broad impact on Austrian national traditions in the popular arts, including film, fashion, music, and other forms of popular entertainment. Traditions act as filters that are hegemonically determined and hierarchically configured and form sociocultural alliances having distinct qualities of time and space. Traditions, like the markets in which they move and in which they are negotiated, are a "contested field of power" (compare Dilley 1992: 5). American traditions have been transplanted to Austria, for example, the musical as a form of entertainment and rock music as a genre of cultural expression. They have transformed traditional cultural forms of music like the *volkstümliche* and the *Schlager* and have spawned transnational forms such as Austropop and the new folk music.[1] They have

---

1. *Volkstümliche* refers to commercialized alpine folklore music. *Schlager* refers to a hit tune. The term is rooted in the German verb *schlagen*, or "to hit," and was first used to denote the

also led to the industrialization of cultural production, distribution, and consumption, with Austria participating on the periphery of a global division of labor. This has marginalized Austrian contributions, in the words of Said (1993: 324), as "a kind of unimportant provinciality," while directing certain symbols and forms signifying "power, legitimacy, balance and authority" to the center or mainstream.

The "Colonization" of Austria

It is fashionable to use the metaphor of Austria as a colony (Fabris 1990) or a subcolony (Wagnleitner 1991) in characterizing the asymmetrical relationship of Austria to both Germany and the United States. The metaphor is based on the penetration of Austria by advertising and commercial culture, by the dominance of German economic and media conglomerates (Scherb 1990; Morawetz 1990; Atzenhofer 1990; Fabris 1990), which ultimately undermined the ability of its citizens and the state to enact sovereign decisions affecting vital areas of society, and by the reliance of Austrians on the consumption of styles, symbols, and cultural artifacts and images of popular culture from outside their borders to construct their identities.

The nationalized industries were once the pillar of Austrian economic sovereignty. They arose from the policy of nationalizing the formerly German-controlled industries in the Nazi era to avoid Soviet reparation demands and have now weakened due to a large-scale sell-off to German economic interests. As a result, 80 percent of direct investments are transferred out of the country as management and license fees, which has had economic repercussions and has affected the ability of the political parties to wield economic power through management appointments in the nationalized industries. The Austrian economy is now effectively dominated by Germany (Scherb 1990: 29). The state-controlled Creditanstalt bank has sold off large holdings in the glass, machine tools, and automobile parts industries to West German interests, primarily MAN (Maschinenfabrik-Augsburg-Nürnberg) (Morawetz 1990: 93). Also, the Önorm (Österreichisches Normeninstitut), which granted preferential treatment in bids on state construction projects to Austrian firms (Morawetz 1990: 93 and 105), was rescinded in preparation for Austrian membership in the European Union. These policies were carried out in the 1980s and 1990s, but even in the 1940s and 1950s American occupation authorities and Austrian politicians sought to maintain the export-oriented basic industries initiated by the Nazis (Mathis 1995: 170), while

---

most popular songs on the market in the late 1800s. At first all types of popular dance tunes could be called *Schlager*, but the term gradually was applied to a particular musical genre using German folk and popular elements.

preventing domestic-oriented and consumer-goods sectors from developing independently of the German and West European markets (Hofbauer 1992: 160). Economist Inge Morawetz (1990: 108) argues that the Austrian economic and political elites have either voluntarily subordinated the economic base to German interests or have capitulated in the face of German pressure.

In the mass media, German penetration and hegemony have accompanied increasing tendencies toward commercialization and reliance on advertising for financing the state-operated electronic media. Also, the push by private interests in the print media for the introduction of private radio has led to the demise of the party press.

Advertising already accounted for 49 percent of the income for Austrian Radio (ORF) in 1992, compared to 42 percent from license fees, and for the first time became the prime income generator for the state public-service broadcaster. Advertising in 1993 could not exceed 20 minutes per day for television and 120 minutes per week for radio. By the year 2001, advertising will reach a peak of 42 minutes per day for television and 172 minutes per week for radio (Luger and Steinmaurer 1993: 184–86).

These guidelines were part of a broader pact among the major media players, above all the West German-dominated print media in Austria, especially the KroKuWaz concern Mediaprint, which consists of the tabloids *Krone* and *Kurier* and the Westdeutsche Allgemeine newspaper group. Mediaprint led efforts by the Association of Austrian Newspaper Editors and Publishers (VÖZ) to gain entrance to the electronic media and dissolve the state monopoly of broadcasting by the ORF (Luger and Steinmaurer 1993: 180). An agreement between the ORF and the VÖZ in 1985 permitted an increase in the amount of time allotted for advertising, including previously excluded Sundays and holidays.

The *Regionalradiogesetz*, passed in 1993, permitted Austrian citizens, legal entities, and corporations based in Austria to operate private local radio stations as of 1 January 1994 and allowed advertising for up to 15 percent of daily programming, not to exceed 90 minutes daily (Luger and Steinmaurer 1993: 182). Advertising has diluted the cultural mission of the ORF laid out in the *Rundfunkgesetz* of 1974, which aimed at providing objective news reports, diverse and critical views on community and public issues, and programs for youth and adult education that presented "impeccable entertainment." Inherent in this advertising shift is a move from the concept of "audience-as-public," based on a hypothetical but normative, culturally educated audience, to the concept of the "audience-as-market" (Ang 1991: 31). The shift creates the need for statistically measuring audience response and for placing people into "stable taxonomic categories for institutional control," albeit "under constant pressure of reconstruction whenever they turn out to be imperfect weapons in the quest for control" (Ang 1991: 40).

A series of measures were introduced at the ORF reflecting these changes. Program choices are now made on the basis of audience surveys, which have been refined by new methods of measuring audience responses that have been introduced into electronic broadcasting. In 1991, the ORF changed its method for tapping the reach of its television programs from written diaries among 900 adults and 150 children to an electronic measurement system encompassing 1,500 adults and 200 children (Luger and Steinmaurer 1993: 195). In 1992, the ORF pop-music network Ö3 introduced computerized music programming, which reduced the opportunity for moderators to have influence over this important function. In 1990, Ö Regional was renamed Ö2 and expanded its local programming. Also, in the beginning of the 1990s, all three networks of the ORF began to provide twenty-four-hour service. Finally, on 1 May 1992, Blue Danube Radio, which had originally been an English-language broadcasting service for UN diplomats in Vienna, became a high-tech service available throughout the country (Luger and Steinmaurer 1993: 195).

The print media comprise one of the primary motors of commercial culture in Austria. The early 1990s witnessed the almost complete demise of the party press, including the former SPÖ newspaper *Arbeiter Zeitung* (*AZ*) and the Communist Party newspaper *Volksstimme* in 1991, as well as several regional newspapers of the ÖVP. While the end of the *Volksstimme* was predicated on the loss of subsidies and advertising from Eastern Europe, the *AZ* lost its advertising base as a result of severing ties with the SPÖ, which meant that advertisers were no longer enticed by the prospect of sustaining connections with the politicians through the paper. Between 1987 and 1990, the advertising revenues of the *AZ* dropped from 54 to 26 million schillings (Bruck and Melcher-Smejkal 1993: 65). Thus from 1986 to 1991 the total market share of the party press sank from 17 percent to 3 percent (Bruck and Melcher-Smejkal 1993: 71).

In addition to the KroKuWaz creation Mediaprint, other West German firms entered the Austrian media market, particularly the Axel-Springer publishing group, which in 1988 helped initiate *Der Standard*, the first of several recently founded daily newspapers in Austria. This step initiated a competitive upgrading of the entire Austrian press landscape and created the new media category "quality national daily press." It not only forced a substantial revamping of the conservative Viennese newspaper *Die Presse* but led to the expansion of the regional *Salzburger Nachrichten* into national distribution. In 1989 Springer bought a 45 percent interest in the *Tiroler Tageszeitung*. The market share for the German-owned daily press rose from 27 percent in 1988 to 31 percent in 1991 (compare Bruck and Melcher-Smejkal 1993: 77).

The book market, too, is highly dependent on the German market. While German unification brought increased orders for Austrian printers and bookbinders serving the newly enlarged German market, experts expect that Austrian entry into the European Union will facilitate a larger presence of German publishers on the domestic market (Panzer 1993: 281–82). A further problem with the small size of the Austrian book market is the attraction of publishing in Germany for Austrian authors. In the hopes of selling more books through the more efficient distribution system in Germany, Austrian authors submit their manuscripts to German publishers, who reexport them in the form of manufactured books into Austria, which negatively affects the Austrian trade balance (Panzer 1993: 283). It is therefore no surprise that Austrian publishers are barely represented among the top one hundred in the German-speaking regional book market. The largest Austrian publisher is the state-run Österreichischer Bundesverlag, which is in fifty-ninth place on the list, the privately owned Ueberreuther is eightieth, and the Veritas publishing house, formerly owned by the diocese of Linz but now owned by Bavarian interests, is ninety-sixth (Panzer 1993: 283–84). German publishers dominate the Austrian book market to the tune of 80 percent. Between 1986 and 1991 Austrian book imports from Germany rose from 1.727 to 2.383 million schillings, whereas book exports to Germany rose only from 692 to 788 million schillings (Panzer 1993: 284). Ownership of publishing houses in Austria tends to be dominated by institutions, chiefly the church or the state. German ownership of Austrian publishers has been a way of life since the 1980s, fueled by such conspicuous acquisitions as the Orac publishing house by the Bertelsmann-owned Kremayr and Scheriau (Panzer 1993: 286). Bertelsmann owns, in addition, the Donauland book club, which after buying up the Deutscher Bücherbund in 1992, became the largest book club in Austria with over a million members (Panzer 1993: 295). According to Panzer (1993: 289), a majority of Austrian publishers would go bankrupt if they had to exist solely from sales of their books.

Austropop as an Innovative and Ambiguous Transnational Practice

I now turn to the impact of Americanization on popular music by analyzing the emergence of Austropop, a transnational music tradition in the 1970s, and the new folk music of the late 1980s and early 1990s. For a variety of reasons, the year 1955 represents a good starting point. It was politically significant as the year of the Austrian State Treaty, which ended Allied occupation of Austria. In addition, by then disposable household income was rising enough to begin trickling down to the realm of consumer goods and daily life. This period thus is crucial for the formation of "fictive ethnicity" in Austria, whereby individuals are "nationalized" or "socialized into the dominant form of national belonging" (Balibar 1990: 94 and 96). Using the examples of Austropop and the new folk music, I will show how popular music has contributed to *ethnicizing* and *naturalizing* the Austrian people through lineage based on history and territory. I use the concept of tradition as a form of national "collective narrative" (Balibar 1990: 93) to show how the two types of music help constitute "the community which recognizes itself in advance in the institution of the state, and recognizes that state as 'its own' in opposition to other states, and in particular, inscribes its political struggles within the horizon of that state" (Balibar 1990: 93). According to Balibar, the two competing paths toward this end are language and race. His analysis becomes especially salient because Austrian identity was strengthened during this period (Reiterer 1988), and being "Austrian," which represents a historically constructed variable, has become a central precondition for the acceptance of artistic achievements:

> One behaves tolerantly toward Austrian art, but if the label "Austrian" is successfully put to doubt, then the level of tolerance sinks proportionally. The opposite is also true: If someone is successful in presenting a certain artist or a group as sufficiently "Austrian," the level of acceptance increases. (Botz and Müller 1995: 37)

In the face of German economic domination and cultural hegemony, Austrians must rely on their historical repertoire of images, symbols, meanings, and values to construct their identities. But they must also accommodate the hegemonically driven predominance of images and symbols transmitted into the country from the United States and Germany. This is a feature Austrians share with other nations that must use their cultures to construct identities and "position themselves in relation to the cultural frames affirmed by the world system" (Ang 1990: 253). This means that identities are historical constructs that form battlegrounds of "intense struggle between a plurality of cultural groupings and interests inside a nation," which make them "fundamentally a dynamic, conflictive, unstable and impure" phenomena (Ang 1990: 252). The development of both Austropop and the new folk music reflects this nonessentialist view of constructing national identities by means of culture and tradition. They represent historical responses to both the constraints and opportunities created by producers of popular music in Austria, who as consumers and constructors of identity were influenced by a wide range of external and internal forces.

Before Austropop could emerge in the early 1970s as a transnational music tradition and form of discourse about popular music produced in Austria, two previous encounters with American and British music were necessary prerequisites. During the first period, which began in the 1950s, only a handful of the cultural avant-garde among Austrian youth consumed rock and roll. Not only were there almost no Austrian rock-and-roll bands with appreciable popularity that would achieve prominence later, but the German *Schlager* industry maintained its hold during this period, successfully incorporating rock-and-roll styles into productions for vocalists like the Austrian Peter Kraus or the Germans Conny Froboess and Ted Herold. One exception was the Bambis, a group of four musicians — two German and two Austrian — who copied, imitated, and modeled their vocal identities on original artists whose music was played on the Radio Luxemburg hit parade. Their popularity coincided with major transformations underway in the music industry, above all the shift from printed notation to the engineered "sound" of the music, which had the effect of "de-skilling" both the musician, who was no longer required to read music, and the arranger, who needed to duplicate the sound in order to achieve success. Austrians contributed to the German-dominated *Schlager* industry by providing recording-studio space for the German majors, primarily Polydor, which hired vocalists to remake American hits in German or in "Americanized" German, which was performed by former American soldiers Gus Backus and Bill Ramsey, as well as German singers, and contained additions to the lyrics like "baby," "darling," and "teenager."

This period, which also featured other pop forms like "folk music" made famous by the Kingston Trio ("Tom Dooley") and other groups, came to an end in 1963 and 1964 with the rise of the Beatles. In the new era, *imitation* became the primary form of youth popular music, as large numbers of middle-class young people started playing the guitar, drums, and other instruments in the Beatles fashion, utilizing English lyrics, dressing accordingly, and performing in front of live audiences composed of peers with similar interests. In contrast to the audiences for rock and roll in the 1950s, which were marginalized and stigmatized by the criminal justice system and the moral guardians of society, audiences for "beat" music grew to such an extent that they were ultimately successful in competing for legitimacy and space within the music industry and the general music market. They performed in the latter half of the 1960s in trade-union halls, church community centers, schools, and commercial establishments, creating networks of production and consumption that formed the basis for the later flourishing of Austropop. A further path to music making for youths was initiated by American and British commercial folk music, typified by Bob Dylan, Donovan, Pete Seeger, and Peter, Paul, and Mary, who served as models for members of student subcultures to imitate. One of the most successful groups was Jack's Angels, a group of folk-music aficionados organized by Jack Grunsky, an Austrian-Canadian studying in Linz. Other groups include the Milestones, who tended to copy folk and folk-rock models with English lyrics, as well as Misthaufen and the Worried Men Skiffle Group. Both the beat-influenced and the folk groups had a common denominator: they relied on English-language lyrics and copied the styles of groups like the Beatles, Rolling Stones, Animals, and Chicago.

The merger of these two styles in the late 1960s and early 1970s was a major step toward Austropop, which was accompanied by a substantial opening of the recording industry and the mass media to the youthful musicians and their cooperative networks. In 1968, the ORF instituted Ö3, which marked the first time a major state-run network in the German-speaking countries dedicated a large proportion of its broadcasting to international popular music. In another development, several of the youthful musicians moved on to related occupations in popular-music production, most notably Peter Jürgen Müller. Müller left his group the Mimes to set up a studio for recording his friends' music and was ultimately hired by Polygram to find and record groups for the newly formed Atom label. Müller has since become one of Austria's most prominent producers and recording engineers, recording some of the most popular groups like the Erste Allgemeine Verunsicherung, Opus, Wolfgang Ambros, and Rainhard Fendrich. Thus, the emergence of Austropop was ultimately connected to an increasing division of labor within the industry and increasing opportunities for young artists to perform and record, plus a kind of "asymmetrical globalization," which gave musical groups greater opportunity to communicate with their audiences.

The turning point in the development of Austropop came in 1971 with the huge popularity of two records, Wolfgang Ambros's *Da Hofa* and a song by the group Waterloo + Robinson called "Hollywood." Ambros, the son of a grade-school principal in Pressbaum, had achieved notoriety by performing as a guitarist and vocalist in the Atlantis student club in Vienna. The lyrics to the song were written by his friend Josef Prokopetz, and the song was recorded in the studio of Peter Jürgen Müller. Müller told me that the two were quite drunk during the recording session and were somewhat astounded that the song would achieve such a large degree of popularity in the ensuing months.

The song was celebrated as a socially critical condemnation of a hypocritical society. The lyrics relate the story of a mentally unstable social outcast who is blamed for the death of a person found lying in the gutter. Upon discovering the corpse, a crowd gathers in front of the house of the presumed culprit, demanding that he appear and be held accountable. Instead of the "Hofa," the landlord appears and explains to the crowd that it is impossible for the Hofa to appear because he is the corpse. The implication is that those most responsible for crimes against social outcasts, the weak, and the powerless are the "respectable citizens" who scream the most about law and order. This typifies most of the lyrical repertoire of Ambros/ Prokopetz: playing with the ambiguities of social behavior and taking the side of the weak while satirizing the powerful. A title on the first LP in 1972,

Alles andere zöht net mehr (Everything else doesn't count anymore), deals ironically with a landlord/building superintendent "Franz Pokorny" who "is a respected/respectable person." The second LP is entitled *Es lebe der Zentralfriedhof* (Long live the central cemetery) and is the epitome of double meanings and irony: "Long live the central cemetery, and all of its dead." On this LP, Ambros/Prokopetz resurrect past figures of Austrian cultural life for a party of death that satirizes "dead" cultural life in present-day Austria: "Am Zentralfriedhof is Stimmung wias seit Lebtag no net woa" (in the central cemetery there is a good time like there never was during life). The Ambros/Prokopetz lyrics repeatedly use death to characterize either Austrian society or outsiders or to stand in juxtaposition to a commercial culture that emphasizes vitality, youth, and activity.

While Ambros represents the alternative, more critical direction of Austropop, the second group, Waterloo + Robinson, personifies its commercial, more affirmative tendency: these contradictory, competing, and ambiguous currents of Austropop persist to this day. Waterloo + Robinson, who come from Styria, built their careers slowly but surely on German-language titles of the drippy-syrupy *Schlager* variety. Many of these titles fell under a decree of the superintendent of the ORF Ö3 network that banned German *Schnulzen* from the Austrian airwaves.[2] English lyrics provided a way of circumventing the decree. Their first successful foray in this respect was the title "Hollywood," which was arranged by Christian Kolonovits, the pianist and arranger for the group Milestones. It was recorded in Müller's studio with Jack Grunsky, jazz musician Kurt Haunstein, and with musicians recruited from some of the most popular groups of that time, like the Schmetterlinge, a left-wing political folk-rock band. The slow, lamenting song "Hollywood" mourns the loss of the big movie stars like Errol Flynn, Gary Cooper, Shirley Temple, and Jane Mansfield by asking: "Did you ever see the movie, where [the respective star] had played?" The refrain laments: "Good old Hollywood is dying, good old Hollywood is dying, good old Hollywood is dead." The arrangements include horns and strings.

Although it appears to be just imitating English lyrics, Austropop represents a qualitatively different level of popular-music development. For the first time, lyrics in dialect found a legitimacy in modern Austrian popular music that was usually a domain of *Volksmusik* or the *Wienerlied*. This distinguishes Austropop from the German *Schlager* and its Austrian clones, which generally used standard German lyrics. The use of English in the lyrics of Austrian groups reflects the experiences of that generation of musicians and their respective audiences, which were based on hearing language

2. *Schnulzen* are highly sentimentalized and drippy *Schlager* and usually involve unrequited love or the yearning to return home.

not as a component of verbal communication but as a structural element of the *music*. Since then, a linguistic dichotomy in the usage of English and German lyrics in popular songs has evolved in the German-speaking countries. English is generally considered to be an artistic language, much as was Italian in operas of nineteenth-century German composers, and putting it to music represents a high level of artistic achievement for a nonnative English speaker or lyricist. Vocalists or lyricists who use it make an implicit assertion about their competitive viability on the international English-language market. The irony is that English is generally used for productions that place the music, rhythm, melody, and entertainment in the foreground and subordinate the communicative function of the lyrics. Using dialect lyrics suggests that the singer/songwriter has something substantial to communicate to the audience. This requires more mental attention and work on the part of the audience to be successful and means placing the message of the lyrics in the foreground.

I call this phase of Austrian popular music "deanglicization" because it represents a new level of control over production by both the musicians and their audiences. They achieved substantially more influence within the recording industries and broadcasting services over performances, recordings, and programming. In addition, they have initiated new forms based on continuity with older traditions of popular music. New composers, arrangers, musicians, studios, and broadcasting outlets developed to serve the new styles of music. By the late 1970s, Austropop moved from the periphery to the core of popular music in Austria when a second generation of singer/songwriters achieved prominence: Rainhard Fendrich, Stefanie Werger, the folk-rock group STS, and the cabaret rock group Erste Allgemeine Verunsicherung. These musicians used the same technical apparatus and some of the same themes in their lyrics as the first generation. In addition, they accommodated a similar institutional aesthetic as a part of their sound. A further reason to treat Austropop as a part of the core traditions of popular music was its ability to sustain production and popularity in the face of the influx of punk and new wave and disco and subsequent dance styles. Austropop also projected a similar image in its stage personae: truthful, open, intimate, sensitive, and rebellious. Personal relations developed between the first and second generation of Austropop artists, and they also embarked on a series of collaborative recording projects, which confirms the view that Austropop may be considered an "art world" comprised of "all of the people whose activities are necessary to the production of the characteristic work which that world ... define[s] as art" (Becker 1983: 34). It represents "an established network of cooperative links" based on "a body of conventional understandings embodied in common practice and in frequently used artifacts" (Becker 1983: 34–35).

The expansion of Austropop into a second generation entailed new nego-tiations of identities by the artists. For example, the first time Stefanie Werger performed as a supporting act together with Wolfgang Ambros she was almost booed off the stage by the Ambros fans. This second phase of Austropop involves a reethnicization due to its ability to "establish its own historical lineage and heritage, spawn its own aesthetic concepts, principles, sounds or ideologies and art worlds" (Larkey 1993: 202). The second gen-eration of Austropop proved that it represented not just a *tactical* but also a *strategic* response to the influx of Anglo-American popular music in the sense that it "postulates a place that can be delimited as its own and serve as the base from which relations with an exteriority composed of targets or threats … can be managed" (Certeau 1984: 36).

One of the primary features of Austropop is that it represents a discourse by both the electronic and print media to delineate the Austrian contribu-tion to the popular music distributed throughout the 1970s. The ORF moderator Eva-Maria Kaiser told me that she coined the term Austropop during a live performance of musicians in Graz in 1972. But a new period-ical called *hit* was marketed in the early 1970s that focused its attention on Austrian popular music. It produced a regular feature entitled "Austropop Lexikon." In addition, the newspaper *Rennbahn-Express*, originally pub-lished by students of a high school in Salzburg, developed into a nationwide, mainstream publication throughout the 1970s that helped to delineate the core of Austrian music for youth. This magazine is now a part of the Medi-aprint concern and has superseded the German-produced *Bravo* as the most popular youth/music magazine in Austria.

The discourse of Austropop has persisted as a marketing category and classificatory device for appropriating global forms of music and incorpo-rating them into the Austrian mainstream as defined by the ubiquitous hit parades or chart listings first established in Austria in the 1960s by the Ger-man-dominated *Schlager* industry. With the advent of the Ö3 pop network, Austrian airwaves were inundated by products of the international Ameri-can/British music industry, against which the Austropop discourse resisted, or at least attempted to establish its own identity. As a result, Ö3 has main-tained a separate *Austroparade* radio show to feature Austrian groups. One of the peculiarities of the hit parades and chart listings is their ability to legit-imize core-periphery relations by quantifying qualitatively different styles and genres of music in terms of record sales. They are thus not just com-mercial marketing mechanisms for selling recordings but help to determine what constitutes both the "popular" and the "national" in popular music. On the basis of the hit parade, groups of musicians are transformed into bands, the noise of the music transmutes into the "sound," and the listeners become the "audience" with varying qualities of emotional engagement and investment as "fans." As the music diffuses through society, the context of the performances and the sales take on symbolic value, which forms the basis for its further diffusion.

Currently, Austropop consists of a variety of musicians and music, including the rock-based Ostbahn-Kurti und die Chefpartie, the cabaret rock group Erste Allgemeine Verunsicherung, the *Schlager*-influenced Jazz-Gitti, the folk-rock trio STS, plus Wolfgang Ambros, Rainhard Fendrich, Stefanie Werger, and Georg Danzer of the first and second generations (compare Renger 1993: 402). While there have been a series of debates and conflicts on the continued legitimacy and viability of Austropop as a discourse strategy, most of the musicians included in the designation refuse to be classified as such. Furthermore, my informal surveys of Viennese high-school students in 1991 revealed that there is no one criterion or even group of criteria that can be uniformly applied to define Austropop productions. Neither the sound, nor the use of language, nor the nationality of the singers, nor the regional background, nor social class seem to be delineating factors, which prompts the assessment that Austropop is primarily a discourse strategy in the sense of Botz and Müller (1995: 37), that is, it provides a political category for aesthetic judgment.

New Folk Music: Counterhegemonic Discourse as World Music

Crafting a "non-German" cultural identity in the face of German hegemony has been of prime importance for most Austrian governments since the end of World War II. The tourist industry, one of the economic motors of Austrian society, caters to a predominantly German clientele; Germans control much of what is published inside Austria; and German publishers are preferred by Austrian authors both inside and outside of their country. The broadcasting and entertainment industries of Germany dwarf those of Austria and offer Austrian performers, producers, and consumers greater opportunities beyond the narrow confines of their own domestic market.

The post-World War II Austrian *Heimatfilm*, which painted city life as evil and glorified rural life, and the popularization of *volkstümliche* have been mainstays of Austrian cultural exports to Germany. These conjure up images of pristine idyllic landscapes in Alpine vacation wonderlands, in which personal conflicts are harmoniously dissolved and the *Volk* is reified into ahistorical, homogeneous, "authentic," easy-going, albeit somewhat dim-witted, characters. This is perhaps most poignantly illustrated in the popular television show *Musikantenstadl*, which is coproduced with the German ARD public-television network, and features highly stylized performances of folk music, folk dancing, singing, and comic sketches staged against a backdrop of a beer tent. The show features large live audiences, the most popular of the *volkstümliche* performers, and prerecorded music "lip-synched" in play-back fashion.

There have been periodic attempts to deconstruct the mythological *Volk* and culture of the tourist-oriented folkloric industries that drew on a wide variety of regional underdog folk figures like actor Helmut Qualtinger's bit-ingly satirical title character in the show *Herr Karl* in the 1950s and 1960s. Anglo-American folk music was also an avenue of cultural resistance against an uncritical commercial Austrian folklore in the 1960s, which grew into a socially critical song movement, using dialect known as the *kritische Lieder-macher*. Even the legendary *Da Hofa* by Ambros can be considered an effort in deconstruction. The increased dependency and integration of Austria into Western Europe under German economic hegemony, the expansion of the EU with Austrian membership, and the breakdown of cold-war barriers to Eastern Europe have expanded critical discourse in Austria on issues of cultural and national identity and created a stronger need for self-assertion and relegitimization of Austrian identity within the confines of global cul-ture and economy.

While resistance to German hegemony seldom takes the form of politi-cal movements, narratives of resistance frequently appear in popular genres. For example, a four-part television drama called the *Piefke-Saga* (Mitterer 1991) draws on the Austrian pejorative term for a German (*Piefke*) and satirically portrays the sellout and ultimate downfall of a Tyrolian mountain village to winter ski tourism dominated by German interests.

Popular-music adherents who grew up with the internationalizing, glob-ally distributed Anglo-American music of the 1960s and 1970s have tradi-tionally been the fiercest opponents of the *volkstümliche* genre. Students and academically trained musicians typically focused their critique on the inabil-ity of the *volkstümliche* genre to portray real problems in Austrian society. My own research has found that urban high-school students in particular express the highest degree of opposition to *volkstümliche* music (Larkey 1993). But the totalizing discourse of this genre makes it the primary focus for strategies of opposition. Many of the Anglo-American-influenced pop-ular-music producers and bands testify that the *volkstümliche* genre has a solid, "authentic" audience in the Austrian countryside. Also, its immense popularity undermines the domestic cultural legitimacy of musicians who promote other forms of "popular" music.

Some Austrian popular musicians and audiences have carved out a criti-cal niche in the popular-music industry by producing musical narratives of resistance against the discourse of the German-dominated tourist industry as well as the official Austrian national discourse. These employ musical components found in the international recording industry but also draw on elements of Austrian regional folklore and music to construct their identities and traditions. While some new forms of popular music represent a subcultural opposition to and repudiation of tourism folklore, other forms attempt to capture domestic entertainment from the international recording industry with a regional music that is still subordinated to this industry but manages to subvert its original totalizing, hegemonic discourse. This is a familiar strategy for recontextualizing and reappropriating styles of popular music, like the *volkstümliche* in Austria and polka and blues in the United States. As ethnomusicologist Steven Feld argues, "dominant stylistic tendencies can and must be utilized in order to ambiguate and deny old meanings and to suggest and legitimate new ones." To do this, "dominant stereotypes can and must be accepted, restated, and centrally available in order to be potentially eclipsed" (Keil and Feld 1994: 219).

This kind of music may be termed "local" music in the sense of Guilbault (1993: 36), that is, "a subset of world music ... that ... emerged in the 1980s ... [and is] mass distributed world-wide yet associated with minority groups and small or industrially developing countries ... [and combines] local musical characteristics with those of mainstream genres in today's transnational music-related industry." As a form of world music, the new Austrian folk music "takes advantage of the skills and resources of the dominant traditions" (Guilbault 1993: 37) to produce a market and distribute its music. By using many mainstream musical characteristics found on the global market, Guilbault (1993: 37) concludes that "a kind of a lingua franca" develops that is recognized by many different people and "renders the output of the small locals clearly identifiable." According to Guilbault (1993: 39 and 43), these musicians "show that they are cosmopolitans who function in and out, at will, of what has been traditionally perceived as the totalizing 'system' [controlled by the dominant cultures]," and represent a desire for recognition and participation in world global economics and for power.

I want to highlight three strategies for framing and constructing the relationship between the global and the local through what I shall term the "new folk music." I focus on three groups: the rock-influenced band Hubert von Goisern, the folk/hip-hop/hardcore duo Attwenger, who utilize rural-based Upper Austrian traditions, and Roland Neuwirth, who draws on the *Schrammel* tradition of the Viennese urban song that was popular in the late nineteenth and early twentieth centuries but had become "orphanized" in the immediate postwar period (Larkey 1997). The productions of all three groups combine regional with international traditions in their efforts to deconstruct and reinterpret reified folkloric images and narratives. They represent highly ambiguous, historically contingent tactical responses to the hegemonic conditions of the global popular-music market in Austria (Certeau 1984: 37).

Although their dialect song lyrics strive toward authenticity, they do not mean to exclude nondialect speakers from their audiences but merely provide an identifying marker to distinguish the identities and distinctions.[3] The artists actively seek to de-construct musical clichés propagated by the industry while reviving and reinterpreting them in the process. For them, the accordion constitutes not just a symbolic but an actual reference to regional Austrian music traditions that until now were primarily identified with tourism folklore. The lyric content contains critical reflections on the subordination of Austrian culture to tourism and alienated urban life-styles. Their use of electronically amplified instruments and blues and pop-music elements signifies a self-conscious participation in the global popular-music industry and indicates a rejection of purist or secessionist attitudes. Also, they include traditional dance tunes like the *Schleiniger*, ländler, and waltz, which suggests that they come from a generation that has been raised on international pop, yet alienated by generational and symbolic differences with its newer adherents.

It is also significant that these artists have not crossed over from the pop domain or merely included single songs into their otherwise pop repertoires and identities. Just as with the "covering" of the rock-and-roll tunes in the 1950s, by which the original popular tunes were sung by different groups or vocalists, it becomes important which vocalist or group originally popularized the tune. Many pop musicians and groups, notably Wilfried Scheutz and even the highly successful Erste Allgemeine Verunsicherung, have critiqued *volkstümliche* music through the ironic use of its styles in their repertoire. In contrast, the new folk music represents a less sporadic and more programmatic effort to sustain a "strategic" critique in the sense of de Certeau (1984: 35ff.). This means that the critical perspective occupies some center of power, certain spaces in cultural discourse, and the necessity to negotiate and compete for legitimacy within the field of music traditions. These are not just occasional critical expressions of a group otherwise located squarely in the *volkstümliche* tradition: they represent a multivocal critique of the dominant discourse on Austrian cultural identities that is nonessentialist and historically contingent.

Hubert von Goisern, a pseudonym for band leader Hubert Achleitner, is a group of musicians named after the Upper Austrian spa city of Bad Goisern. The group is by far the most commercially sounding of the three. To establish their musical identity and profile, they have relied on melodies from old American favorites like "Georgia on My Mind" ("Goisern") and "Cocaine Blues." They gave the first song a perhaps ironic text in Austrian dialect about returning to their beloved Goisern ("Goisern, Goisern, it is

3. In the discussion that follows, I have retained the idiosyncratic spellings given in the liner notes of the CDs of Hubert von Goisern, Attwenger, and Roland Neuwirth.

really bad, every once in a while I must return to you/otherwise I can bear no more"). While their first CD, *Alpine Lawine* (Alpine avalanche) (COL 46264 2), released as an LP in 1988, included several songs with English lyrics ("It's All Over Now," "Cocaine," "Me No Got No," and "Striptease Dancer"), their second recording, *Aufgeigen stått niederschiassen* (Play it up, don't shoot it down) (BMG 262 752–222), released in 1992, contains, programmatically, no more English-language lyrics. The title "Cocaine" on the first LP/CD can also be found on the third CD, *Omunduntn* (Above and below) (BMG 74321 18962 2), but in a German/Austrian rendition.

Most of the Goisern tunes are derived from typical Austrian "traditional" dance melodies like the ländler and the *Schleiniger* and utilize four-liner verses called *G'stanzl* as lyrics, which are derived from the traditions of wandering musicians during earlier periods of orally transmitted culture. These humorous oral narratives, once considered the sole domain of the *volkstümliche* music, are, in the new folk music, incorporated into the repertoire of those previously opposed to this type of music. The Goisern song "Landlertanz," for example, is a typical example showing this new relationship of folklore to global pop music. The narrative explains how "Peppi" goes to San Francisco to proselytize in a "psychedelic disco" against rap and for ländler music "so that you can feel something in your balls." The song starts with a rock beat. With the refrain on the ländler—"Landlerisch tanzn kann net a niada, i kanns selber nit guat aber meine brüader" (dancing the landler is something not everyone can do, I can't do it myself very well, but my brothers can)—the song breaks into a four-part harmony and yodeling with a traditional ländler melody, broadly supported by a rock base line and electric rhythm guitar. Each new visit of Peppi takes him to another location where the international music is rooted, for example, Africa, where there is supposed to be "a little action" in dancing and drumming, only to learn that their music is already "out." A trip to Japan, where the music is copied, provokes the conclusion that "it somehow sounds like *The Sound of Music*." One of the verses of the refrain is: "you were there yesterday, today again, if you come everyday you'll become something again," implying that these are the roots to which all internationalized Austrians will return.

Goisern, in contrast to Attwenger, makes concrete references to political events and criticizes, for example, in the song "Iawaramoi," the shooting between Serbs and Croats: "ob krawaten oder serbn/alle müaßen sterben./ob serb oder krawat, um an jeden is schad" (whether Croat or Serb/all must die/whether Serb or Croat/it is too bad for all). The same song critiques simplistic views that attribute increased crime in Austria to foreign immigrants and asylum seekers. This is a reference to a referendum held in 1994 that was defeated by the electorate and provoked by right-wing Freedom Party boss Jörg Haider's call to "leave Austria to the Austrians" and expel the refugees and immigrants. Another politically motivated tune by Goisern is their rendering of the famous anthem from Habsburg times: "Gott Erhalte, Gott Beschütze" (God keep, God protect). This solemn tune, the only one with standard German lyrics on the *Omunduntn* CD, is adapted from Haydn and resembles the German national anthem. They produce it with a heavy/speed metal sound and with lyrics that parody present-day Austrian society, thus "modernizing" the old anthem while at the same time offering a critique of nostalgic longings for the Habsburg period: "gott erhalte, gott beschütze/uns den traum vom himmelreich/pippi langstrumpf, wurstel-prater,/jedem goldfisch seinen teich" (God keep, god protect/for us the dream of heavenly kingdom/pippi longstockings, Prater amusement park/ for every goldfish its own pond).

Hubert von Goisern provides cultural opposition *within* the mainstream by using rock and folk, English and German in its song productions. In contrast, Attwenger places itself uncompromisingly within the cultural opposition *outside* the mainstream. Their songs and instrumental productions accommodate neither standard German, nor English, nor popular forms of music, except for rap and hardcore riffs from the global music industry that are hardly "popular" in the standard commercial sense of the word. In contrast to the Goisern lyrics, the Attwenger productions contain no direct references to any concrete political or social events except in metaphor version by depicting a "modernized timelessness" of rural village life. Other people, unpleasant ones, are generally all referred to as "de leid" (those people) or "d' goscherten leid" (the stupid people).

Paradoxically, the duo uses the most extreme of the modern pop and world music traditions—rap, hardcore, and hip-hop—to maintain the most stubbornly traditionalist stance and assertions of authenticity for rural folk music. For instances, the fable *kosz* (what's it cost) tells the rather vulgar story of a boy who wants to kiss a girl "where she pisses." The girl replies that of course he may, "and just kiss my ass." The moral of the story is: "Where is the ass, where is the face?"

As titles they use simple words from rural peasant daily life: *luft* (air), *most* (juice), and *pflug* (plow), which indicates a refusal to participate in the pop-music industry's game of metaphor creation in its productions. Instead of producing with any of the major recording companies in Austria or Germany (as Goisern does with BMG Ariola), it uses the alternative German Trikont label. Also, unlike both Roland Neuwirth and Hubert von Goisern, the group does not supply standard German translations of its lyrics in the liner notes, defiantly challenging non-Austrian audiences to decipher them for themselves.

In contrast to Hubert von Goisern, whose primary aim is to provide danceable entertainment while incorporating the plays on words with dialect lyrics in a variety of *G'stanzl* forms, many of the Attwenger texts foreground these devices in their own right. On the *luft* LP, for instance, the title "wos nu" (what now) features rhymes and word plays on the term "wirr-war" (confusion): "waun i wieder weniga wirr wa waun i wissad wia ma daun wa wan i wieda weniga wirr wa & des wirrwarr ned so irr wa & des wa ma daun vü lieba waun des wirr warr weniga irr wa."[4] Each new rhyme scheme is introduced by the refrain, whose rhythm then slows down to quarter the otherwise breakneck speed of the lyric passage: "Und wos nu." A more conventional form is found in the rhymes of the *G'stanzl* "rahm" (cream), an extreme example of sexual innuendo and double meanings, which extends for nine verses: "wer koan rahm ned hod der kau koan rian,/wer koa heisl hod braucht kane dian/wer koa hemd ned hot der braucht koan krogn/wer nix sogn wü der braucht nix song" (whoever doesn't have any cream can't churn it/whoever has no house doesn't need a girl/whoever has no shirt, needs no collar/whoever doesn't want to speak, doesn't need to say anything).

Both Attwenger and Hubert von Goisern incorporate musical styles of rural Austria into the global music industry and frame their music productions within this context either within the production (Goisern) or by juxtaposing their productions to the international sound (Attwenger). In contrast, the productions of Roland Neuwirth reflect the urbanity, cosmopolitanism, and modernist tradition of Vienna, Austria's capital city and a major historical center of German cultural life.

Neuwirth draws from an urban song tradition situated around the numerous wine restaurants (*Heurige*) and cafés in and around Vienna that saw their heyday in the late nineteenth and early twentieth centuries. These restaurants featured a peculiar type of musical quartet made famous through the Schrammel brothers, Johann (Hans) and Joseph. The Schrammel quartet consisted of a contraguitar, two violins, and either an accordion, called a *Knopferlharmonika*, or a clarinet, in addition to an upper voice and a lead singer (Endler 1985: 115–16). This music may also be used to play dance rhythms such as the waltz and the polka and is fairly quiet and sedate, which helps to highlight the satirical and parodistic types of lyrics typical of the genre. Neuwirth's three recordings under discussion run the gamut from old-time *Schrammel* sounds to pop ballads, especially on the LP recording *Guat Drauf* (On top of it all), to blues, particularly a title for which he has achieved a certain popularity, the *Fußpilz-Blues* (Athlete's foot blues). Contrary to the music of Attwenger or Hubert von Goisern, Neuwirth relies primarily on acoustic instruments. While Attwenger generally satirizes the "other people" in the style of Till Eulenspiegel, Neuwirth generally includes himself when satirizing the weaknesses of the Viennese.

---

4. "if i were less confused i'd know what we do if i were still less confused and the confusion were not so great and what we do would be better if the confusion was less confusing."

Neuwirth's lyrics conspicuously adopt the inclusive "we" in talking with the audience. This device serves to include himself and his audience in the group of people whose behavior is the object of satire or parody, while creating ironic distance with his audience with respect to the behavior described in the song. One example of this is the song "So Samma und so Bleimma" (That's the way we are, and that's the way we'll stay), which parodies an audience member at an event like the *Musikantenstadl* who in the course of the evening gets progressively drunk and ends up spending several hours lying in a pissoir. This song on the live CD is all the more poignant due to the improvisations of the lyrics in the face of what the liner notes ironically and euphemistically call the "indisposition" of the singer, whose own drunkenness becomes increasingly evident during the performance. Another example of the inclusive "we" as an ironic device is used with the song "Die Herrn vom Praterstern," which is about drinking "boys" who get their kicks out of getting drunk and beating up people, notably long-haired ones like himself. The refrain does not talk about them as "de leid," as in the lyrics of Attwenger, or even in the first person singular. Instead, Neuwirth's refrain sings: "Wir sind die stårken Herrn, vom Praterstern ..." (We are the strong men of the Praterstern).

This ironic inclusivity is also featured in the *G'stanzl*-style song *Zinshaus-Ballade*, which is about the screwy occupants of a house in Vienna and their escapades. Each new verse tells about a different neighbor, for instance, a Ms. Keplacek, who was poisoned inexplicably, perhaps by her husband who "bred mushrooms" and has mysteriously disappeared; or little "Pschihalek," whose wife throws him out of the apartment now and then, and who goes around on crutches chasing women; or the "Yugoslav from across the hall," who keeps a crocodile in his apartment. After singing about the other strange personalities living in the house, he describes "a long-haired musician who just can't stop practicing his *Schrammel* music until after midnight" and therefore can't expect to be liked by anyone in the house, a blunt reference to himself.

The *G'stanzl* form, as was the case with Attwenger and Hubert von Goisern, lends itself also to modernization and adaptations. For instance, Neuwirth's song "Fjutscha G'stanzl" utilizes two of the most popular Viennese song lyrics to comment on the threat of nuclear contamination as a result of war. To the tune of *Ich waß a klanes Wirtshaus* (I know a small inn), an old favorite, the story tells about knowing a *Strahlnschutzkeller* (a nuclear shelter) in Ottakring, a former suburb on the outskirts of Vienna now incorporated into the city. The suggestion that one should go to the shelter to quench one's thirst is dictated by the fact that the air is hot and "full of plutonium." The innkeeper, called in the original song a *kreuzfidels Mannderl* (a faithful little man), becomes in Neuwirth's version a *kreuzfidel's Mutanterl* (a faithful little mutant). He uses the tune and refers explicitly to the *Reblaus* song made famous in the 1930s by Hans Moser, with the refrain "Ich muß im frühren Leben eine Reblaus gewesen sein" (I must have been a grapevine louse in my earlier life). The Neuwirth text diverges from the original by referring to the innkeeper (not the singer himself), who if he were not a grapevine louse in his other earlier life wouldn't run around in this one "on his six [!] feet to serve the wine." The last verse of the song nostalgically recalls the time in the past when lung cancer "was just an infant disease."

Conclusion

What impact did Americanization have on Austrian identities and cultural change and how was this manifested in Austropop and the new folk music? It led to a reconfiguration of national popular-music traditions in which American and German-influenced traditions played a prominent role. It also led to a restructuring of Austrian institutions and infrastructure for producing and distributing popular music, for example, the creation and reorganization of the radio channel Ö3, the Ö3 show *Austroparade*, and Blue Danube Radio, which modified the paths through which Austrian and globally distributed music, and the symbolic value attributed to them, circulated and were contested in Austrian society. Finally, Americanization enabled a new generation of musicians with social experiences rooted in consumerist values to emerge and provided a common basis for them to conduct both global and local sociocultural communication and to engage in identity formation.

Austropop and the new folk music are strategies in musical discourse for legitimizing the "Austrian" in the face of homogenizing globalization and embedding the Austrian contribution within the global setting. They both affirm the hegemonic relations while establishing critical distance within them. The two musical discourses reflect reethnicizing strategies rooted in this homogenization and globalization. One of the most striking results of Americanization is the increased use of English as the language of song lyrics because it is considered by many Austrian popular musicians and audiences to be the sole legitimate language for popular music. The self-conscious use of dialect stands in historical opposition to the use of standard German in *Schlager* and *volkstümliche* music and represents an effort to retrieve the intimacy and emotion symbolized in the language of everyday use by Austrians and to counteract the abstractness of both standard German and English lyrics. Both the Austropop discourse and the new folk music manifest how Austrians have incorporated globally available musical symbols and styles into their own repertoires and identities. In this manner, they have legitimized both global and local music as integral components of Austrian cultural heritage and social memory. This process represents a critical modernization of Austrian music traditions. The more commercialized music contains elements that enhance the continued dominance of commercial music and culture. But these very same components may also be employed in oppositional or subaltern discourses to support alternative or contested identities.

Austropop and the new folk music illustrate the different types of emotional musical links of the present to the past with mythic and nostalgic connotations mobilized by Austrian producers, musicians, and audience groups on the basis of American idioms of musical communication. Some of the music is directed against the one-dimensional optimism fostered by the advertising industry and attempts to retrieve the voices of dissent that are continually coopted by the global entertainment industry.

Popular and commercial music from the United States continues to be the point of reference for musical innovations with groups like the Erste Allgemeine Verunsicherung, Ostbahn-Kurti und die Chefpartie, and those of the new folk music. These groups embark on performance tours in Germany for the majority of their schedules, which underscores their efforts to both participate in and distance themselves from German hegemony. More traditional forms of entertainment music in Austria like the German *Schlager* and the *volkstümliche* varieties have been transformed as well, with more emphasis placed on the technological details of producing recordings and the sound, on marketing images of particular groups, and on being integrated into the tourist industry's production of Austrian identities.

The development of Austropop and the new folk music should be seen within the context of the economic control of the Austrian recording market. The five largest companies in the world are the five largest on the Austrian market, with the following market shares in 1992: PolyGram 24.2 percent, BMG Ariola 23.6 percent, EMI 14.5 percent, Warner 13.6 percent, and Sony 12.2 percent (Renger 1993: 401). It is therefore no surprise that "international pop music" dominates the music styles with 75 percent, followed by classical music with 10.5 percent, Austropop with 8.5 percent, and "folk music" with 4.2 percent (Renger 1993: 402). Between 1987 and 1992 the market share for international pop rose from 71.8 percent to 76.8 percent, whereas the share of Austrian pop music sank from 12.2 percent to 8.5 percent and the share of folk music rose from 3.6 percent in 1987 to 4.2 percent in 1992 (Renger 1993: 413). There seems to be a decrease in the popularity of Austrian artists, and a smaller number of artists are responsible for the increases in popularity that have occurred, for example, six of the most popular Austropop artists (Ostbahn-Kurti, Jazz-Gitti, Rainhard Fendrich, EAV, Stefanie Werger, and Ludwig Hirsch) account for two-thirds of the national production (Renger 1993: 402). ORF has, however, increased the share of Austropop to approximately 20 percent (Renger 1993: 403). While the ORF has confronted the net loss in popularity of Austrian artists expressed in net market share, the domination by global conglomerates has not been beneficial for Austrian popular music in its domestic market. The creation of private radio stations will no doubt lead to a further reduction of Austrian national pop on the airwaves.

Further research on Americanization and Austrian identity could focus on how the cultural policies of Austrian federal, state, and local authorities have positioned themselves with regard to the hegemony exerted by both Germany and the United States and on how effective such policies have been. Also, the view of Botz and Müller about the development of "the Austrian" as a political category of aesthetic analysis needs further study, since obviously "the American" and even "the German" contain great symbolic value on the Austrian market, to the point of numerically eclipsing the popularity of domestic recording artists.

References

Ang, I. 1990. "Culture and Communication." *European Journal of Communication* 5:249–63.

———. 1991. *Desperately Seeking the Audience.* London.

Atzenhofer, R. 1990. "Wie das Deutsche Eigentum wieder 'deutsch' wurde." In *In deutscher Hand? Österreich und sein großer Nachbar,* ed. M. Scherb and I. Morawetz, 61–85. Vienna

Balibar, E. 1990. "The Nation Form: History and Ideology." In *Race, Nation, Class: Ambiguous Identities,* ed. E. Balibar and I. Wallerstein, 86–106. London.

Becker, H. S. 1983. *Art Worlds.* Berkeley.

Bogart, L. 1995. *Commercial Culture.* New York.

Botz, G., and A. Müller. 1995. "Identität/Differenz in Österreich. Zu Gesellschafts-, Politik- und Kulturgeschichte vor und nach 1945." *Österreichische Zeitschrift für Geschichtswissenschaften* 6, no. 1:7–40.

Bruck, P. A., and I. Melcher-Smejkal. 1993. "Massenmedien in Österreich. Printmedien." In *Medienbericht. Massenmedien in Österreich 4,* ed. Institut für Publizistik und Kommunikationswissenschaft der Universität Salzburg, 57–91. Vienna.

Campbell, C. 1994. "The Desire for the New: Its Nature and Social Location as Presented in Theories of Fashion and Modern Consumerism." In *Consuming Technologies: Media and Information in Domestic Spaces,* ed. R. Silverstone and E. Hirsch, 48–64. London.

Certeau, M. de. 1984. *The Practice of Everyday Life*. Berkeley.

Dilley, R. 1992. "Contesting Markets: A General Introduction to Market Ideology, Imagery and Discourse." In *Contesting Markets: Analyses of Ideology, Discourse and Practice*, ed. R. Dilley, 1–34. Edinburgh.

Endler, F. 1985. *Musik in Wien – Musik aus Wien*. Vienna.

Ewen, S. 1988. *All Consuming Images*. New York.

Fabris, H. H. 1990. "Medienkolonie—Na und?" In *In deutscher Hand? Österreich und sein großer Nachbar*, ed. M. Scherb and I. Morawetz, 113–30. Vienna.

Guilbault, J. 1993. "On Redefining the 'Local' through World Music." *The World of Music* 35, no. 2:33–49.

Hofbauer, H. 1992. *Westwärts: Österreichs Wirtschaft im Wiederaufbau*. Vienna.

Keil, C., and S. Feld. 1994. *Music Grooves: Essays and Dialogues*. Chicago.

Larkey, E. 1993. *Pungent Sounds: Constructing Identity with Popular Music in Austria*. New York.

———. 1997. "The Orphanization of the 'Wienerlied' in the 1950s." *Modern Austrian Literature* 30, no. 1:69–87.

Luger, K. 1991. *Die konsumierte Rebellion. Geschichte der Jugendkultur 1945–1990*. Vienna.

Luger, K., and T. Steinmaurer. 1993. "Rundfunk." In *Medienbericht. Massenmedien in Österreich 4*, ed. Institut für Publizistik und Kommunikationswissenschaft der Universität Salzburg, 177–243. Vienna.

Maase, K. 1992. *Bravo Amerika*. Frankfurt.

Mathis, F. 1995. "Zwischen Lenkung und freiem Markt. Die verstaatlichte Industrie." In *Österreich in den Fünfzigern*, ed. T. Albrich, K. Eisterer, M. Gehler, and R. Steininger, 169–82. Innsbruck.

Mitterer, F. 1991. *Die Piefke Saga*. Innsbruck.

Morawetz, I. 1990. "Schwellenland Österreich?" In *In deutscher Hand? Österreich und sein großer Nachbar*, ed. M. Scherb and I. Morawetz, 87–112. Vienna.

Panzer, F. 1993. "Buch und Buchmarkt." In *Medienbericht. Massenmedien in Österreich 4*, ed. Institut für Publizistik und Kommunikationswissenschaft der Universität Salzburg, 281–324. Vienna.

Reiterer, A. F., ed. 1988. *Nation und Nationalbewußtsein in Österreich*. Vienna.

Renger, R. 1993. "Audio-Industrie." In *Medienbericht. Massenmedien in Österreich 4*, ed. Institut für Publizistik und Kommunikationswissenschaft der Universität Salzburg, 391–415. Vienna.

Said, E. 1993. *Culture and Imperialism*. New York.

Scherb, M. 1990. "Wir und die westeuropäische Hegemonialmacht." In *In deutscher Hand? Österreich und sein großer Nachbar*, ed. M. Scherb and I. Morawetz, 27–59.

Schou, S. 1991. "Postwar Americanisation and the Revitalisation of European Culture." In *Media Cultures: Reappraising Transnational Media*, ed. M. Skovmand and K. C. Schrøder, 142–60. London.

Sklair, L. 1991. *Sociology of the Global System*. Baltimore.

Thurner, E. 1995. "Die stabile Innenseite der Politik. Geschlechterverhalten und Rollenverhalten." In *Österreich in den Fünfzigern*, ed. T. Albrich, K. Eisterer, M. Gehler, and R. Steininger, 53–66. Innsbruck.

Wagnleitner, R. 1991. *Coca-Colonisation und Kalter Krieg.* Vienna.

_____. 1994. *Coca-Colonization and the Cold War: The Cultural Mission of the United States in Austria after the Second World War.* Chapel Hill: The University of North Carolina Press.

Wallerstein, I. 1990. "Culture as the Ideological Battleground of the Modern World-System." In *Global Culture: Nationalism, Globalization and Modernity,* ed. M. Featherstone, 31–56. Newbury Park, Calif.

LIST OF CONTRIBUTORS

John Bunzl is Research Fellow at the Austrian Institute for International Affairs and Associate Professor of Political Science at the University of Vienna.

David F. Good is Professor of History at the University of Minnesota.

Bernhard Handlbauer is a clinical psychologist and psychotherapist who practices in Salzburg and lectures at the University of Klagenfurt.

Edward Larkey is Associate Professor of German at the University of Maryland Baltimore County.

Maria Mesner is Head of the Department of Social Sciences at the Renner Institute, Vienna, and Lecturer in Contemporary and Gender History at the University of Vienna.

Richard Mitten is Associate Professor of History at Central European University.

Jonathan Munby is Lecturer in American Studies at Lancaster University.

Oliver Rathkolb is Research Director of the Bruno Kreisky Archives Foundation and the Ludwig Boltzmann Institute for History and Society, and Associate Professor of History at the University of Vienna.

Egon Schwarz is Rosa May Distinguished University Professor Emeritus in the Humanities at Washington University.

Jacqueline Vansant is Associate Professor of German at the University of Michigan-Dearborn.

Reinhold Wagnleitner is Associate Professor of History at the University of Salzburg.

Ruth Wodak is Professor of Applied Linguistics at the University of Vienna and Head of the research center Discourse, Politics, and Identity.

INDEX